MEDICAL ASPECTS
of
DEVELOPMENTAL DISABILITIES IN CHILDREN BIRTH TO THREE

Second Edition

James A. Blackman, M.D., M.P.H.

Kluge Children's Rehabilitation Center and Research Institute
Department of Pediatrics
University of Virginia
Charlottesville, Virginia

AN ASPEN PUBLICATION®
Aspen Publishers, Inc.
Rockville, Maryland
1990

Library of Congress Cataloging-in-Publication Data

Medical aspects of developmental disabilities in children
birth to three/[edited by] James A. Blackman.--2nd. ed.
p. cm.
"An Aspen publication."
Includes bibliographical references.
ISBN 0-8342-0107-0
1. Developmentally disabled children--Medical care.
[DNLM; 1. Child Development Disorders--handbooks.
2. Child, Exceptional--handbooks. 3. Health--handbooks WS 39 M489]
RJ135.M43   1989   618.92--dc20   DNLM/DLC
for Library of Congress
89-17808
CIP

The authors have made every effort to ensure the accuracy of the information herein,
particularly with regard to drug selection and dose. However, appropriate information
sources should be consulted, especially for new or unfamiliar drugs or procedures. It is the
responsibility of every practitioner to evaluate the appropriateness of a particular
opinion in the context of actual clinical situations and with due consideration to new
developments. Authors, editors, and the publisher cannot be held responsible for any
typographical or other errors found in this book.

Editorial Services: Jane Coyle Garwood

Library of Congress Catalog Card Number: 89-17808
ISBN: 0-8342-0107-0

Printed in the United States of America

1 2 3 4 5

The second edition of this book is dedicated to the staff of the Infant and Young Child Clinic, Division of Developmental Disabilities, Department of Pediatrics, University of Iowa, and of the Iowa High-Risk Infant Follow-up Program as well as to the children and families they serve. It is from these professionals and families that I learned the importance of the interdisciplinary approach to developmental disabilities and chronic illness.

Table of Contents

Introduction

The health status of disabled children has a profound effect on their development. It is therefore essential that early intervention professionals become knowledgeable about the health and functioning of the children they serve. Without such knowledge, they may be unaware of—or over-estimate—the limitations that particular conditions or treatments can place on a child's progress.

Medical records are sought routinely by early service programs, but often these contain jargon understandable only to members of the health profession. The same may be said of textbooks written by and for physicians. Even individuals with training in the health field may have difficulty keeping up with countless new developments in the diagnosis and management of the various conditions. What is needed—and what this manual seeks to provide—is an accessible, easy-to-understand resource on those conditions, tests, and other health care issues that are relevant to infants and young children with developmental disabilities. Topics—arranged alphabetically for ease of reference—were selected on the basis of a survey of professionals who deliver services in early intervention and early education programs.

This manual is not a resource for educational and therapeutic techniques. Neither is it an exhaustive treatment of any given topic (for this, the reader may want to consult specialized textbooks, journals, or health care professionals). Rather, it is a summary of health information that is important to the care of a particular child—with special emphasis on those aspects of a condition that affect day-to-day functioning. We recommend that this manual be readily available to all professionals—including medical professionals—who work with developmentally disabled children.

Acknowledgments

We wish to acknowledge Marcia Henderson, R.N., M.A., C.P.N.P., Janet R. Mapel, R.N., B.S.N., C.P.N.P., Frederick R. Schultz, M.D., and Gerald Solomons, M.D., for their contributions to the earlier edition of this book; Kathy Breese, Muriel Metz, and Kay Rebec for their assistance in the preparation of the manuscript; Richard Huber for graphics; and Ron Strampe for photography.

Preface to Second Edition

Services in the 1990s for young children with actual or potential developmental problems promise to be very different from those of previous decades. Although there is a long history in this century of gradually increasing emphasis on the welfare of children in general, and on that of disabled children in particular, the passage of Public Law No. 99-457, *1986 Amendments to the Education for All Handicapped Act,* provided the needed impetus for substantial changes in the nation's infrastructure. By mandating coordinated, comprehensive services for children with, as well as at risk for, developmental disabilities but offering few new resources, the United States Congress has forced the many professionals who serve young children to take a fresh look at how their work can become more efficient and effective. Within the context of developing an individualized family service plan, these professionals must understand the health, social, and educational aspects of a child's disability if interdisciplinary efforts are to be successful.

This second edition of *Medical Aspects of Developmental Disabilities in Children Birth to Three* was expanded to meet the health information needs of early service providers. It is hoped that it will make a significant contribution to the continuing development of exemplary services for young children and their families.

Contributors

James A. Blackman, M.D., M.P.H.
Associate Professor
Department of Pediatrics
Kluge Children's Rehabilitation Center and Research Institute
University of Virginia
Charlottesville, Virginia

Patricia A. Smigielski Curry, R.N., M.S., C.P.N.P.
Pediatric Nurse Practitioner
Infant and Young Child Service
Division of Developmental Disabilities
The University of Iowa Hospitals and Clinics
Iowa City, Iowa

James C. Hardy, Ph.D.
Professor
Department of Pediatrics
College of Medicine and
Department of Speech Pathology and Audiology
The University of Iowa
Iowa City, Iowa

Alfred Healy, M.D.
Professor
Department of Pediatrics
College of Medicine and
Division of Special Education
College of Education
The University of Iowa
Iowa City, Iowa

Gerri Kahn, Ph.D., CCC-A
Adjunct Associate Professor
Department of Speech Pathology and Audiology
The University of Iowa
Iowa City, Iowa

Loretta Knutson Lough, L.P.T., M.A., P.C.S.
Adjunct Associate Faculty
Physical Therapy Education
The University of Iowa
Iowa City, Iowa

Arthur J. Nowak, D.M.D.
Professor
Department of Pediatric Dentistry
College of Dentistry
The University of Iowa Hospitals and Clinics
Iowa City, Iowa

David P. Schor, M.D.
Associate Professor
Department of Pediatrics
School of Medicine
Temple University
Philadelphia, Pennsylvania

Elizabeth J. Thomson, R.N., M.S.
Clinical Coordinator
Regional Genetic Consultation Service
Division of Medical Genetics
Department of Pediatrics
The University of Iowa Hospitals and Clinics
Iowa City, Iowa

Mark L. Wolraich, M.D.
Professor
Department of Pediatrics
College of Medicine
The University of Iowa
Iowa City, Iowa

Anemia

DESCRIPTION

Anemia is a condition in which the blood is deficient in either red blood cells (RBCs) or hemoglobin, the oxygen-carrying pigment in RBCs.

CAUSE

Anemia occurs (1) when there is inadequate production of either RBCs or hemoglobin or (2) when the RBCs are destroyed or lost faster than they can be replaced.

Inadequate Production of Either RBCs or Hemoglobin

The production of RBCs or hemoglobin in the bone marrow may be affected adversely by congenital defects that impede the normal division and development of immature cells; by a lack of essential nutrients; or by lead poisoning, drugs, infection, malignancy, irradiation, kidney disease, or any chronic debilitating condition. The most common cause, however, is iron deficiency.

Iron deficiency anemia results from insufficient daily intake of iron or from excess losses of this mineral through bleeding. A full-term infant is born with enough iron in its body to last only a few months; a premature infant has even less. To accommodate rapid growth, there must be adequate iron in the diet. Iron deficiency anemia may occur in the infant who drinks only breast milk for a prolonged period or in one who drinks a commercial baby formula that is not iron-fortified. It may also occur in the toddler who drinks large quantities of whole milk (low in iron) in lieu of other, iron-rich, foods or in the "picky eater" whose food selection excludes iron-rich foods.

At high risk for iron deficiency anemia are infants with developmental disabilities. The difficulty these children often have with chewing and swallowing disrupts the normal shift from milk to various solid baby foods to table foods—a sequence that usually ensures adequate iron even when there is no awareness of proper nutrition.

Iron deficiency anemia occurs most often between ages nine and 24 months in full-term infants, earlier in those who are premature.

Toxic substances such as lead can interfere with the production of RBCs (see "Anemia Due to Lead Poisoning").

Excessive Loss or Destruction of RBCs

Even when the rate of production is normal, RBCs may be lost or broken down faster than the body can replace them. Normally, an RBC lives for about 120 days before it is replaced by a new RBC, which is made in the bone marrow. In a healthy child or adult, about 1 percent of all RBCs are replaced daily. When the loss or destruction exceeds 1 percent, the bone marrow speeds up production.

Excessive numbers of RBCs may be lost through hemorrhaging due to surgery, injury, or parasitic infestations in the gastrointestinal tract. Also, RBCs may break down too rapidly because of abnormalities in their enzymes or membranes or because they have deficient or defective hemoglobin. A common anemia caused by defective hemoglobin is sickle cell disease.

Sickle cell disease is transmitted through autosomal recessive inheritance. That is, both parents must be carriers of a gene responsible for abnormal hemoglobin synthesis, and both must pass the gene on to the child. Eight percent of all American blacks are carriers for sickle cell anemia. When both parents are carriers, there is a 25 percent chance that the offspring will inherit the disease.

Carriers themselves have no difficulty with sickle cell anemia. However, in a person who has the disease, the RBCs have a tendency to assume abnormal shapes, becoming long and thin like a sickle instead of round and concave. The sickled RBCs clog blood vessels and fail to circulate and deliver oxygen to the tissues. When this occurs, affected children are severely limited in their activities; too, they are often in considerable pain and very susceptible to certain serious bacterial infections.

CLASSIFICATION OF ANEMIAS BY CAUSE

Anemias caused by inadequate production of red blood cells or hemoglobin

- Chronic infection or inflammation
- Congenital or acquired aplastic anemias
- Iron deficiency
- Kidney disease
- Lead poisoning
- Malignancy
- Bone marrow damage from irradiation and drugs
- Deficiencies in vitamin B_{12} and folate

Anemias caused by increased destruction or loss of red blood cells

- Certain drugs
- Hemolytic disease of the newborn
- Immune disease
- Certain infections
- Sickle cell disease or other hemoglobin disorders
- Certain toxic substances

DETECTION

Anemia can be detected by passing a small sample of blood through a special instrument that automatically detects and records the number of RBCs and amount of hemoglobin therein. Clinics and offices, however, frequently estimate hemoglobin content by filling a small, thin tube with blood and then centrifuging it to separate the RBCs from plasma and other blood elements. The percentage of the total volume occupied by RBCs (hematocrit) yields an estimate of the amount of hemoglobin in the blood.

Hemoglobin determinations are recommended at nine months (six months for premature infants), then yearly thereafter during routine checkups. In some localities, it has been the practice to screen routinely for the sickle cell trait among populations with a high incidence of the disease, including blacks and certain groups with Mediterranean ancestry.

COURSE

Children with mild anemia do not look or act any differently from other children. Children with moderate anemia, however, appear pale and lose the pink coloration of their gums and lips. They also become less active because of the limited amount of oxygen available to burn calories. With severe anemia, heart and breathing rates increase, even at rest. This condition can cause cardiac failure and even—though rarely—death.

A decrease in hemoglobin below expected levels is an excellent indicator of a serious health problem. Detected, such a decrease often prompts remediation of both the anemia and the underlying cause.

With moderate to severe iron deficiency anemia, increased iron produces notable improvements: in 24 hours there is reduced irritability and increased appetite, and within 72 hours new RBCs are released from the bone marrow. The normal amounts of RBCs and hemoglobin usually are attained within one month, but it takes an additional two months to replace the iron stores the infant needs to sustain itself in the event of another period of low iron intake. Supplemental iron is not necessary for all types of anemia; at times it may even be dangerous.

Sickle cell disease is a lifelong condition that may affect longevity. Acute "crises"—characterized by a worsening of the anemia or by pain and swelling of bones, abdominal organs, or other body tissues—may be precipitated by infection or by a reduction of available oxygen; crises may also occur spontaneously for no apparent reason. The most common type is the vaso-occlusive episode, which occurs when abnormally shaped RBCs become trapped in the small blood vessels, depriving tissue of needed oxygen (ischemia) and/or causing the death of small amounts of tissue (infarction). In young children this generally occurs in the bones of the hands and feet. Swelling may also occur around the affected bones. On occasion, sudden, severe anemia may develop, which can be fatal if not treated with intravenous fluids and blood transfusions.

ACCOMPANYING HEALTH PROBLEMS

All types of anemias interfere with the oxygen-carrying capacity of the blood. Therefore, the major effect on the infant is lack of energy to perform the usual developmental tasks of childhood. Iron deficiency anemia can also cause significant listlessness and irritability. If it is prolonged, it may impede developmental progress.

Sickle cell disease may have associated health disorders, the most important of which is an increased susceptibility to serious, potentially lethal infections. Each child should have an individualized health care plan that is carefully developed by parents and medical professionals.

MEDICAL MANAGEMENT

Once anemia has been discovered, its exact cause should be identified prior to prescribing treatment. Iron deficiency anemia can be diagnosed and treated adequately by any primary care physician. Other production failure anemias and the hemoglobinopathies, however, may require consultation with a pediatrician or someone specially trained in blood disorders of children (pediatric hematologist).

A well-rounded diet of all of the basic food groups provides adequate iron except during the first year of life, when iron supplementation is recommended. This is most conveniently supplied in an iron-fortified formula for infants, though it can be provided separately. Supplemental iron for infants exclusively breast-fed is usually recommended despite recent evidence suggesting that the iron content of breast milk, while low, is very well absorbed by the infant. Any child over one year of age with mild anemia and no other health problems may be treated by dietary changes alone; that way, permanent changes can occur in the child's eating habits.

Consultation regarding iron deficiency anemia and dietary management is available from dietitians, nutritionists, nurses, or physicians.

IMPLICATIONS FOR EDUCATION

Children with developmental disabilities, both physical and mental, are at high risk for developing iron deficiency anemia. Education-related professionals can help by encouraging parents to have the child's physician check periodically—and whenever the child is lethargic—for signs of this condition. Educators and therapists can also observe the child for signs of positive response to iron therapy, including increased activity and alertness.

Iron-rich foods should be encouraged both at home and at school. Offer as many of the following foods as possible each day:
- meat, fish, or poultry
- enriched breads and cereals (especially dry baby cereals and cereals fortified with extra iron) and wheat germ
- dried beans and peas (chili, navy, or pinto beans; split peas)
- peanut butter
- dark green, leafy vegetables (spinach, broccoli, chard, kale, beets, turnip greens, dandelion greens)
- dried fruit (raisins, prunes, dates, figs, apricots)

To help the body utilize the iron content of these foods, offer foods rich in vitamin C at the same time. These include oranges, grapefruit, strawberries, melons, green peppers, and selections from the cabbage family.

Children with, or at risk for, sickle cell disease should be referred immediately for medical evaluation whenever they have a fever or other signs of an infection. Irritability or lethargy in young children with this disease should be investigated, since these may be symptoms of a sickle cell "crisis."

There has been recent interest in, and research on, how mild anemia affects learning and development. While results have been equivocal, it is reasonable to assume that a child with optimal health is more likely to benefit from learning experiences. Since moderate to severe (and possibly mild) anemia can influence developmental function and learning, it is important that this condition be recognized, evaluated, and treated promptly.

ANEMIA DUE TO LEAD POISONING

Lead causes anemia by interfering with iron utilization and hemoglobin production. In addition, high levels of lead, which can accumulate in the body over a lifetime, can harm the brain, kidneys, and liver and the reproductive, cardiovascular, immune, and gastrointestinal systems. The risk of lead to fetuses, infants, and children is of primary concern because they are susceptible to lower levels of body lead. At levels once thought to be acceptable, there is now evidence that lead may cause learning and behavioral disorders in children and also may affect growth.

While lead levels in the blood of the population of the United States have dropped as a result of governmental restrictions on leaded gasoline, the banning of lead-based paints, and a reduction in the use of lead-soldered cans for food preservation, there continues to be significant lead exposure from community water supplies with old lead service pipes and water mains, old homes with lead or lead alloy pipes, old homes with lead-based paints, industrial emissions, runoff in mining operations and industrial wastes, and various food sources.

Young children with pica, a craving for unnatural food such as dirt or paint chips, are at particular risk. Public health programs conduct lead screening programs that include environmental investigations if children are found to have unacceptably high lead levels. Lead is detected by checking blood levels of hemoglobin, erythrocyte protoporphyrin, and actual lead. In certain cases, children may require chelation, a procedure that forces excretion of lead into the urine by administration of special drugs. Children with elevated blood lead levels require close developmental surveillance.

Autism

DESCRIPTION

Autism is a developmental disorder with severe distortions of social and language development generally beginning before the third birthday. It is a group of associated symptoms (a syndrome). Extensive criteria are listed in the third revised edition of the American Psychiatric Association's *Diagnostic and Statistical Manual*. This manual specifies that behaviors abnormal for the child's developmental level must occur in each of the following areas:

- qualitative impairment in reciprocal social interaction (example: may seem unaware of others' feelings or even their existence)
- qualitative impairment in verbal and nonverbal communication and imaginative activity (example: does not use words, sounds, hand movements, or even facial expression to communicate)
- very narrow range of activities and interests (example: exhibits repetitive body movements such as flicking the fingers)

Children with mental retardation, developmental language disorders, deafness, or childhood schizophrenia may exhibit a few of these features, but their symptoms in these areas are generally less severe and more likely to respond to treatment. In only rare cases do the features of autism not appear until after the first two and one-half years of life. In these instances, however, there is some controversy over whether the term *autism* is appropriate.

CAUSE

While autism is thought to be due to brain dysfunction that arises before or around the time of birth, most autistic children do not have a brain injury that is detectable by medical assessments. The prevalence of autism is higher among children with recognized brain injuries, however, than in the population as a whole.

INCIDENCE

Autism is a rare disorder, occurring in about one child in two thousand. Individuals born with rubella and those with a chromosomal abnormality called fragile X run a higher risk, as do those with some very rare conditions. It is more common in boys, and the prevalence is significantly increased among siblings of children with autism.

DETECTION

Although there are no specific laboratory tests that detect autism, a medical evaluation for affected children is helpful to search for conditions at times associated with this diagnosis.

The language and social skills of children with autism are not as well developed as their nonverbal cognitive functioning in test or real-life situations. In contrast, the language, social, and cognitive skills of children with mental retardation are all at similar stages of development.

Careful questioning of parents will usually reveal that the child with autism demonstrated an unusual lack of involvement with others at a very young age. For example, parents may recall lack of eye contact or facial expressiveness in infancy. While some children are reported to have developed relatively normally for up to two years before the onset of symptoms, parental anxiety or lack of knowledge has, in at least some of these cases, masked earlier symptoms.

COURSE

Autism is a chronic disorder; that is, it is manifested at birth (or soon after) and is present throughout the individual's lifetime. While some children are able eventually to lead independent lives after intensive professional services, most continue to require some degree of custodial care. The best predictor of a favorable outcome is the development of useful speech by the age of five.

ACCOMPANYING HEALTH PROBLEMS

Seizures, usually associated with an underlying condition or disease, are rare in the first years yet occur in about 25 percent by early adult life.

MEDICAL MANAGEMENT

No specific medical treatment has proven to be effective with autism. Seizures, if present, are treated with medications, just as they are with children who do not have autism.

IMPLICATIONS FOR EDUCATION

Children who have or are suspected of having autism should be observed carefully for possible problems with seeing or hearing. They almost always require special education—focusing on language and self-help skills—along with a systematic and individualized program aimed at modifying inappropriate behavior and improving interaction with others. These efforts are often intensive, and progress can be slow.

Although the autistic child's speech may be complex—these children may have normal or above-normal rote memories—it is unorganized; when an adult's response is equally complex, the child is unable to comprehend. Some guidelines for communication: keep it simple and direct; use objects or actions in conjunction with words; emphasize functional language (e.g., have the child ask for something by naming it rather than by pointing); and give the child opportunities to interact with younger children, who have a more comparable level of language development. In managing behavior, include tangible rather than social reinforcers, and establish predictable routines regarding the sequence of events, the language and gestures you use, and the components of the physical environment.

Parents of children with autism need access to respite care as well as ongoing contact with available, supportive, knowledgeable personnel. They need, especially, assurance that the autism was not caused by a lack of love or attention on their part.

With autism, good communication among parents, educators, and other professionals is particularly important; not only does it facilitate the child's present learning, but it may also reduce or eliminate typical behavior problems that can stand in the way of future development.

SEE ALSO

Hearing Impairment and *Mental Retardation*

ADDITIONAL RESOURCE

Coleman, M. "Young Children with Autism or Autistic-Like Behaviors." *Infants and Young Children* 1, no. 4 (1989): 22–31.

Bowel and Bladder Management

Many infants and young children with developmental disabilities have complex needs related to their bowel and bladder function. Management of constipation, intestinal ostomies, and clean intermittent catheterization is discussed.

CONSTIPATION

Description
Constipation means hard, rocklike bowel movements that may cause painful straining during defecation. If stools are infrequent, but soft, it is not constipation. A young child should have a bowel movement at least once every three days.

Cause
Infants and young children with developmental disabilities may not be as physically active as other children because of developmental delay, motor impairment, or immobilization following orthopedic procedures. Because of their inactivity, these children are more likely to become constipated. Certain medications and feeding difficulties may also predispose these children to constipation. Children with spinal defects such as spina bifida have neurogenic bowels (lack of voluntary bowel control), which decrease the movement of food through the intestines, leading to constipation.

Incidence
Most children whose disabilities involve central nervous system dysfunction experience some degree of constipation.

Accompanying Health Problems

Constipation should be prevented because it can cause abdominal discomfort, decreased appetite, and irritability. Straining to pass the hard stool may cause hemorrhoids, fissures (cracks around the anus that may bleed), and—rarely—rectal prolapse (bowel tissue forced out through the anus). If constipation becomes severe, stool may become impacted (intestinal obstruction), causing a medical emergency that requires special medical—and sometimes surgical—correction.

Medical Management

Diet

Dietary methods of treatment should always be used first to treat and/or prevent constipation before medications are used. Extra fluids in the form of water or fruit juices should be offered frequently. A small amount of prune juice on a daily basis may prevent constipation, since prune juice acts as a natural laxative.

Children should also be given a high-fiber diet. Fiber absorbs water in the intestines, which results in bulkier, softer stools. Infants over six months of age should be offered daily servings of strained fruits and vegetables. Strained prunes (up to three tablespoons a day) may be especially helpful. In addition, bran flakes can be softened with formula and added to the baby's regular cereal, or one or two teaspoonfuls of dark Karo syrup can be added to each four ounces of formula or milk. High-fiber foods for toddlers include raw and cooked fruits and vegetables, and whole-grain breads and cereals. Foods high in fat, such as milk, cheese, and ice cream, may be constipating and should be limited. Intake of milk or formula should be limited to one quart (32 ounces) per day unless recommended otherwise by the child's physician.

Stool Softeners/Laxatives

If dietary management of constipation has been unsuccessful, a stool softener or laxative may be considered. Many stool softeners or laxatives can be purchased without a prescription, but they should be recommended by a physician. Bulk-forming agents (e.g., malt/barley extracts; psyllium) or stimulants (e.g., senna), or a combination of the two, are safest and most effective for young children. Wetting agents or lubricants, such as milk of magnesia or mineral oil, are not generally recommended for children under three. Stool softeners come in powder, liquid, or granular form and therefore can be added easily to the child's feeding. These preparations should be given on a regular basis (every day or every other day) to prevent constipation.

Suppositories

Suppositories are rarely needed on a regular basis if a stool softener and high-fiber diet are used. Children with paralysis (e.g., spina bifida), however, may require the additional assistance of suppositories since they lack normal anal function. Any child who is immobilized after surgery or has an illness resulting in decreased fluid or food intake may require suppositories on a temporary basis. Glycerin suppositories are the most common type used with young children and come in a child-size form. Liquid glycerin preparations are also available for rectal insertion.

Enemas

Enemas are indicated only when there is severe constipation. Enemas should never be given to an infant or young child without the recommendation of a physician. Too many enemas may disturb the chemical balance in a child's body.

Problems

A physician should be contacted in the following situations:

- The treatment measures are unsuccessful.
- The child has not had a bowel movement in five days.
- The child's abdomen is hard and distended.
- There is blood or mucus in the stool.
- There is persistent diarrhea.

INTESTINAL OSTOMIES

Description

Children who are born with abnormalities of the lower digestive tract and those who develop bowel diseases may require the surgical formation of an ostomy. An ostomy is an artificial opening made through the abdomen into the intestine. It enables waste products to bypass part of the child's digestive tract. An ostomy may be temporary or permanent.

A stoma is the part of the intestine that is seen at the ostomy site (see illustration below). Stool is diverted through the stoma into a pouching system. This is usually a disposable plastic pouch that is held in place over the stoma by self-sticking adhesive. A stoma is bright red to pink. It is not painful, since intestinal tissue does not have nerves that sense pain. With an ostomy, a child does not feel a normal urge to have a bowel movement since stool does not pass through the rectal/anal muscles.

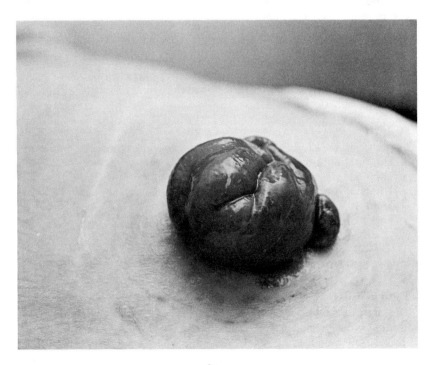

Stoma

An ostomy is named after that portion of the intestine where the ostomy is placed. The small intestine consists of three consecutive sections: the duodenum, jejunum, and ileum. Therefore, an ostomy in the jejunum is called a *jejunostomy*; an ostomy in the ileum is called an *ileostomy*; and an ostomy in the large intestine, or colon, is called a *colostomy* (see illustration). The care of the ostomy is the same no matter where the location. The only difference between the sites is in the character of the stool. Waste products become increasingly more solid as they pass through the digestive tract. Stool from an ileostomy will be liquid and highly erosive to the skin, whereas stool from a colostomy will be semisolid and less irritating. A pouching system should be used in all cases to protect the skin.

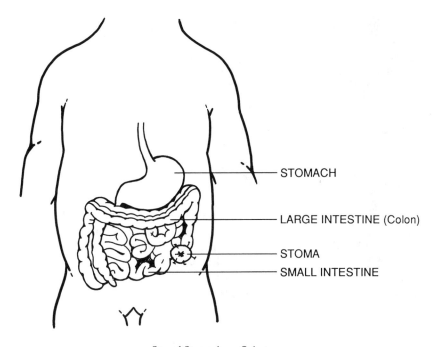

STOMACH

LARGE INTESTINE (Colon)

STOMA

SMALL INTESTINE

Site of Stoma for a Colostomy

Cause

Some of the most common reasons for a colostomy/ileostomy in a young child are listed below.

Hirschsprung Disease

Hirschsprung disease is characterized by a congenital absence of the nerve endings that signal the intestine to propel stool through the colon, rectum, and anus.

Imperforate Anus

Imperforate anus is a congenital malformation of the anus and/or rectum so that there is no exit for stool.

Necrotizing Enterocolitis

Necrotizing enterocolitis is an inflammatory bowel disease found primarily in premature infants of low birth weight who experience other complications, such as respiratory distress or infection. Necrotizing enterocolitis can occur anywhere in the small or large intestine and results in dysfunctional segments of intestine.

Incidence

Both Hirschsprung disease and anal/rectal malformations occur in approximately one in five thousand live births. The occurrence rates of other diseases that necessitate an ostomy vary.

Course

Most ostomies in young children are temporary, lasting a few months to a few years. When the primary condition is alleviated, the bowel is reattached and the ostomy is closed. Surgical correction for Hirschsprung disease and anal/rectal malformations is usually done when the child weighs 20 to 25 pounds (one to one and a half years of age). Once the bowel is reconnected, only a small abdominal scar remains. Stool patterns gradually become normal and toilet training can be accomplished.

Medical Management

Elimination

Both an ileostomy and a colostomy require a one- or two-piece pouching system to collect the stool and protect the skin. This system usually consists of a flexible skin-barrier wafer that is placed around the stoma and a disposable collection pouch that snaps onto or sticks to the wafer.

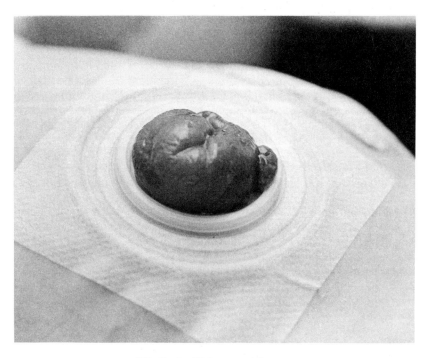

Skin-Barrier Wafer around Stoma

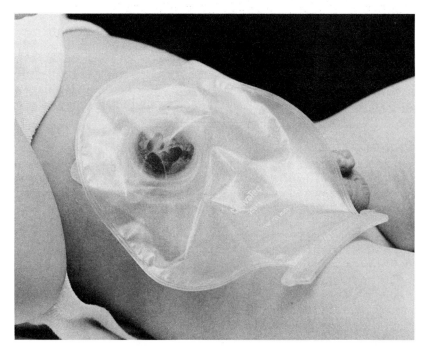

Pouching System on Child

The pouch is open on one end to allow for emptying. A clamp or rubber band keeps it closed during use. The collection pouch is emptied and rinsed three to five times a day. The pouching system itself is changed when it becomes loose or leaks (approximately every two to three days). The skin around the stoma is cleansed with mild soap and water and dried thoroughly before another skin-barrier wafer and pouch are attached. If the child has a temporary colostomy, the lower bowel continues, despite disuse, to secrete mucus. As a result, there may be drainage from the rectum, which diapers or underwear are sufficient to absorb.

Diet and Fluid Intake

The diet of a child with an ostomy should include enough fiber for stool formation. It will be evident which foods the child cannot tolerate and should therefore avoid. Certain vegetables, for example, may cause diarrhea or excessive gas. Small, hard particles of food such as popcorn, nuts, and corn-on-the-cob should be eliminated for toddlers because these foods may cause blockage. Since fluids may be lost quickly because of decreased absorption from the colon, the child needs to drink plenty of liquids. A child with an ileostomy has a precarious fluid and electrolyte balance; a mild case of diarrhea can progress to a life-threatening situation in only a few hours.

Skin Care

Skin care is an important concern while a child has an ostomy. Leaking of intestinal contents is perhaps the most frequent problem. Any itching or burning under the pouching system means there is leakage and the system needs to be changed. The system should be inspected routinely whenever the pouch is emptied to ensure that the pouching system is tightly sealed. If a rash develops or the skin becomes irritated, a physician should be consulted and karaya powder may be prescribed. If leaking persists, assistance should be sought from a public health nurse or at the child's medical center to evaluate the leaking and obtain a new type of pouching system if necessary.

Odor and Gas

Some odor and/or gas is fairly common with a colostomy. The new pouching systems rarely transmit odor from gas or stool unless there is leakage. The plastic snap-on type of system can be opened easily a crack to release gas. Offensive odors can also be controlled by regular changing of the system and thorough cleaning when emptying the pouch. Some families use deodorants specifically designed for these pouching systems.

Activities

The colostomy and ileostomy present no physical limitations. The child may lie on his or her stomach and may be held and handled the same as any other child. Any comfortable clothing may be worn that is not tight around the stoma, since excessively tight clothing may cause irritation or bleeding of the stoma. One-piece suits are recommended for small children to prevent them from purposefully or accidentally dislodging the pouching system during play. The pouch can also be tucked into the child's diaper. The child can be bathed with or without wearing the ostomy pouch. Although swimming is permitted, the edges of the pouching system should be secured with waterproof tape. The child who is at an appropriate developmental level may be involved in the care of the colostomy by handing equipment to the caretaker or by helping to empty the pouch. Such involvement may enhance the child's self-esteem and sense of control.

Problems

The following signs and symptoms should be reported to the parent or primary caretaker, who should then contact the child's physician:
- stoma that appears gray, dark blue, or black
- stoma that is flush with the skin or sunken below the level of the skin
- any unusual outpouching (prolapse) of the stoma
- bleeding from the stoma that lasts longer than five minutes
- redness and/or abrasion of the skin surrounding the stoma
- large amount of watery stools
- no passage of gas or stool from the stoma for 12 to 24 hours
- pencil-thin stools
- bloating (abdominal distention), pain, tenderness, fever, vomiting, or increased irritability

CLEAN INTERMITTENT CATHETERIZATION

Description

Clean intermittent catheterization is a procedure during which a thin tube, or catheter, is inserted into the bladder through the urethra (see illustration of urological anatomy) to empty urine. It is a clean, rather than sterile, procedure. It is done intermittently (four to six times a day) rather than leaving the catheter in place permanently.

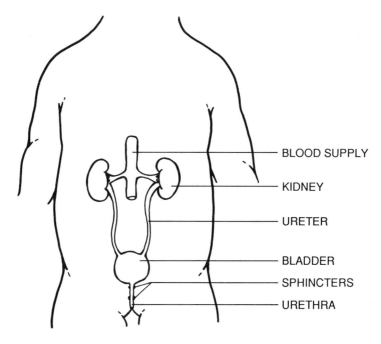

BLOOD SUPPLY

KIDNEY

URETER

BLADDER

SPHINCTERS

URETHRA

Urological Anatomy

The goals of clean intermittent catheterization are as follows:
- *Preserve kidney function.* When the bladder is continually full, pressure forces urine into the ureters (the tubes leading from the kidneys to the bladder), which in turn may create pressure that can damage the kidneys. Catheterization helps to prevent this problem by regularly emptying the bladder.
- *Prevent urinary tract infections.* Urine retained in the bladder provides a warm, dark, moist environment in which bacteria can easily grow.
- *Achieve social continence.* Catheterization helps to avoid the social problems that may be created by constant wetness. Many children can experience dryness with the catheterization procedure.

Cause

The nerves that enable a person to control urination voluntarily are located in the lower part of the spinal cord. Children with spinal cord problems (i.e., spina bifida or spinal cord trauma) usually do not have voluntary control of their bladders. Because the nerves controlling the bladder do not work, the child is said to have a neurogenic bladder. This can lead to retention of urine, which puts pressure on the kidneys and causes urinary tract infections. Over time, these problems may lead to kidney damage. Since these children cannot control urination, they may also be constantly wet and cannot be toilet-trained in the usual way.

Incidence

Spina bifida occurs in approximately three out of every one thousand children. About 90 percent of children with spina bifida have neurogenic bladders. Of those children, a substantial number are eventually managed by clean intermittent catheterization.

Medical Management

Procedure

Good handwashing and clean supplies are necessary before beginning the catheterization procedure. The child's genitals are cleansed with soap and water. A catheter is then inserted into the urethra or urinary opening. (Most children who require catheterizations have decreased sensation in this area so this is not a painful procedure.) The catheter is threaded into the body until urine flows out, indicating that the catheter is in the bladder. When the urine flow stops, the catheter is removed. Some physicians recommend an instillation of antibacterial medication into the bladder before the catheter is removed. The catheter is rinsed with soap and water and can be reused if boiled in water for ten to 15 minutes. The procedure takes five to 15 minutes to complete and needs to be done approximately every four hours during daytime. Although some children stay dry with catheterizations alone, other children require medication in order to avoid wetness between catheterizations.

Self-Catheterization

Children can learn to catheterize themselves when they are between 5 and 12 years of age. Although the age of beginning self-catheterization varies with each child, the average age seems to be around eight years. Mental retardation, visual problems, and fine-motor problems may prevent self-catheterization from being accomplished.

Alternative Treatment

Credé Method. Another method to empty urine from the bladder is manual expression, or Credé method. The Credé method should not be performed on a child unless prescribed and demonstrated by a physician. It involves manually pressing or massaging the lower abdomen over the bladder until urine is expressed. In most cases, catheterization is preferable to the Credé method.

Cutaneous Vesicostomy. A young child who has a high-pressure neurogenic bladder that is not responsive to catheterizations may require a cutaneous vesicostomy. This is a small opening from the bladder through the surface of the abdominal wall. Unfortunately, urine draining directly onto the skin will irritate the abdomen. This problem can be alleviated by having the child wear an ostomy appliance.

Problems

If a urinary tract infection is suspected, the child should be seen by a physician who can do a urinalysis and urine culture. The following can be signs and symptoms of a urinary tract infection:
- persistently cloudy urine
- abnormally smelly urine
- blood in urine
- persistent diaper rash
- fever, chills, irritability, abdominal pain

IMPLICATIONS FOR EDUCATION

Bowel and bladder problems of children can interfere with educational or therapy services. If a young child is constipated, he or she may be quite irritable, making learning activities difficult. Placing an infant in a prone position may provoke crying if that child has a hard, distended abdomen. In addition, feeding intervention may be futile if constipation is contributing to a decreased appetite. A leaking ostomy bag due to improper fit can also make sessions with a child quite unpleasant. If a child is being catheterized, therapy or teaching times may need to be scheduled around the child's catheterization times. Service providers in early intervention may be involved in identifying children who are constipated or who have problems related to their ostomies or catheterizations. They may also be asked to participate in the medical management (i.e., do catheterization) and monitor the effects of that management.

Note: This chapter was adapted, in part, from the chapter entitled "The Colostomy and Ileostomy" by Marcia Henderson and Janet Mapel in the first edition of this book. The author also wishes to acknowledge the assistance of Laura Phearman, R.N., Division of Pediatric Surgery, University of Iowa Hospitals and Clinics.

SEE ALSO

Myelomeningocele

ADDITIONAL RESOURCES

ConvaTec. *Children with Ostomies.* Princeton, N.J.: ConvaTec, 1988. Videotape. Telephone (201) 359-9260.

Learner Managed Designs, Inc. *Clean Intermittent Catheterization.* Lawrence, Kans.: Learner Managed Designs, Inc. 1988. Videotape. Telephone (913) 842-9088.

Bracing

Braces, also known as orthoses, are generally used to assist the child in standing and walking and to prevent contractures or malalignments of joints. Most typically, braces for standing and walking are worn during the day, and those for preventing loss of motion or poor alignment of joints are worn at night.

If a child needs braces, they will be prescribed by an orthopedic specialist, frequently following consultation with a physical therapist. Prescription is based on a variety of factors, including the type and degree of disability, the child's ability to perform functional skills, and his or her age and social-intellectual development.

Recent years have brought many advances in orthotics. New materials and new styles are now available. Lighter, more cosmetic, plastic molded braces are often used in place of the conventional metal designs or are used in combination with limited metal components. In some cases, factors such as growth, material stress, and skin sensitivity make metal braces more desirable. Styles and preferences vary across the country and around the world. The devices described in the next few pages are representative of commonly used braces.

THE SWIVEL WALKER

The swivel walker, such as that designed by the Orthotic Research and Locomotor Assessment Unit in the United Kingdom, is a rigid body brace mounted on swiveling feet. It is used to encourage early standing and walking without crutches or a walker. This brace is prescribed primarily for children with high-spinal-level myelomeningocele or paraplegia, who have little or no use of the muscles of the lower extremities and who often have muscle weakness in the trunk.

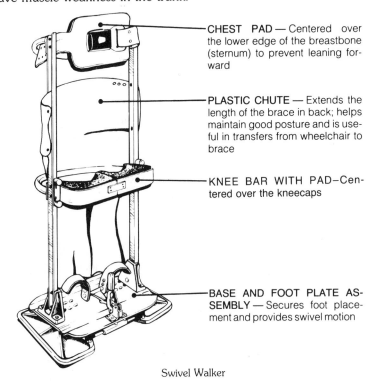

CHEST PAD — Centered over the lower edge of the breastbone (sternum) to prevent leaning forward

PLASTIC CHUTE — Extends the length of the brace in back; helps maintain good posture and is useful in transfers from wheelchair to brace

KNEE BAR WITH PAD—Centered over the kneecaps

BASE AND FOOT PLATE ASSEMBLY — Secures foot placement and provides swivel motion

Swivel Walker

The child can walk with a swivel walker brace, without crutches, by shifting the body weight from side to side. As weight is shifted to one side, the opposite foot plate rises and rotates forward. Swinging the arms with the weight shift increases speed. While a swivel (pivoting) gait pattern is most common, crutches can be used on uneven surfaces with a swing-to (child swings up to the crutches) or a swing-through (child swings past the crutches) gait pattern.

There are no locks at the hips or knees of the swivel walker; therefore, sitting is not possible. However, one experimental variation of the swivel walker combines the base plate assembly of this brace with a parapodium (described below), which does have hip and knee locks. This combination is sometimes used with children who already have parapodiums and are accustomed to being able to sit while in the brace.

THE PARAPODIUM

The Canadian parapodium, a body brace mounted on a platform base, is used for standing and walking with the aid of crutches or a walker. Like the swivel walker, it is worn primarily by children who have high-spinal-level myelomeningocele or paraplegia and, therefore, flaccid or semiflaccid lower extremities and trunk. Hip and knee locks work simultaneously to allow sitting. (The Rochester, New York, variation of the Canadian parapodium allows independent hip and knee joint operation.)

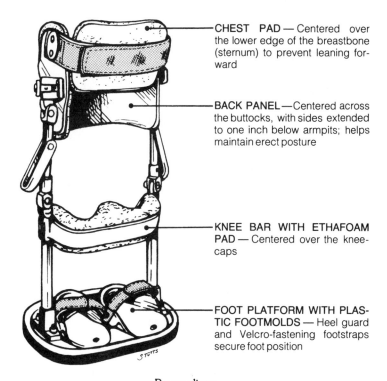

CHEST PAD — Centered over the lower edge of the breastbone (sternum) to prevent leaning forward

BACK PANEL—Centered across the buttocks, with sides extended to one inch below armpits; helps maintain erect posture

KNEE BAR WITH ETHAFOAM PAD — Centered over the kneecaps

FOOT PLATFORM WITH PLASTIC FOOTMOLDS — Heel guard and Velcro-fastening footstraps secure foot position

Parapodium

The child may first pivot-walk with the help of an adult and later be taught to use a walker or crutches to execute a swing-to or swing-through gait pattern. A few children will learn to pivot short distances without the aid of an adult, crutches, or a walker.

Some centers secure polypropylene to the bottom of the parapodium to increase the ease of swivel walking. The standard parapodium has rubber molding on the bottom.

THE RECIPROCATING GAIT ORTHOSIS

The reciprocating gait orthosis (RGO), a plastic molded brace, was first conceived in Canada and later redesigned at Louisiana State University Medical Center. Like the swivel walker and parapodium, it provides the necessary support for children with high-spinal-level myelomeningocele or paraplegia. It has also been tried with some success on children who have other muscular or neuromuscular problems. Unlike the swivel walker and parapodium, the RGO has a cable coupling system connecting two separate leg supports. This allows independent leg motion (reciprocal walking) with a walker or crutches. Other special features of the RGO are the pelvic band design and the composite insert at the ankle.

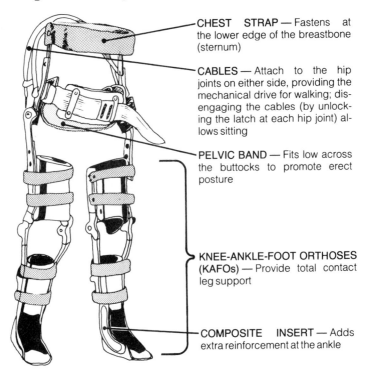

CHEST STRAP — Fastens at the lower edge of the breastbone (sternum)

CABLES — Attach to the hip joints on either side, providing the mechanical drive for walking; disengaging the cables (by unlocking the latch at each hip joint) allows sitting

PELVIC BAND — Fits low across the buttocks to promote erect posture

KNEE-ANKLE-FOOT ORTHOSES (KAFOs) — Provide total contact leg support

COMPOSITE INSERT — Adds extra reinforcement at the ankle

Reciprocating Gait Orthosis (RGO)

To ambulate, the child shifts the body diagonally forward; the resultant traction in the cables causes the opposite leg to swing forward. Weight is then shifted forward onto that leg and the reciprocal pattern of walking progresses. Use of the RGO is perhaps best preceded by use of the parapodium and/or the swivel walker for children with paraplegia from birth. Children should developmentally be at or close to age three before beginning training in the RGO. In contrast, the parapodium or swivel walker is prescribed around a developmental age of one year.

THE HIP-KNEE-ANKLE-FOOT ORTHOSIS

The metal hip-knee-ankle-foot orthosis (HKAFO), as shown below, is composed of long leg braces with a pelvic band. The HKAFO provides support or control at the major joints of the lower extremities—the hip, knee, ankle, and foot. This brace traditionally is attached to high-top shoes but can work with oxford-style shoes. It is used for children with a variety of developmental disabilities (including high-spinal-level myelomeningocele and cerebral palsy) to stretch muscles or other soft tissues or to assist in standing and walking.

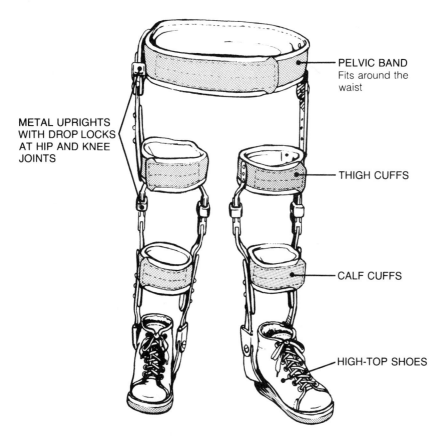

Hip-Knee-Ankle-Foot Orthosis (HKAFO)

Various locks and joint designs are prescribed according to individual needs. The knees are usually locked when the child is standing or walking. The child may use a swing-to, swing-through, or reciprocal (one-leg-at-a-time) gait pattern.

This brace design has been replaced in many facilities with more modern designs using polypropylene and standard street shoes.

KNEE-ANKLE-FOOT ORTHOSES

Knee-ankle-foot orthoses (KAFOs), also known as long leg braces (without pelvic band), are generally used with children who have less functional impairment than children using HKAFOs. Like HKAFOs, KAFOs are used for stretching as well as for standing or walking.

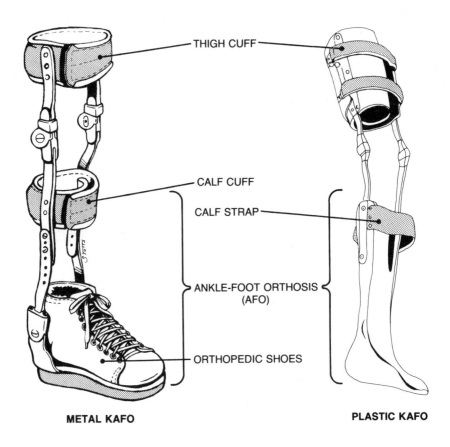

THIGH CUFF

CALF CUFF

CALF STRAP

ANKLE-FOOT ORTHOSIS
(AFO)

ORTHOPEDIC SHOES

METAL KAFO

PLASTIC KAFO

Knee-Ankle-Foot Orthoses (KAFOs)

KAFOs may be made of metal or plastic. While plastic braces are lighter and more cosmetic (they are less bulky and can often be worn inside regular shoes), metal braces can be lengthened and adjusted more easily for growth. The physician and physical therapist will determine which is suitable for an individual child. A swing-to, swing-through, or reciprocal gait pattern may be used with these braces.

ANKLE-FOOT ORTHOSES

Ankle-foot orthoses (AFOs), commonly called short leg braces, are used with a child who has muscular control at the hip and knee but not at the ankle. They are also used with children who threaten to lose joint motion because of spasticity or poor muscle control at the ankle.

The metal AFO has an ankle joint that can be adjusted to control the up-and-down motion of the foot. Styles vary. One design may look like the lower portion of the metal KAFO in the previous figure. The plastic AFO, such as the one shown below, was traditionally molded in a fixed position, at a 90 degree angle. The setting of the ankle joint on either brace can influence motion of the knee joint as well as the ankle. Either brace can be adapted to provide medial-lateral ankle support if needed.

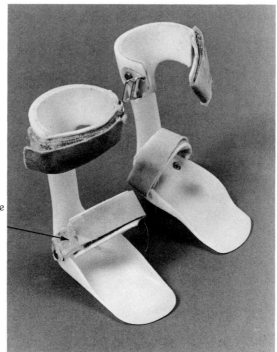

ANKLE STRAP—Secures the heel within the brace

Fixed Molded AFO

Despite the fixed, molded design of these AFOs, the narrow posterior component of these AFOs allows some flexibility at the joint. Many fixed, molded AFOs extend further forward around the ankle.

AFOs may be used for reasons other than walking. When they are used for walking, the child typically walks in a reciprocal pattern with or without crutches or a walker.

Alternative designs of polypropylene AFOs have been made that allow more flexibility at the ankle joint. The appropriateness of these designs for a given child will be decided by the physician and physical therapist. A polypropylene AFO, which supports the foot in a normal position and has localized areas of pressure application and relief, has been called a tone-reducing ankle-foot orthosis (TRAFO). When appropriately designed, TRAFOs are thought to reduce muscle tone in spastic muscles. Whether they act by reducing muscle tone or merely by improving foot mechanics has not been demonstrated. Most AFOs now incorporate the concepts of design used in TRAFOs. Increasingly orthotists (brace makers) can design polypropylene braces according to the child's needs.

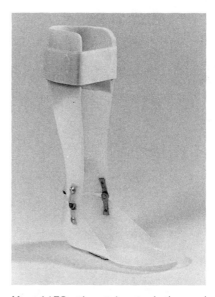

Hinged AFO with unrestricted motion upward and stopped downward motion at a 90 degree position

Hinged AFO with partial motion both up and down

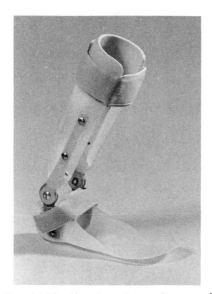

Hinged AFO with spring-action motion upward

Three Designs of Hinged Polypropylene AFOs

TWISTER CABLES

Twister cables are tightly woven coils in a plastic housing used to control the rotation—either inward or outward—of the legs. (Excess inturning of the legs is common in children with cerebral palsy; out-turning is common in children with midlumbar-level myelomeningocele.)

Reciprocal walking with or without crutches is typical with these braces.

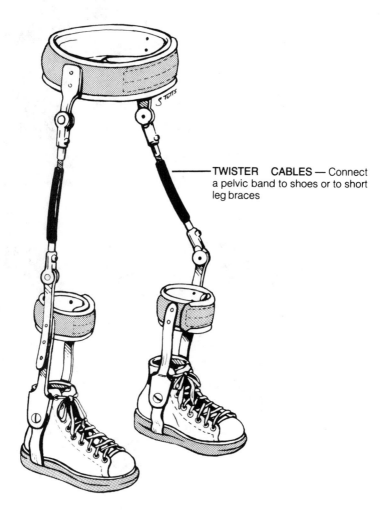

TWISTER   CABLES — Connect a pelvic band to shoes or to short leg braces

Twister Cables with
Pelvic Band and Short Leg Braces

FOOT ORTHOSES

Foot orthoses (FOs) are used with children who primarily need control of medial-lateral, sideways motion at the ankle or foot. There are no joints built into the brace. Motion up and down is possible to a lesser or greater extent depending on the FO design.

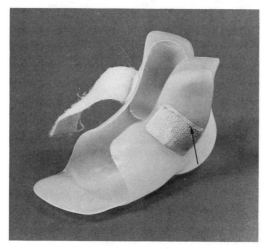

ANKLE STRAP—Restrains the heel in the brace

Supramalleolar FO. *This orthosis goes above the ankle bones (supramalleolar) and therefore could be considered an AFO. Unlike most AFOs it is not intended to control motion up and down; it restricts medial-lateral motion. The extensive lateral support, ankle strap, and anterior projection of the plastic give more support against medial-lateral ankle motion than the other FOs shown.*

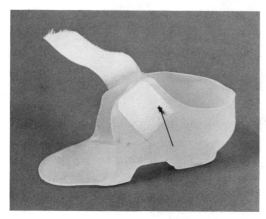

ANKLE STRAP—Restrains the heel in the brace

FO with Low-Cut Side Support. *If the child has a mild foot valgus with weight taken on the inside of the foot, this FO should suffice. It provides less support against undesired medial-lateral motion than the supramalleolar FO.*

FO or Shoe Insert without Side Support. *This FO is sometimes recommended for flat feet or very mild ankle valgus.*

THE BODY SHELL

The total contact body shell is most commonly used with the type of scoliosis caused by neuromuscular disease. This brace is one of a number of devices (thoraco-lumbar-sacral orthoses) designed to prevent progressive spinal deformity.

The body shell is made of plastic or acrylic materials and may be padded on the inside. The one shown here has two pieces—a front and a back shell—that fasten at the sides with Velcro. Many body shells are one-piece devices that open in the front or back and extend higher or lower on the chest. Either type can be worn with other braces and may be used during the day or night or both.

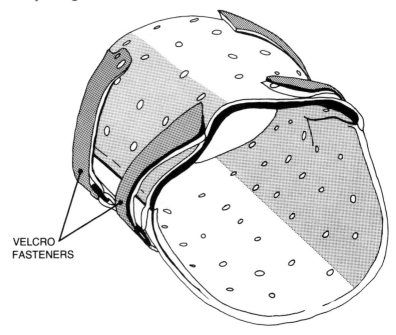

VELCRO
FASTENERS

Body Shell

THE POPE NIGHT SPLINT

Pope night splints help prevent heelcord tightness and joint contractures, which may be caused by muscle imbalance from spasticity or weakness. They are generally worn at night and during naps and are set at 90 degrees (other angles are sometimes recommended).

If a child is wearing a metal or polypropylene AFO during the day, the physican may have the parent apply the same brace at night as an alternative to ordering a second brace.

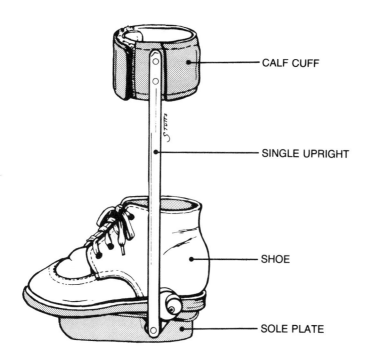

CALF CUFF

SINGLE UPRIGHT

SHOE

SOLE PLATE

Pope Night Splint

THE LORENZ NIGHT SPLINT (ABDUCTION SPLINT)

The Lorenz night splint separates the legs to stretch the adductors, the muscles that bring the legs together. It is usually worn at night and during naps to prevent hip dislocations or partial dislocation (subluxations) in children at risk for malalignments of the hip joints or in children who have had hip surgery. Thigh and pelvic bands are connected by a metal bar that is flared to separate, and sometimes flex, the legs, bringing the thigh bone (femur) and the hip socket (acetabulum) into proper alignment. The brace is generally flexed at the hip for the child who has had hip dislocations from birth (congenitally dislocated hips). In contrast, the child who develops dislocations from muscle imbalance about the hip should be positioned in the brace with the legs separated but not flexed. Flexion contractures are too easily developed in these children. As with most night braces, the Lorenz night splint may be worn for several months or all through the growing years.

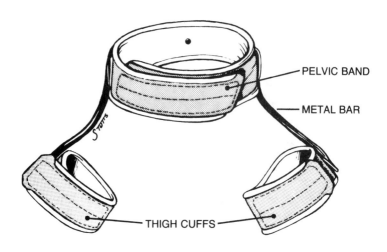

PELVIC BAND

METAL BAR

THIGH CUFFS

Lorenz Night Splint

THE VARIABLE ABDUCTION HKAFO

The variable abduction HKAFO, developed at the University of Rochester, has a specially designed hip joint that can be adjusted to keep the legs apart, together, or at any desired angle between the two extremes. When set to keep the legs apart, this brace (like the Lorenz night splint) promotes good hip alignment. When set to keep the legs together, it can be used as a frame for standing with assistance, but not for walking. Extensions below the knee help maintain full knee extension and neutral foot alignment. The variable abduction HKAFO is often used for several hours at a time—usually at night. It is appropriate mostly for younger children with myelomeningocele.

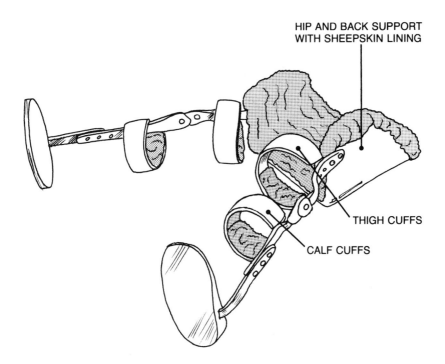

Variable Abduction HKAFO

THE DENIS-BROWNE SPLINT

The Denis-Browne splint (bar) is commonly applied following serial casting in the treatment of clubfoot. It has also been used to treat twisting (torsion) of bones in the legs or feet, although the benefits of such treatment have not been documented. The length of the bar separating the legs can vary, as can the inward or outward direction of the shoe attachment. Special shoes are attached if necessary.

Denis-Browne Splint

SPECIAL SHOE COMPONENTS

Shoes, which ordinarily provide protection from the elements and irregular ground surfaces, are sometimes modified in an attempt to restore foot support and balance during standing or walking. The benefits of special shoes or shoe inserts for the child with a disability have not, however, been confirmed.

Shoes may be specially designed, or regular shoes may be altered, either internally or externally. Common modifications in children's shoes include the addition of components that support the arch or shift body weight laterally. Three such modifications are the Thomas heel, the medial wedge, and the cookie insert.

The Thomas Heel

The Thomas heel is an external modification used with children who have valgus alignment, and outward turning of the feet and bear their weight on the medial foot surface. The medial extension of the heel supports the longitudinal arch, helps rotate the foot inward, and shifts body weight to the center during walking. (A reverse Thomas heel has an extension on the lateral heel surface. It is used for foot varus—inward turning of the feet.)

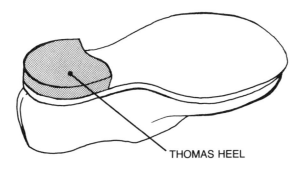

THOMAS HEEL

Thomas Heel

The Medial Wedge

The medial wedge is an external addition to the heel, sole, or both to provide lateral weight shift for treatment of foot valgus. Lateral wedges shift weight medially for treatment of foot varus.

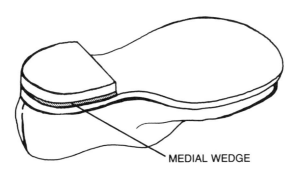

MEDIAL WEDGE

Medial Wedge

Cookie Insert (Arch Insole or Scaphoid Pad)

The cookie insert, an internal modification made of leather or firm sponge material, is placed in the shoe under the inside arch borders to provide support for the longitudinal arch.

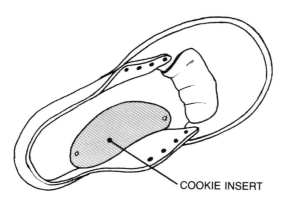

COOKIE INSERT

Cookie Insert

INHIBITIVE CASTING

Inhibitive casting has been used by some physical therapists as an adjunct to dynamic treatment; the cast keeps the foot in normal alignment and inhibits unwanted reflexes or muscle tone, allowing the therapist to focus on developing normal movement patterns throughout the rest of the body.

Inhibitive casts are used most for children with cerebral palsy, just before they begin to walk. They are replaced by TRAFOs or AFOs once the child is walking. Since alternative AFO designs have been developed, the use of casts has decreased. Physicians and physical therapists may choose to order AFOs from the beginning.

Inhibitive Casting

IMPLICATIONS FOR EDUCATION

The use of braces, shoes, or casts is only one facet of a therapeutic program for children with disabilities. It is generally accompanied by regular range-of-motion exercises and other physical therapy treatments.

Systematic training in ambulation and in performing functional skills—applying and removing ("donning" and "doffing") the brace, rolling over, and attaining a standing position—is best done by a qualified physical therapist. Educators may be asked to ensure that new skills are put into practice in the classroom.

While a brace can assist a young child, caution is necessary to prevent problems. For instance, metal components of braces should not remain in contact with the skin. Also, because a new brace can cause redness or irritation, it should be applied for gradually increasing time periods until the child develops brace tolerance—a process that may take a few weeks. This is especially important if the child has a sensory deficit. The child's skin should be inspected for reddened, irritated, or ulcerated areas, and any skin problems should be reported immediately. Braces should be checked for correct fit every four to six months, depending on the child's growth rate, by an orthopedic physician or a physical therapist.

Brain Imaging Techniques

COMPUTERIZED TOMOGRAPHY

Computerized tomography (CT) scanning is a radiological technique that allows for precise examination of internal body structures. With ordinary X-ray, a single beam passes through the body and strikes an X-ray film, producing a photographic negative. In contrast, a CT scanner passes multiple X-ray beams through the body at different angles, generating, with the use of a computer, a composite image. A series of images generally is made, displaying numerous cross-sections ("slices") of any part of the body. This technique makes it possible to focus clearly on structures as small as two millimeters thick.

Continuous CT images (cine CT) are used to assess moving structures such as the airway during the respiratory cycle.

A child or infant must remain perfectly still during the scanning procedure. Initially, this took up to 20 minutes, and children had to be sedated with medication; some even required a general anesthetic. CT scanners now operate much more rapidly—about three seconds per slice. However, sedation with medication (with possible, though rare, complications or side effects) is still necessary with children who are likely to move. Depending on the degree of sedation required and the period of time necessary for it to wear off, these children may need to remain at the scanning facility for up to several hours. At times, particularly with small infants, hospital admission may be advisable. Occasionally, dye is injected through a vein to enhance the CT image.

CT scanning, like an ordinary X-ray, is painless. While the amount of radiation associated with this technique exceeds that of an ordinary X-ray, the small amount of tissue exposed keeps the dosage within an acceptable range.

CT scanning of children has been used primarily for quick identification of abnormalities in the brain and its coverings, including tumors, bleeding, infection, hydrocephalus, or various congenital abnormalities.

CT scanning has to a large extent replaced other, more complicated radiographic procedures, such as pneumoencephalography (which involves injecting air into the spaces within the brain) and cerebral angiography (which involves injecting X-ray contrast materials into blood vessels going to the brain).

Besides being rapid and accurate, CT scanning imparts much more information than is attainable from ordinary X-rays. Too, the results are available immediately. CT scanning is not painful and carries considerably less risk of complication than do procedures such as pneumoencephalography and cerebral angiography.

MAGNETIC RESONANCE

The magnetic resonance (MR) technique is based on the tendency of hydrogen ions in body tissues to "line up" when placed in a strong magnetic field. When lined up, the ions react in a predictable manner to various radio frequencies. This produces a "map" of hydrogen ion densities, which, when processed by a computer, creates pictures of the scanned portion of the body. A major advantage of MR scanning is that there is no radiation exposure. Also, the same equipment can create several different diagnostically useful images simultaneously.

ULTRASONOGRAPHY

Ultrasonic waves, sound waves that vibrate at such high frequencies that they are not audible to the human ear, are bounced off body tissues (a particular organ, a tumor, a developing fetus). Their "echoes" are transmitted electronically to a screen, creating a realistic image that can be photographed or viewed directly. This technique is used for determining gestational age, for prenatal diagnosis of birth defects, and for detecting bleeding into the brain and resultant hydrocephalus in premature infants. There is no radiation (X-ray) exposure with ultrasound. Used appropriately, it is considered to be quite safe.

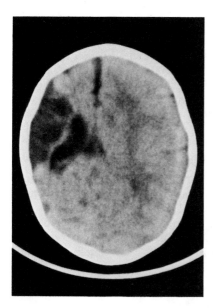

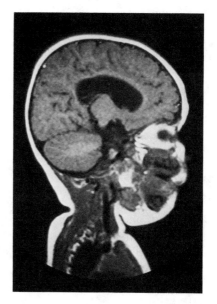

CT Scan. *The dark area in the upper left (parietal) area of the CT image represents tissue death and scarring from a prenatal stroke. The child was left with a hemiplegia of the opposite side of the body.*

Magnetic Resonance Image. *This child experienced severe birth asphyxia with resultant brain atrophy (shrinkage) and enlargement of the fluid-filled spaces (ventricles) in the center of the brain (dark area).*

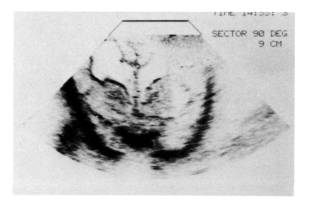

Head Ultrasound. *This premature infant sustained a grade IV intraventricular hemorrhage with resultant destruction of brain tissue and formation of a fluid-filled porencephalic cyst (the light round area in the upper left portion of the ultrasound image).*

BRAIN MAPPING

Multiple electroencephalogram (EEG) electrodes and computerized analysis of the EEG signals are used to generate maps of frequency and voltage (evoked potential). Areas of abnormality show up in shades of gray or a color different from that of normal areas. This relatively new technique holds promise as a clinical tool in the evaluation of children with behavioral and developmental disorders.

POSITRON EMISSION TOMOGRAPHY

Like CT scanning, positron emission tomography (PET) scanning visualizes brain "slices." However, this technique has an added advantage: it measures the metabolism of each small area of the brain. With PET scanning, physicians may be able to determine which parts of the brain are affected during various disease states, thereby learning more about such conditions as epilepsy, metabolic diseases, and certain psychiatric disorders.

Brain Malformations

Although alterations in brain development can result from a variety of genetic and metabolic diseases, this discussion covers only major structural defects that can occur during embryonic and fetal life. Such congenital malformations of the nervous system comprise a spectrum of disorders ranging from anencephaly, a lethal condition, to microscopic alterations in brain structure, which are generally compatible with life but may cause anything from mild learning disorders to severe mental retardation.

ANENCEPHALY

Evident at birth, anencephaly is characterized by the absence of the cerebral hemispheres and the overlying bones of the skull. Infants with this condition usually are either stillborn or alive for only a few days.

HYDRANENCEPHALY

With hydranencephaly, the cerebral hemispheres are absent, and the space is filled with fluid. At birth the infant may look normal; however, if a light is held next to the head in a dark room, much of the fluid-filled skull will be illuminated. The brain stem, responsible for the basic processes of life (such as breathing), is well formed and operational. Without higher cortical functioning, however, there can be no voluntary motor or intellectual development. Also, seizures may occur. These infants often die before reaching one year of age, though a few survive beyond that time in a very primitive state of functioning.

HOLOPROSENCEPHALY

Among the numerous defects that may occur during the process of differentiation and growth of the cerebral hemispheres is holoprosencephaly. Children with this condition have a single cerebral sphere instead of the usual paired structures. As a result, they have severe motor and mental defects and rarely survive past infancy. Some children with holoprosenecephaly have been found to have chromosomal abnormalities.

AGENESIS OF THE CORPUS CALLOSUM

Normally, the two cerebral hemispheres are connected by a midline fiber tract called the corpus callosum. The child in whom this structure fails to form may have difficulty transferring information from one cerebral hemisphere to the other. This may become more problematic with age, as it becomes necessary to process information requiring input from both hemispheres. In some individuals, agenesis of the corpus callosum is associated with other severe central nervous system malformations that may cause seizures, developmental delay, and hydrocephalus. This disorder is typically diagnosed using computerized tomography.

PORENCEPHALIC CYST

A cystlike expansion of the lateral ventricle, a fluid-filled space in the brain, can result from a defect in the development of the cerebral mantle (cortex) or from local damage to the brain during fetal life or early infancy. Depending on the size and location of the cyst, a child may have motor, sensory, or visual defects. If the cyst is in one hemisphere only, these problems are evident on the opposite side of the body. For instance, a child with a left porencephalic cyst might have muscular stiffness (spastic hemiplegia) on the right side.

ENCEPHALOCELE

A malformation that occurs very early in the development of the nervous system is encephalocele, a condition similar to myelomeningocele in that there is a defect in the skull through which the brain, brain covering (meninges), or both, extend. This defect is usually at the back of the head but may occur in other parts of the skull as well. Unlike other defects in brain development, encephalocele can usually be repaired surgically—unless there are other major malformations.

Encephalocele may be accompanied by hydrocephalus, which necessitates a shunt. If only the meninges protrude through the skull, there is a 60 percent chance the infant will have normal intelligence and motor function. If the brain is involved also, chances for normal intelligence drop to 10 percent.

MICROCEPHALY

Developmental abnormalities or destructive processes in the fetus or newborn may result in poor growth of the entire brain, a condition that is not treatable. A head circumference that is less than two standard deviations below the mean suggests abnormality; one that is three or more standard deviations below is a clear indication. Causes for microcephaly include recessive inheritance, chromosomal abnormalities, certain teratogens (e.g., radiation, alcohol), intrauterine infections (e.g., rubella), anoxia at birth, and severe malnutrition.

MEGALOCEPHALY

Megalocephaly is a rare condition in which there is excessive brain growth resulting in unusually rapid enlargement of the head. The growth is due to an increase in supportive tissues rather than an increase in the brain cells themselves. Megalocephaly must be differentiated from hydrocephalus and certain metabolic diseases that also cause excessive enlargement of the head. Severe mental deficiency is common.

SEE ALSO

Brain Imaging Techniques, Hydrocephalus, Myelomeningocele, and *Teratogens*

Bronchopulmonary Dysplasia

DESCRIPTION

Bronchopulmonary dysplasia (BPD), sometimes called chronic lung disease of the premature infant, is a condition characterized by chronic lung changes in infants who had respiratory distress syndrome and/or required prolonged mechanical ventilation and high concentrations of oxygen. Full-term infants with meconium aspiration, pneumonia, or other causes of respiratory distress may develop BPD. Infants with BPD require oxygen for at least 28 days, and their chest X-rays show the typical abnormalities.

CAUSE

BPD results both from the initial injury to the lungs and from its treatment. Irritation to the lungs from inflammation is compounded by the repeated pounding pressures delivered by a ventilator for weeks to months. Extra oxygen, while needed to maintain adequate blood levels, can itself further damage the lungs. Thus, a vicious cycle is set in motion whereby continuing mechanical ventilation and supplemental oxygen are necessary but further exacerbate the disease. Nevertheless, these treatments must continue until the infant's lungs heal and new, normal air sacs (alveoli) grow.

INCIDENCE

The more preterm the infant at birth, the more likely the development of BPD. As many as 80 percent of infants born weighing less than 1,000 grams (2.2 pounds) will develop BPD, in contrast to only 10 percent of those weighing over 1,500 grams (3.3 pounds). The mortality rate for infants with BPD is about 20 percent in the first year of life. Most affected infants die while in the hospital, but 8 percent die after discharge. Common causes of death include irreversible damage to the lungs and heart, lower respiratory tract infections, and sudden death with no apparent cause. Although improved early treatment of all causes of respiratory distress in newborns may reduce the incidence and severity of BPD, prevention efforts must focus on cutting the high rate of preterm births.

DETECTION

The most common symptom of BPD is an increased respiratory effort and rate. Listening to the lungs one hears wheezing, honks, and crackles. Infants on ventilators have periodic episodes of blue spells that require increases in oxygen delivery and respiratory support. They tend to retain carbon dioxide in the blood and need supplemental oxygen, often for long periods after hospital discharge. Chest X-rays show signs of chronic inflammation and scarring, overexpansion because of air trapping, and sometimes an enlarged heart because of the extra work it has to do to pump blood through damaged lungs.

COURSE

BPD, by definition, is a chronic disease lasting many months to years with manifestations that can be mild to severe. An infant with mild disease may be discharged from the hospital when other problems, such as feeding, have resolved. In severe cases, the child may remain in the hospital for over a year. With moderate disease, the child may go home but require a high level of medical support, sometimes provided by the parents alone or in conjunction with home nursing assistance. As the child improves, the features of BPD improve, but very gradually. Setbacks are common.

ACCOMPANYING HEALTH PROBLEMS

BPD is one of the most complex health conditions because so many body systems are affected by the disease and its treatments. In addition to the complications of prematurity or other perinatal events discussed in other chapters of this book, there are health problems specifically related to BPD.

Infection

Infants with BPD are particularly susceptible to lower respiratory tract infections (especially with respiratory syncytial virus). Recurrent otitis media (ear infections) may lead to conductive hearing loss.

Kidney Stones

BPD is treated commonly with diuretics such as furosemide (Lasix), which leads to calcium deposition and stone formation in the kidneys.

Fragile Bones

Because of feeding problems and some of the medications used, the bones may not mineralize as they should and thus are susceptible to fractures. Rickets, a bone disease caused by insufficient calcium and vitamin D, is commonly seen on X-ray.

Abnormalities of the Trachea

Infection and irritation from the tube placed in the trachea to ventilate the infant mechanically may cause narrowing and collapse. A tracheostomy (an opening through the tissues of the neck into the trachea) is placed if the child has difficulty moving air through the damaged trachea or if it is anticipated that the child will need prolonged ventilator support.

Vomiting and Feeding Problems

Infants with BPD often have gastroesophageal reflux; that is, the highly acid stomach contents back up abnormally into the esophagus, causing irritation, pain, and the risk that they will back up far enough to spill into the trachea, producing aspiration pneumonia. Treatments include positioning, thickened feedings, or at times a gastrostomy and Nissen fundoplication to prevent reflux. Infants who have been fed for long periods by tube (either nasogastric or gastrostomy) and have had unpleasant oral experiences (e.g., suctioning and tubes) frequently resist attempts at oral feedings.

Poor Growth

Because of feeding problems, food intolerance, repeated setbacks from infections or respiratory complications, and excessive caloric needs for increased energy expenditures and "catch up" growth, infants with BPD will tend to fall and remain well below the fifth percentile on weight and weight-for-length growth charts. Persistent attention to growth is needed to avoid possibly permanent injury to tissues, especially those of the central nervous system.

High Blood Pressure

Damage to the kidneys and lungs predisposes to high blood pressure. This should be monitored on a regular basis.

Psychosocial Problems

Family stress may be caused by the health problems associated with BPD and contribute to them. Inattention to this issue will increase the risk of a poor outcome for the child. Not the least of concerns is the financial support needed to maintain an infant with BPD in the hospital and the home.

Development at Risk

The list of possible reasons why a child with BPD may lag in development is lengthy. Preconceptual factors and complications of pregnancy, delivery, early postnatal life, and treatment are major risk factors for poor developmental outcome. However, with a chronic disease such as BPD, the environment must be optimized so as to minimize the negative effects of the disease process, which will continue throughout the most important developmental years. Creative ways must be sought to allow a child tied to a ventilator to move and interact with people without jeopardizing respiratory status, to allow a child a variety of experiences outside the hospital room, and to allow a child opportunities for attachment and healthy emotional development. It is in this area where the most regrettable, avoidable damage can be done if heroic efforts are not made to normalize the environment insofar as possible.

MEDICAL MANAGEMENT

Optimal health care requires a coordinated effort among medical specialists, nurses, therapists, and other support professionals. When the child with BPD is discharged, interaction must occur between community service providers and the hospital team. Planning for discharge should begin early so that the transition is smooth and the child's health is never compromised. Health issues to be addressed include nutrition, respiratory status, oxygen therapy, medications, cardiopulmonary resuscitation, and routine health maintenance.

IMPLICATIONS FOR EARLY INTERVENTION

Children with BPD have the same needs as other high-risk children but have ongoing medical complexity superimposed. The needs in BPD apply to the family as well as the child. Assistance is needed with coordination of care from many sources, finances, respite care, and emotional support. Developmental support must be begun in the hospital and integrated into the general care plan even during periods of health instability, which may last for months. The community developmental team should participate in discharge planning, becoming familiar with the safest and most effective ways to encourage interaction with people and the environment. In-service training on monitors, ventilators, oxygen equipment, gastrostomies, and tracheostomies will afford more comfort in dealing with medically complex infants and toddlers. Not all early intervention professionals will be expected to handle equipment; but knowing what it is, how it works, and what it does for the child can help make suggestions on developmental support more meaningful and realistic.

ADDITIONAL RESOURCES

Ahman, E. *Home Care for the High Risk Infant*. Rockville, Md.: Aspen Publishers, Inc., 1986.

American Lung Association. *BPD: Parent Guide to Bronchopulmonary Dysplasia*. Available from local chapter of the American Lung Association.

Cerebral Palsy

DESCRIPTION

Cerebral palsy, sometimes called chronic, nonprogressive, neurological injury, is a disorder of muscle control or coordination resulting from injury to the brain during its early (fetal, perinatal, and early childhood) stages of development. The major functional problems experienced by individuals with cerebral palsy are difficulties in mobility and communication. There may be associated problems with intellectual, visual, or other functions.

With cerebral palsy, the problem lies in the brain's inability to control the muscles; the muscles themselves and the nerves connecting them to the spinal cord are perfectly normal. The extent and location of brain injury determine the type and distribution of cerebral palsy.

Spasticity

Stiffness of the muscles (hypertonia) occurs when the injury is on the brain surface (motor cortex) or when it involves those nerves leading from the surface through the substance of the brain (corticospinal, or pyramidal, tract) and into the spinal cord. Spasticity is present in about 60 percent of all cases of cerebral palsy.

Dyskinesia

Dyskinesia, which accounts for roughly 20 percent of all cases of cerebral palsy, is caused by injury to the basal ganglia area, the brain's motor switchboard. *Dyskinesia* is a term describing the unwanted, involuntary movements of cerebral palsy. These include slow writhing movements, particularly of the wrist and fingers (athetosis), which may be accompanied by more abrupt and jerky movements (choreoathetosis). Another form of dyskinesia comprises slow, rhythmic movements involving the trunk or an entire extremity (dystonia). All three forms are more prominent with voluntary activity or emotional stress. Dyskinesia is sometimes accompanied by increased muscle tone, or "tension," which also varies with body position and emotional state.

Ataxia

Occurring by itself in about 1 percent of all cerebral palsy, ataxia is characterized by a broad-based, lurching gait with primary balance difficulties. The injury is in the cerebellum.

Mixed

Approximately 30 percent of individuals with cerebral palsy have a combination of spasticity and dyskinesia or ataxia, with one type predominating.

With the spastic type of cerebral palsy, the following terms are used to denote which parts of the body are affected:

- *diplegia*—involvement of the trunk and all four extremities (the legs more so than the arms)
- *hemiplegia*—involvement of one side of the body only
- *paraplegia*—involvement of the legs only
- *quadriplegia*—involvement of both arms, both legs, the head, and the trunk

There are also cases of *monoplegia*—involvement of one extremity—and *triplegia*—involvement of three extremities, but these are unusual.

Some children with cerebral palsy have severe disabilities; others have barely detectable problems with muscle control. There is no universally used, objective method by which physicians or therapists can adequately categorize patients as having mild, moderate, or severe degrees of motor dysfunction. Such estimates are usually made subjectively.

CAUSE

Cerebral palsy results from brain dysfunction due to events such as stroke during fetal life, lack of oxygen at birth, or intracranial hemorrhage or meningitis during infancy. Up to 40 percent of cases of cerebral palsy may occur in low-birth-weight infants or preterm births. Another 25 percent are attributable to perinatal asphyxia in term infants. The remaining causes include congenital and perinatal infection, genetic factors, brain malformation, endocrine disorders, and in utero exposure to toxic substances. At times, an exact cause cannot be pinpointed. Some cases, attributed to complications at birth, actually had their origins prenatally. A newborn infant, for example, may have difficulty breathing because of an injury to the brain sustained during the previous nine months of gestation.

The type of cerebral palsy is related to three factors: the causal event, the timing of this event, and the location of the damage. For example, an intracranial hemorrhage in a susceptible premature infant may damage the corticospinal and associated tracts, causing spasticity. Or high levels of bilirubin—a product of the breakdown of red blood cells—may damage the basal ganglia in newborns, resulting in athetosis.

INCIDENCE

The incidence of cerebral palsy varies with different studies. The most often quoted figure is 1.5 to 2 per thousand live births. The incidence is higher in areas where there is inadequate prenatal care and accompanying prematurity.

DETECTION

The diagnosis of cerebral palsy is made on the basis of a history of delayed achievement of motor milestones, observation of abnormal movement, and abnormal findings in the physical examination (e.g., stiffness, very active knee jerks, persistent primitive reflexes).

Spasticity or dyskinesia are not always evident during the first few months of life. However, most cases of cerebral palsy can be detected by 12 months, nearly all by 18 months. Some children with abnormalities of posture and movement in the early months reportedly outgrow them; but this, except in mild cases, is rare.

Infants who experienced a significant lack of oxygen or were extremely small at birth may not show clear signs of neuromotor involvement in early infancy when the nervous system is immature. Such infants require careful periodic assessment from birth to detect the first signs of cerebral palsy, if they occur, so that the affected child may be introduced to early intervention services in a timely manner. The majority of the "at risk" infants, however, will not have cerebral palsy. Newer neurobehavioral assessment techniques may assist in distinguishing between those infants with transient motor abnormalities and those who will have persistent difficulties.

Other factors besides insufficient age can make the diagnosis difficult. These include the following factors.

Prematurity

An infant born too early or too small must be given extra time to achieve certain skills. For example, the infant born two months early may be normal but just not sitting up within the normal range of expected times for full-term infants.

Extremes of Normal Range

Some babies sit at four months, others not until nine months; yet both groups may fall within the normal range. Only when the skill is not being performed after the outer limits of "normal" are reached or when there is a constellation of abnormal signs can we infer that something is wrong.

Quality of Performance

Some infants have the ability to manipulate objects at the expected age, yet the manner in which they do so may indicate an abnormality. That is why experienced examiners must observe *how* as well as *when* infants perform motor activities. Since the diagnosis of cerebral palsy is based on clinical judgment and not on blood tests, X-rays, or the like, the observations of skilled examiners are necessary to make or confirm the diagnosis during infancy.

Effects of Motor Impairment

Children with cerebral palsy, like infants with general developmental delay, often do not perform expected motor tasks at age-appropriate times. It is critically important, however, to differentiate between these two groups of children. The basic indicator is that the generally developmentally delayed child's abilities are depressed in all areas, whereas the child with cerebral palsy may be very depressed in motor activities yet have good socialization and receptive language skills.

The Belief That "They Will Grow Out of It"

At times, parents are falsely reassured that, given time, an infant's motor delays will resolve on their own. Also, the physician may be reluctant to make a firm diagnosis of cerebral palsy on the basis of one office visit, particularly if the child is very young. If there is doubt, the wisest course is to re-examine the child at frequent intervals or to make a referral to persons highly experienced in developmental and neurological assessment. The advantages of early treatment if the child does have cerebral palsy— or the relief and reassurance if the child does not—are well worth the extra effort.

COURSE

During infancy, the manifestations of brain injury often change. The initially floppy (hypotonic) baby, for example, can later show signs of spasticity. Sometimes athetosis is not evident until the child is older. For this reason, diagnosis may not be exact in early infancy but may be revised as the child's neuromotor status evolves.

Cerebral palsy is the result of a permanent brain injury and is therefore lifelong. While the brain damage itself is nonprogressive, the resultant muscle control problems are not. However, their progress can be halted— or at least postponed—with proper therapy, including frequent elongation of stiff muscles and proper positioning. In some cases, surgery is necessary to release tight muscles and tendons, particularly of the ankles and hips, or to treat dislocations of the hips. Other orthopedic disorders, such as scoliosis and contractures of the joints, may become more problematic as the child gets older.

When appropriate therapy is available during the child's developing years, the parents can expect to see continued gains in muscle control, strength, and awareness of how certain motor skills are performed; such gains will result in improved ability to move, feed, dress, toilet, or communicate. The rate of this improvement, however, is greatly dependent upon the type of cerebral palsy, the way it is distributed, the degree of muscle involvement, and the presence of associated problems.

Children with cerebral palsy—provided they have comprehensive evaluation, care, and treatment—can look forward to an average longevity. All previous data supporting a shortened life span have been faulted by the inclusion of large numbers of individuals who, at an early age, were placed in institutions where they received less than adequate care.

ACCOMPANYING HEALTH PROBLEMS

Events causing brain injury around the time of birth are seldom so site-specific that they bring about only one kind of clinical problem. There are often injuries to different areas of the brain, each of which controls different functions. Associated problems include the following.

Behavior Problems

Some children may be inactive and unresponsive; others may over-react to mild stimulation. Exaggerated startle responses or other tonic reflexes, feeding difficulties, and routine illnesses contribute to difficulties in caring for and nurturing the young child with cerebral palsy.

Constipation

Inactivity and lack of dietary bulk result, commonly, in constipation. This may result in irritability and poor feeding. This problem usually responds to added fiber intake and/or stool softeners.

Dental Disease

Although dental cavities are not more common among children with cerebral palsy (provided they are exposed to fluoride), malocclusions, dental irregularities, and fractured teeth can be found. Of most importance, lengthy and prolonged bottle feedings of milk or juice promote the decay of the primary upper front teeth and first molars.

Eating Disorders and Feeding Problems

Because the motor disorder in cerebral palsy involves the muscles of the tongue, lips, jaws, and the upper esophagus, many children with cerebral palsy have biting, chewing, and swallowing disorders. These disorders often require the evaluation and generation of special eating or feeding programs by therapists trained in these disorders.

Hearing Impairment

Cerebral palsy, particularly the type associated with brain damage due to excess bilirubin, may produce hearing deficits. Hearing ability should therefore be carefully monitored. Also, children with motor problems may spend a large percentage of their time in a recumbent position; this makes them more susceptible to middle ear infections and persistent fluid in the middle ear, which can cause a conductive hearing loss.

Mental Retardation

Around 60 to 70 percent of all children with cerebral palsy are mentally retarded. This problem is seen less often with spastic diplegia.

Musculoskeletal Problems

Abnormalities of muscle tone (hypertonicity and imbalance of tone between antagonistic muscle groups) affect development of the musculoskeletal system. Potential problems in young children include shortening of the Achilles tendon (the feet are held in a downward position), shortening of the hip adductors (the legs cannot be spread apart), dislocation of the hips, and scoliosis (spinal curvature).

Seizures

The brain injury that results in cerebral palsy often causes scarring on the cortex, a source of chronic irritation that may precipitate seizure activity in 35 to 45 percent (some studies report 60 percent) of persons with cerebral palsy. All types of seizures are reported, grand mal the most frequently.

Visual Impairments

As many as 50 percent of all children with spastic cerebral palsy have an eye muscle imbalance problem; refractive errors are almost as common.

MEDICAL MANAGEMENT

The Interdisciplinary Approach

Because the problems associated with cerebral palsy are numerous and complex, treatment involves the integrated efforts of specialists from many disciplines.

The physical therapist works to facilitate motor development, to prevent or slow orthopedic problems (such as limited range of motion or dislocation of joints), and to improve posture and positioning so that the child may engage more profitably in other types of interventional activities.

The occupational therapist teaches parents to handle the child's daily living activities, such as toileting, feeding, and dressing.

Both the physical and occupational therapists may help select appropriate equipment, such as special chairs and eating utensils, to facilitate independence and learning.

The speech pathologist monitors the child's progress in speech and language skills. While it is unlikely that speech therapy per se will be initiated before age three, this specialist counsels parents and other therapists on how to stimulate language development and may also work with the occupational therapist in managing feeding problems.

The psychologist or social worker can assist the family in managing behavioral concerns as well as family stress. With very medically complex children, help is needed in interpreting the input from many health and therapeutic service providers.

Also important is the primary physician, who treats the usual childhood disorders and helps prevent many health problems from occurring. Depending on the nature of the associated problems, a variety of physician subspecialists may also be involved with the child: an orthopedist to prescribe braces or perform surgical procedures, an ophthalmologist to treat crossed eyes (strabismus), a neurologist to help control seizures.

Muscle Relaxants

Certain drugs are helpful in cases of hypertonia. The three most commonly used are diazepam, dantrolene, and baclofen. Diazepam (Valium) acts on the central nervous system rather than directly on the muscle. This drug is useful for treating spinal cord injury as well as cerebral palsy.

Dantrolene (Dantrium) works directly on the muscle, reducing contraction. It is especially useful with children whose care is made difficult by prolonged muscle contraction and who will not be troubled by a reduction in voluntary muscle power. This drug may affect liver function; therefore, frequent tests of liver function should be performed.

Baclofen (Lioresal) acts mainly on the spinal cord to relieve increased muscle tone and muscle spasms. It is used primarily with spinal cord lesions and occasionally for cerebral palsy. The most common side effect is sedation, which tends to disappear a few days after the initial doses.

Controversial Therapies

Neurodevelopmental therapy, the most widely used method of physical therapy; sensory integrative therapy; patterning; relaxation and biofeedback; and electrical stimulation of muscles, spinal cord, and cerebellum are examples of approaches toward reducing the effects of damage to the central nervous system. All have a theoretical basis, but, unfortunately, none is supported by controlled studies that document long-term efficacy despite the positive claims by proponents. Parents and professionals should be cautious and skeptical about treatments until there is scientifically derived evidence of their efficacy. There are many examples in history of therapies thought to be efficacious that ultimately were shown to be harmful.

Selective dorsal (or posterior) rhizotomy is a neurosurgical procedure in which certain sensory nerve roots adjacent to the spinal cord in the lumbosacral (lower back) area are cut. This reduces the sustained muscle contraction or spread of that contraction to other muscle groups seen in spasticity. The best candidates appear to be those children with pure spasticity (no dyskinetic components), especially spastic diplegia, who have no orthopedic contractures. Although initial results appear promising, controlled long-term studies are necessary before this procedure can be accepted as an appropriate treatment for some children with cerebral palsy.

IMPLICATIONS FOR EDUCATION

Some children with cerebral palsy have normal intelligence, which is masked by severe motor impairment. (With motorically handicapped individuals, accurate assessment of cognitive abilities can be difficult.) Most, however, have some degree of cognitive delay. Both groups require a program and environment that is optimal for learning. When devising a home- or center-based learning program, educators need to consider the limitations brought about by the child's motor and possible cognitive deficits; unrealistic expectations can be frustrating to both child and parents. Educators need to be especially patient with these children; studies show that they require a longer than usual period to respond to a request.

Most children with cerebral palsy should avoid constant sitting, especially "W" sitting; instead they should assume different positions in order to prevent further tightening of muscles. Too, they need proper equipment to facilitate eye-hand coordination, necessary for learning and for the performance of self-help skills. Application of assisting technology can be of significant help to persons with cerebral palsy. Communication, mobility, environmental control, and other activities of daily living can be enhanced through fabrication of appropriate augmentative communication devices, powered wheelchairs, and computer-assisted educational aids. Attention to proper posture, positioning, and seating is a prerequisite to construction or fitting of any adaptive equipment or functional device. Only after a comprehensive evaluation of the child's posture, type of motor disability, associated health problems, communication abilities, cognitive capacity, and potential arm/hand or other available "motors" can a child receive maximal benefit from a communication or other assisting device.

Educators who have regular contact with the child and family can reinforce the advice of therapists and other service providers.

SEE ALSO

Bracing, Neurological Examination, Orthopedic Problems, Perinatal Injury, Positioning and Handling, and *Seizure Disorders*

ADDITIONAL RESOURCES

Scherzer, A.L., and I. Tscharnuter. *Early Diagnosis and Therapy in Cerebral Palsy: A Primer on Developmental Problems.* New York: Marcel Dekker, 1983.

Thompson, G.H., I.L. Rubin, and R.M. Bilenker, eds. *Comprehensive Management of Cerebral Palsy.* New York: Grune & Stratton, 1983.

Child Abuse and Neglect

DEFINITION

The definition of child maltreatment is a legal one and varies from state to state. It can include physical or emotional abuse or neglect and sexual abuse. A broad definition is found in the Child Abuse Prevention and Treatment Act, Public Law No. 93-247: "The physical or mental injury, sexual abuse or exploitation, negligent treatment or maltreatment of a child under the age of eighteen . . . by a person who is responsible for the child's welfare. . . ."

Incidence

In the United States each year over a million children are the victims of abuse or neglect, according to a recent government survey. Physical abuse is the most common type followed by emotional and sexual abuse. With respect to neglect, educational is most frequent, then physical and emotional. As many as 1,500 children die each year from child abuse. Though the incidence of physical abuse increases with age, when the youngest children are abused, they are more likely than older children to experience fatal injury.

Child abuse occurs at all socioeconomic and educational levels, though it is more often reported among lower socioeconomic groups. Parents are not the only abusers; others include step parents, boyfriends, babysitters, and foster parents. Around 60 to 90 percent of abusers have been victims themselves. Less than 10 percent are severely emotionally disturbed.

ABUSE AND NEGLECT OF THE CHILD WITH DISABILITIES

Child abuse is more likely to occur when (1) there is stress and strain in the family; (2) parents have unrealistic expectations of the child; or (3) parents are emotionally and socially isolated. Usually, one particular child in the family serves as a scapegoat, receiving the brunt of the abuser's animosity. Low-birth-weight infants, while they comprise only 10 percent of newborns, make up a higher than expected percentage of the physically abused population. A major factor here may be impairment of maternal-infant attachment.

Children with disabilities are also particularly vulnerable. The mere physical care of a disabled child can be exceedingly taxing—physically, emotionally, and financially. When these stresses are compounded by parental anger, denial, and guilt—and by long periods without child-care relief—the potential for abuse increases dramatically.

Approximately one-third of abused children have signs of central nervous system damage, one-half to two-thirds have intellectual impairment, and one-third are below the normal range for height and weight. While many children are already disabled prior to being abused, the abuse itself frequently results in developmental disabilities, including neurological impairment. The effects of neglect can be just as devastating as those of physical abuse.

All maltreated children have serious long-term psychosocial problems. In a recent study in a cerebral palsy clinic, issues of child abuse were important considerations in deciding on the custody of 36 of 86 children. Nearly one-half of this group (17 of 36) were injured severely enough by abusers in the home to warrant custody by the state.

There is significant potential for abuse by those caring for handicapped children, including medical and education-related professionals. The professional also wields tremendous power over children with handicaps and their families by determining the type, nature, and extent of services received and even whether some children will be excluded from services. When trying to develop the maximal potential of the handicapped child, care should be taken not to trigger abuse and neglect by raising unrealistic expectations for performance or by otherwise altering a climate of acceptance in the family.

SIGNS OF CHILD ABUSE/NEGLECT

Physical Abuse

The following should alert the professional to possible physical abuse:
- unexplained injuries, scars, or bruises
- implausible explanation of injury
- inconsistency between explanation offered and actual injury or developmental level of the child
- fuzzy or changing details of how injury occurred (Normally, parents know the exact moment and place of the injury.)
- delay in seeking medical attention
- unusual sites or shapes of injury (e.g., bruises confined to the back or buttocks, rounded burns as from a cigarette, hand prints, linear marks from a belt, choke marks around the neck)

Caution: A normal, slate-blue patch over the back, buttocks, or other body areas, called a *mongolian spot*, may be confused with a bruise. It is a common finding in dark-complexioned infants of all races and disappears by age four. A bruise will turn greenish and fade, whereas a mongolian spot stays the same.

Physical or Emotional Neglect

The following signs may indicate physical or emotional neglect:
- poor growth (While there are specific medical causes of "failure to thrive," insufficient caloric intake or environmental deprivation is the most common cause.)
- failure to obtain routine medical care or to comply with treatment recommendations
- bald spot on back of infant's head from infant lying in one position excessively
- poor hygiene
- poor attendance at school program

Sexual Abuse

Sexual abuse should be suspected if any of the following are seen:
- sexually transmitted diseases in the young child
- evidence of injury to the genital area (e.g., bruises or lacerations)
- vaginal discharge or blood
- blood in diaper or underwear

Munchausen Syndrome by Proxy

Munchausen syndrome by proxy describes instances in which a child's illnesses are fabricated or induced by parents. Children are usually under six years of age and are too young to understand or reveal the deception. The induced symptoms lead to unnecessary hospitalizations and treatments. Suspicion of this condition should be reported to Child Protective Services to prevent the child's being taken to other facilities or the parents' administering fatal treatments when confronted with the evidence.

Shaken Baby Syndrome

Over 95 percent of serious head injuries during the first year of life are the result of abuse. Violent, whiplash-type shaking followed by dropping or throwing the infant onto a hard surface result in serious bleeding in the brain. Hemorrhages in the retinas of the eyes (seen with an ophthalmoscope) are the hallmark of this kind of injury; rarely are they found with accidental head injury. Frequently no skull fracture is evident. Victims of this injury, if they survive, usually have significant motor and mental impairments.

REPORTING CHILD ABUSE

Every state has a law requiring health and other professionals to report child abuse whenever it is suspected. In many states there are penalties for professionals who fail to report. These include a jail sentence and/or a fine of several hundred dollars; in some cases the professional who fails to report child abuse can be liable for damages resulting from subsequent injury to the child.

Know your state law in detail, particularly the definition of child abuse and neglect; know also the reporting procedure if you are a mandatory reporter and the legal consequences if you do not report. Utilize the child abuse law as a means of getting help early to a family in need. And, most important, be compassionate, sympathetic, and understanding. Under certain circumstances, many of us could become child abusers.

ADDITIONAL RESOURCE

Gabarino, J., P.E. Brookhouser, and K.J. Authier. *Special Children, Special Risks: The Maltreatment of Children with Disabilities.* New York: Aldine De Gruyter, 1987.

Cleft Lip and Palate

DESCRIPTION

During the sixth through the 13th weeks of fetal life, the roof and upper front of the mouth are formed by development and fusion, mostly in the midline, of soft tissue and bony processes. Interruption of this formation results in a group of disorders known as clefts.

The specific forms and severity of clefts vary, and these variations are usually attributed to the timing of the interference with normal development.

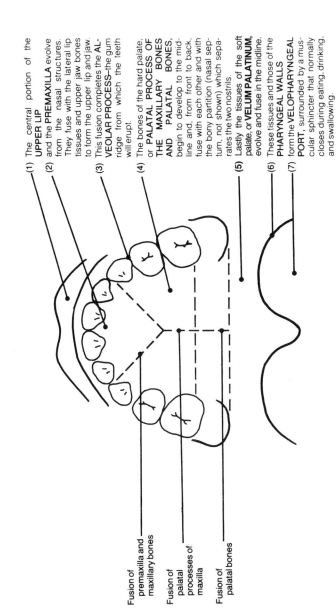

(1) The central portion of the **UPPER LIP** and the **PREMAXILLA** evolve from the nasal structures. They fuse with the lateral lip tissues and upper jaw bones to form the upper lip and jaw.

(2) This fusion completes the **ALVEOLAR PROCESS**—the gum ridge from which the teeth will erupt.

(3) The bones of the hard palate, or **PALATAL PROCESS OF THE MAXILLARY BONES AND PALATAL BONES**, begin to develop to the midline and, from front to back, fuse with each other and with the bony partition (nasal septum, not shown) which separates the two nostrils.

(4) Lastly the tissues of the soft palate, or **VELUM PALATINUM**, evolve and fuse in the midline.

(5) These tissues and those of the **PHARYNGEAL WALLS** form the **VELOPHARYNGEAL PORT**, surrounded by a muscular sphincter that normally closes during eating, drinking, and swallowing.

Fusion of
premaxilla and
maxillary bones

Fusion of
palatal
processes of
maxilla

Fusion of
palatal bones

Normal Development of the Lip and Palate

Cleft of the Lip Only

Interference during the initial stages of development is likely to result in a cleft of the lip only. This malformation may include as little as the border of the lip or it may extend upward and into the nostril (as shown).

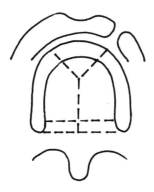

Cleft of the Lip Only

Clefts of the Lip and Palate

Clefts of both the lip and palate appear to result from an impediment to normal development that spans weeks six through 13 of fetal life.

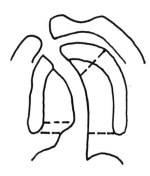

Unilateral Cleft of the Lip and Palate. *The premaxilla and the maxilla fuse on one side only, as do the bones of the hard palate and the nasal septum. There is a cleft of the tissues of the soft palate.*

Bilateral Cleft of the Lip and Palate. *Neither side of the premaxilla, the maxilla, or the palatal bones fuses together.*

Clefts of the Palate Only

Interference during the later stages of development may result in clefts of palatal tissues only.

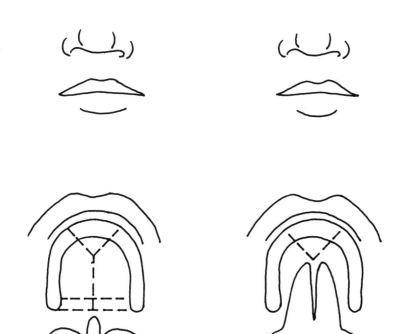

Cleft of Both the Hard and Soft Palates   Cleft of the Soft Palate Only

Normal development of the lip and the hard and soft palates is essential to proper eating and speech production. The front lip helps control liquids and foods during drinking and eating and helps create a suction to assist in moving liquids and foods to the back of the mouth for swallowing. The hard palate provides a partition between the mouth and nasal passages. The muscles of the soft palate normally act in conjunction with those of the walls of the upper throat (pharyngeal walls) to close the opening between the posterior oral and nasal cavities (velopharyngeal port) during eating, drinking, and speaking.

Therefore, the chewing, drinking, and swallowing behaviors of infants and very young children with clefts may require special attention. Feeding techniques will be quite different for a cleft of the lip than for a cleft of the palate. With the former, the infant cannot close the mouth around the nipple to create suction; with the latter, liquids and foods frequently are forced into the nasal cavity, sometimes to the extent of liquids being expelled from the nostrils. Special techniques may be required to move food and liquids to the backs of these children's mouths for swallowing. The development of compensatory swallowing patterns is common. Moreover, the child may have to be kept on soft foods for an extended period of time because of problems in the development of speech.

An opening between the nasal and oral cavities has two adverse effects upon speech production. First, the quality of speech is likely to be offensive; the voice has a "nasal" quality when the air in the nasal cavity is set into vibration along with the air in the throat and oral cavity. Second, and most important, the buildup of air pressure within the oral cavity that is necessary to produce many consonant sounds is negated by the leak through the nasal cavity. In addition to causing speech impediments, an opening between the oral and nasal cavities leads to increased susceptibility to upper respiratory infections.

Clefts of the palate also may affect hearing. Normal hearing is dependent upon proper functioning of the eustachian tubes, which provide an opening between the middle ear and the posterior nasal cavity. With a cleft palate, the eustachian tube is exposed to foods and liquids, predisposing it to inflammation. Also, the frequent upper respiratory infections common in children with clefts increase the likelihood of eustachian tube and middle ear infections.

The congenital anomaly of clefting, then, may result in the following problems, the presence or severity of which depends on the specific characteristics of the cleft and the particular child:

- serious dental problems, including inappropriate alignment of the teeth and/or a faulty relationship between the upper and lower teeth (malocclusion)
- susceptibility to upper respiratory infections
- middle ear disease and associated hearing impairment from eustachian tube dysfunction

- significant eating difficulties and subsequent nutritional problems in early life
- problems of speech development
- psychosocial problems and low self-esteem due to (1) strained parent-child relationships, (2) facial disfigurement, (3) a speech problem, and/or (4) a hearing impairment
- educational difficulties due to health, speech, hearing, and psychosocial problems

Babies with clefts may have additional congenital anomalies, such as heart defects and extra fingers or toes.

CAUSE

There is no comprehensive, definitive explanation for cleft lip or palate. Certain families may have a history of clefts, especially clefts of the palate only. Even for that subgroup, however, the exact pattern of genetic transmission is not usually clear. A number of environmental factors are also believed to result in clefting, including German measles, drugs, and vitamin deficiencies in the mother. Any genetic pattern for, or predisposition to, clefts is compounded by the possible presence of these factors.

INCIDENCE

Known racial differences make general overall incidence figures meaningless. For example, in Caucasians, cleft lip, cleft palate, or both occur in one of every 550 live births; in blacks, they occur in only one of every 2,500 live births.

DETECTION

A cleft can usually be detected at birth. Exceptions are submucous clefts of the palate, in which the posterior portion of the palatal bones is not fused. With this condition, the tissue of the dysfunctional soft palate may appear normal anatomically, and the cleft may not become evident until an eating or a speech development problem appears.

COURSE AND INTERDISCIPLINARY MANAGEMENT

Proper management of cleft problems requires highly specialized interdisciplinary efforts.

Cleft Treatment Centers

Infants with clefts should be referred to one of the numerous cleft treatment centers that have been established throughout the nation. (Locations of interdisciplinary cleft lip and palate treatment centers may be obtained by contacting the American Cleft Palate Educational Foundation, 331 Salk Hall, University of Pittsburgh, Pittsburgh, PA 15261.)

The staffs of cleft treatment centers usually provide a variety of services.

- Surgeons repair the cleft.
- Otolaryngologists diagnose and treat ear disease and eustachian tube dysfunction.
- Pediatricians diagnose any additional birth defects, evaluate general health status, and provide general medical treatment.
- Orthodontists anticipate and work to prevent problems of dental occlusion.
- Prosthodontists construct any needed intraoral appliances to provide missing teeth and/or a partition between the oral and nasal cavities.
- Pedodontists oversee dental development and hygiene.
- Speech-language pathologists advise and plan programs relative to speech development.
- Audiologists assist the otolaryngologist in determining the presence and type of hearing impairment and recommend hearing aids when appropriate.

In addition to these specialists, treatment centers often have sophisticated radiology services that provide documentation of the effects of growth as well as surgical and dental procedures. They may also have psychologists, social service workers, and appropriately trained nurses to assist parents and other family members with potential problems. The cleft palate team will make recommendations for specific management techniques, since these vary with the individual.

Management

Though it is desirable to close clefts surgically as soon as possible, surgery during the first or second month of life may interfere with the growth of the maxillofacial structures. Surgical closure of clefts of the lip may be done when the infant is three to six months old. Initial surgery of the palate may be delayed until the child is 12 to 18 months old. To allow for complete growth, the final surgeries to bring about optimal cosmetic results may not be performed until adolescence.

In general, the management goals for clefts of the lip and palate, and for clefts of the palate only, are to make the oral cavity structurally sufficient to reduce both eating difficulties and hearing problems by the time the child is three to four years old. However, more adequate velopharyngeal function is required to prevent nasal resonance and to permit impounding intraoral air pressures during speech production. Therefore, for a great number of cases, achieving adequate palatal function (velopharyngeal competence) for speech production must await secondary surgical procedures and/or prosthetic management during the early school years.

During the formative period of speech development, the child who is unable to produce a number of speech sounds because of a cleft of the palate may learn inappropriate compensatory speech production patterns. While those components of speech that are deviant because of mislearning may change as a result of management by a speech-language pathologist, the child still may not be able to eliminate completely the speech production problems until the cleft treatment team is able to restore adequate palatal functioning.

IMPLICATIONS FOR EDUCATION

There is a strong possibility that the school performances of children with clefts will be below their potential. Problems of self-esteem and social interaction may be the basis of that difficulty. Parents may need to be involved in efforts to alleviate a child's feelings of "being different."

Because of increased susceptibility, unnecessary exposure to upper respiratory infections should be avoided. However, precautions should not extend to excluding the child from early educational experiences that may be beneficial. Certain modifications in the environment (e.g., increased humidity in the classroom) may help reduce the extent and severity of these infections.

A child should receive remedial assistance for any speech problem that is present.

In cases where there is hearing loss, educational methods appropriate for the hearing impaired should be employed.

Parents of children with clefts need to have professionals with whom they can discuss their ongoing concerns about health, growth, and development; they also need continuing support to offset guilt reactions and other negative feelings.

SEE ALSO

Middle Ear Disease (Otitis Media)

ADDITIONAL RESOURCE

American Cleft Palate and Craniofacial Abnormalities Association. A telephone hot line has been established where callers can obtain information about services in their locales: 1-800-24C-LEFT.

Congenital Heart Disease

DESCRIPTION

Congenital heart disease (CHD) includes cardiovascular malformations that are present and usually evident at the time of birth but may not be recognized until months or even years later.

The body is dependent upon the heart to pump oxygen and nutrients to all its tissues; therefore, physiological, anatomical, or electrical defects are debilitating and potentially life-threatening. The more common heart defects include the following.

Aortic Stenosis

In aortic stenosis, the aortic valve between the left ventricle and the aorta is narrowed.

Atrial Septal Defect

In atrial septal defect, blood leaks through a hole in the atrial wall from the left to the right side, enlarging the right atrium and ventricle as well as the pulmonary artery.

Atrioventricular Canal

Sometimes referred to as an endocardial cushion defect, an atrioventricular canal results from lack of separation of the heart's four chambers and incomplete formation of the valves between the atria and corresponding ventricles. There is only one leaky valve between the atria, which have a large hole in the wall between them, and the ventricles, which also have a large hole in their wall. This defect is common among children with Down syndrome.

Coarctation of the Aorta

In coarctation of the aorta, a narrowing of the aorta causes the left ventricle to pump harder, raising the blood pressure above the constricted part and lowering it in the blood vessels below. Surgery relieves the narrowing.

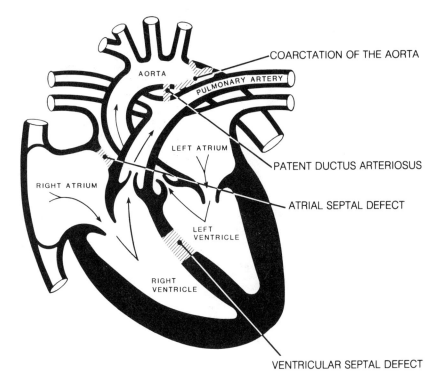

COARCTATION OF THE AORTA

AORTA

PULMONARY ARTERY

LEFT ATRIUM

PATENT DUCTUS ARTERIOSUS

RIGHT ATRIUM

ATRIAL SEPTAL DEFECT

LEFT VENTRICLE

RIGHT VENTRICLE

VENTRICULAR SEPTAL DEFECT

Common Heart Defects

Hypoplastic Left Heart

In the hypoplastic left heart abnormality, the left side of the heart is underdeveloped. Since the left ventricle is small and nonfunctional, the right ventricle must pump blood both to the lungs and to the rest of the body. Most infants with this disorder die; some are candidates for heart transplantation.

Patent Ductus Arteriosus

The duct used to bypass the lungs in the fetus, the ductus arteriosus, remains open after birth in this defect. Oxygenated blood from the left side of the heart flows across the duct, back into the pulmonary artery; this makes the left ventricle work harder and floods the lungs. Sometimes a patent ductus arteriosus can be closed with medication; otherwise, the duct is closed surgically.

Pulmonary Stenosis

In pulmonary stenosis, the pulmonic valve (between the right ventricle and pulmonary artery) itself or tissue above or below the valve is narrowed, preventing unoxygenated blood from reaching the lungs. The narrowing must be relieved or an alternate pathway provided for blood to go to the lungs.

Tetralogy of Fallot

In the tetralogy of Fallot, a combination of four defects causes deoxygenated blood to mix with oxygenated blood and be carried to the body. Temporarily, connections may be made to allow blood to bypass the narrowed pulmonary valve (Blalock-Taussig, Waterston, Potts shunts). After successful total correction, the child should have no symptoms and can lead an unrestricted life.

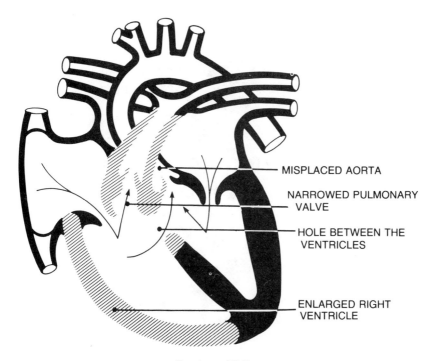

MISPLACED AORTA

NARROWED PULMONARY VALVE

HOLE BETWEEN THE VENTRICLES

ENLARGED RIGHT VENTRICLE

Tetralogy of Fallot

Total Anomalous Pulmonary Venous Return

In total anomalous pulmonary venous return, the pulmonary veins, which should bring blood back to the left side of the heart from the lungs, have developed abnormally. Oxygenated blood from the lungs may drain back into the right atrium or into the large vein (inferior or superior vena cava), where it circulates right back to the lungs. The only way for oxygenated blood to get to the left side of the heart, and thus out to the rest of the body, is through a defect, sometimes created surgically. Whereas if untreated the prognosis is poor, surgical correction in some cases may result in a good outcome.

Transposition of the Greater Arteries

In transposition of the greater arteries, the aorta and pulmonary artery are attached to the wrong ventricles. Deoxygenated blood is carried to the body; oxygenated blood, to the lungs. A patent ductus arteriosus and septal defect, if present, allow some oxygenated blood to reach the rest of the body, making life possible. Newborns with this defect usually require immediate palliative surgery prior to definitive correction. The Mustard and Senning procedures reverse the abnormal blood flow patterns.

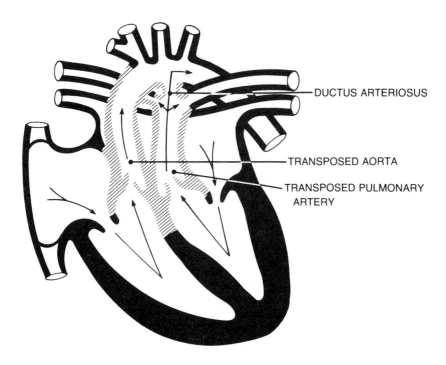

DUCTUS ARTERIOSUS

TRANSPOSED AORTA

TRANSPOSED PULMONARY ARTERY

Transposition of the Greater Arteries

Tricuspid Atresia

The valve (tricuspid) between the right atrium and right ventricle has failed to develop in tricuspid atresia, thus allowing no passage of blood through this normal route. Temporary and permanent surgical procedures, such as the Fontan operation, are necessary to allow blood to bypass this obstruction.

Ventricular Septal Defect

In ventricular septal defect, blood leaks through a hole in the wall between the ventricles, usually from left to right. Large defects may strain both ventricles, particularly the left.

CAUSE

When the embryo is just 23 days old, the heart begins to beat. The rapidly developing heart is particularly susceptible to deleterious influences during early fetal life. In most cases the specific cause for CHD is not identifiable. There is a suspected association with teratogens—that is, agents or factors (viruses, drugs, excessive radiation)—which cause physical defects in the developing embryo. However, there are cases of identical twins in which one developed CHD and the other did not, even though both presumably were exposed to the same environment in the uterus. CHD may also be caused by new gene mutations and other genetic factors. (It is linked, for example, with a number of chromosomal abnormalities, including those responsible for Down and Turner syndromes.)

INCIDENCE

About eight out of every thousand people have cardiovascular malformations. The chances of having a second child with a heart defect is 2 to 5 percent; they may be even greater if two children in one family are already affected. The prevalence of malformations among children whose parents have CHD is 3 to 4 percent.

DETECTION

Serious CHD is often recognizable at birth; the newborn shows breathing difficulties and remains blue despite the administration of high concentrations of oxygen. While the physical examination, chest X-ray, and tracing of the electrical activity of the heart (electrocardiogram) may indicate the presence of CHD, other, more sophisticated, tests are often necessary to determine the type. One newer, useful diagnostic technique is echocardiography: sound waves are bounced off the heart to produce an image of its structures on paper or a television screen. It is sometimes necessary to obtain an exact outline of the heart structures and to chart the flow of blood through it by a procedure called cardiac catheterization, which involves injecting dye into the heart via a tube threaded through blood vessels.

COURSE

How seriously the child will be affected by CHD depends upon the type and severity of the problem. Some defects (atrial septal defect, ventricular septal defect) may be so minor that the child will tolerate them well and no specific corrective procedures will be necessary. In such cases, the child's condition is followed very closely, and corrective procedures are considered only if there are signs of worsening. Severe malformations, however, such as those in which the blood bypasses the lungs (tetralogy of Fallot, transposition of the greater arteries), can be life-threatening unless treated early. If because of small size or poor health the child is not able to withstand major corrective surgery, it may be necessary to perform temporary surgical procedures that allow for adequate oxygenation of the blood.

ACCOMPANYING HEALTH PROBLEMS

During the first few years of life, children with significant heart defects are often in and out of the hospital, where they are treated not only for the heart condition but also for secondary medical problems, such as pneumonias, poor feeding, or infections. Other secondary problems are of particular importance. Among these is congestive heart failure, a condition in which the heart, having to work extra hard, becomes strained and does not pump as efficiently as it should, causing fluid to back up into the lungs, liver, and other organs. Drugs such as digitalis and water pills (diuretics) are generally effective in preventing and treating this complication.

The altered anatomy of the heart, including narrowed valves or holes between heart chambers, is conducive to the growth of bacteria, which can damage the heart even further. Clumps of bacteria may even break off and lodge in the brain, causing abscesses. Such serious complications must be identified and treated with antibiotics as quickly as possible.

The degree of severity of CHD determines the effects it will have on growth and development. The incomplete oxygenation of blood and extra caloric expenditure that accompany the most severe forms of this condition result in poor growth of tissue, causing the child to be small and underdeveloped. Serious conditions also cause poor appetite (with resultant inadequate caloric intake) and frequent hospitalizations for surgery and secondary illnesses. The less severe types of heart defects, on the other hand, are not likely to interfere significantly with normal growth and development.

MEDICAL MANAGEMENT

The main features of management include early identification, medical and physical stabilization prior to corrective surgery, rehabilitation following surgery, and—of special importance—nutritional and developmental assessment and treatment before, during, and after surgery.

IMPLICATIONS FOR EDUCATION

Oftentimes, frequent hospitalizations, coupled with the unstable medical conditions of children with CHD, divert attention away from learning and development. It is almost impossible to determine the potential for children in such circumstances. Nevertheless, growth of the brain and other tissues is rapid during the first several years, and attention to developmental needs cannot be postponed until after surgery and medical management are complete. Thus, early intervention professionals in home- or center-based programs must work closely with the medical team to determine how the child's development can be coordinated most efficiently with medical management. Once early intervention personnel understand both the nature of the heart condition and the rationale for treatment, they can bring their performance expectations in line with the child's physical limitations. They can also observe the child for fatigue, poor appetite, or other warning signs of setbacks or complications. CHD is a good example of how important it is for medical and education-related professionals to work together for the child's optimal treatment in the early years.

SEE ALSO

Down Syndrome, Low Birth Weight, and *Teratogens*

ADDITIONAL RESOURCE

Fink, B.W. *Congenital Heart Disease.* Chicago: Year Book Medical Publishers, Inc., 1985.

Congenital Infections

Congenital infections comprise a group of diseases acquired either before or during birth through exposure to viral, bacterial, or protozoan organisms. Besides causing illness and death in the newborn period, they may result in chronic physical, sensory, and mental handicaps. Most is known about the so-called TORCH-S or STORCH infections. The letters stand for Syphilis, Toxoplasmosis, Other infections, Rubella, Cytomegalic inclusion disease, and Herpes. Acquired immune deficiency syndrome (AIDS) is discussed under the "Other infections" category.

SYPHILIS

Syphilis is a sexually transmitted infection caused by the bacterium *Treponema pallidum*. Untreated syphilis in the mother, whether contracted during pregnancy or years before, may be transmitted to the fetus. In 25 percent of cases, untreated syphilis in a pregnant woman results in the death of the fetus, usually during the second trimester. An additional 25 percent die soon after birth. Of those who live, about 25 percent show signs of jaundice, anemia, pneumonia, skin rash, and bone inflammation. The remaining 75 percent may show no signs of infection at birth yet later manifest such problems as abnormalities of the teeth, blindness, skeletal anomalies, mental retardation, and sensorineural deafness.

The exact incidence of congenital syphilis is dependent upon the incidence of untreated syphilis in pregnant women. With the advent of effective antibiotics, this figure had been decreasing; however, there is once again an upward trend in the number of cases. Since early treatment may help prevent defects, it is important that all pregnant women have a blood test for syphilis in the early stages of pregnancy. Once the mother has been treated adequately, there is no risk in future pregnancies (unless she becomes reinfected with syphilis).

Whenever a newborn has general signs of infection, the possibility of syphilis in the mother should be investigated. The diagnosis of congenital syphilis is confirmed by a special blood test (called Venereal Disease Research Laboratory [VDRL] or fluorescent treponemal antibody [FTA]) or, less commonly, by viewing the organism under a microscope. If the results suggest congenital syphilis, treatment with appropriate antibiotics, usually penicillin, should begin immediately. These infants must be followed closely for at least 12 months to ensure that the treatment is effective. More specific medical management is dependent upon the organ systems affected.

Because children with congenital syphilis may require special education for their sensory or mental handicaps, it is important for educators to understand which organ systems are primarily affected. If the infant has been treated appropriately, there is no risk of infection to those caring for the child.

TOXOPLASMOSIS

Toxoplasmosis is an infection caused by the protozoan organism *Toxoplasma gondii*. Although this organism infects many animals, including humans, the cat is the most widely recognized vector of transmission. Cysts containing the organism are passed through the animal's feces to the soil, which becomes potentially infective. Toxoplasmosis can also be contracted by ingesting the raw meat or eggs of infected animals. Since an infected individual is usually without symptoms, the organism may pass through the placenta of an unsuspecting pregnant woman and into the fetus.

Toxoplasmosis may result in spontaneous abortion or premature delivery. Affected infants are characterized by low birth weight, a large liver and spleen, jaundice, and anemia. Congenital defects include hydrocephalus, microcephaly, and calcifications in the brain. Some of the problems that may become manifest later are mental retardation, seizures, cerebral palsy, and diseases of the retina with resultant blindness.

The approximate incidence of congenital toxoplasmosis is about one to two per thousand live births. This condition should be suspected in any infant who shows signs of congenital infection. Diagnosis is confirmed by a specific blood test or, rarely, by isolating the organism from body tissues. Antiprotozoan drugs, although their efficacy has yet to be proven scientifically, are used to treat the disease in the newborn period in hopes of preventing further damage by the organism.

Because toxoplasmosis is not normally transmitted from person to person, individuals caring for affected infants are not in danger of catching it. Once the mother is treated, there is no danger to the fetus during a future pregnancy.

The severity of this disease calls for individualized educational programs involving many professionals.

OTHER INFECTIONS

Acquired Immune Deficiency Syndrome

Not long after acquired immune deficiency syndrome (AIDS) was first recognized in homosexual men and intravenous drug users in the early 1980s, cases were reported in children. Caused by the human immuno-deficiency virus (HIV), symptoms in children relate to a damaged immune system (lymph gland, liver, and spleen enlargement; recurrent infections with both common and unusual organisms; poor growth [i.e., failure to thrive]; and fever). Furthermore, there may be disease of the brain resulting in developmental delay, deterioration of motor skills and intellectual abil-ities, and behavioral abnormalities. Malignancies appear less common in children affected with AIDS than in adults. The majority of children with AIDS die; those diagnosed in the first year of life have the worst prognosis.

Most children under three will contract AIDS from the mother who is infected with HIV. The virus is transmitted to the child during pregnancy, at the time of birth, or possibly through breast milk, but not through the type of intimate contact that goes on among family members after the child is born. A congenital AIDS pattern, suggesting transmission of the virus early in pregnancy, has been described in which affected infants are born with microcephaly (small head), a boxlike forehead, wide-spaced eyes, short nose, and prominent lips.

While the number of new cases in some high-risk populations may be leveling off, AIDS among children is increasing. If the mother is infected with HIV, there is approximately a 50 percent chance that the infant will be infected. Because maternal antibodies to HIV cross the placenta and enter the fetus' blood stream, it may be difficult to determine whether a newborn infant has AIDS since the antibodies from the mother persist in the child's blood for up to one year. In young infants, therefore, the diagnosis of AIDS will hinge on typical signs of the disease and positive cultures for the virus rather than on the usual blood tests.

There is no evidence that HIV is transmitted by normal, casual, and nonsexual contact in home, school, day care, or foster care settings. The American Academy of Pediatrics Task Force on Pediatric AIDS, therefore, has made the following recommendations:

1. HIV-infected children should be admitted to day care if their health, neurological development, behavior, and immune status are appro-priate. Most infected children, particularly those too young to walk, pose no risk to others. HIV-infected children who persistently bite others or who have oozing skin lesions theoretically may transmit the virus, although such has not been demonstrated conclusively. Medical evaluation should be ongoing, to evaluate changes in the child's health.
2. If the child's personal physician is uncertain as to the efficacy or safety of placement within a school or group setting, consultation should be sought with individuals or groups having particular expertise re-garding HIV infection and AIDS.

3. Where available, day care centers that are designed to meet the specific needs of children infected with HIV may represent an acceptable alternative placement, particularly to provide a supportive environment for the children, but these centers are not necessary for reasons of infection control. This alternative should not be used to isolate or segregate infected children.

4. Some children may be infected with undiagnosed HIV or other infectious agents, such as hepatitis B virus; these agents may be present in blood or body fluids. Thus, responsible individuals in all day care and foster care settings in high-prevalence areas, and individuals in any day care center in which there is a known infected child, should adopt precautions for blood spills from all children. All child care personnel and educators should be informed about these procedures. For example, soiled surfaces should be cleaned promptly with disinfectants, such as household bleach (a 1:10 to 1:100 dilution of bleach to water prepared daily). Disposable towels or tissues should be used whenever possible and properly discarded, and mops should be rinsed in the disinfectant. Cleaning personnel should avoid the risk of having their mucous membranes or any open skin lesions exposed to blood or blood-contaminated body fluids (by using disposable gloves, for example).

Hepatitis B

Formerly called *serum hepatitis* because the main route of transmission is through exposure to the blood of an infected person, hepatitis B can be passed from mother to fetus during pregnancy. Persons of Asian, Pacific Island, and Alaskan Eskimo descent; some persons of Hispanic descent; and persons born in Haiti or sub-Saharan Africa have high rates of chronic hepatitis B virus carriage. Thus newborns in these groups may be born with the disease. Another risk group includes infants of mothers who are prostitutes or drug abusers, since the virus can be spread by sexual intercourse or sharing contaminated needles. Steps have been instituted to check pregnant women for hepatitis B; if present, the newborn receives special treatment to eradicate the virus. Symptoms include jaundice (yellowness of the skin and whites of the eyes), decreased appetite, nausea, and fatigue. The brain is not usually affected by the virus even when the infection occurs during gestation. Individuals with chronic carriage of hepatitis B virus are at risk of developing cirrhosis or cancer of the liver.

Persons caring for young children with chronic hepatitis B carriage (e.g., children exposed prenatally who were not treated at birth) are at low risk of acquiring the infection provided good hygienic practices are followed. It is not recommended that chronic carriers be excluded from group care settings, but care should be taken that the blood of infected individuals not come in contact with open wounds of children or adults. A vaccine is available for those who have frequent exposure to blood containing hepatitis B virus; usually this would be in a health care setting but could be in a group care setting serving children with high carriage rates. The local health department is a good source of current information and advice.

Other Agents

Other infectious agents, including influenza virus, chickenpox, various enteroviruses (such as coxsackievirus and echovirus), and parvoviruses are suspected of causing damage to the fetus; but since their effects are still uncertain, they are not discussed in this chapter.

RUBELLA

Rubella, commonly called German measles, is caused by a virus that usually produces only mild upper respiratory symptoms and rash in the infected individual. It can, however, cause severe damage to the fetus— in some cases resulting in spontaneous abortion. When women are infected during the first month of pregnancy, there is a 35 percent chance that the fetus will be affected. This figure decreases to 25 percent in the second month, 16 percent in the third. When women are infected after the fourth month of pregnancy, damage to the fetus is uncommon.

Recently, there has been an average of only 20 new cases of congenital rubella in the United States per year. This represents a drop from previous years, presumably as a result of recent mass immunization for rubella. If the immunization rate decreases, however, or if the immunity achieved from immunization in infancy proves to wear off in adulthood, the incidence figure could rise. While there is no specific treatment for the infection, it can be prevented through effective immunization of everyone.

Rubella in the newborn should be suspected whenever an infant shows the general signs of a congenital infection, particularly if the mother has had a flulike illness during pregnancy; the diagnosis is confirmed by isolating the virus and by blood tests. Affected newborns may also have a low birth weight, a large liver and spleen, and a peculiar rash (petechiae), caused by the leakage of minute amounts of blood into the skin. Typical congenital malformations include heart defects, microcephaly, cataracts, and small eyes (microphthalmia). Later complications may occur in infants who are asymptomatic at birth. Thus, it is possible to trace to congenital infections a hearing loss that manifests itself months or years after birth. Other later complications may include mental retardation, seizures, thyroid disease, and diabetes.

Infected infants may continue to excrete the virus for up to 12 months. Therefore, susceptible personnel who are pregnant should avoid contact with infants with proven rubella. In addition, all women of childbearing age who have contact with young children, particularly with children who have a high prevalence of congenital infections, should have a blood test to determine their immunity to rubella. Susceptible women should avoid contact with such infants or be immunized at a time when there is no risk of pregnancy.

CYTOMEGALIC INCLUSION DISEASE

Cytomegalic inclusion disease (CID), the most common of the congenital infections discussed in this chapter, is caused by cytomegalovirus (CMV). About 1 percent of newborns are infected with CMV acquired in utero; but, fortunately, only about 10 percent of these manifest the signs and symptoms of CID: low birth weight, jaundice, rash (petechiae), anemia, large liver and spleen, and encephalitis. Those with encephalitis usually are mentally retarded and have motor impairment. Inflammation of the retinas may result in varying degrees of visual loss. Of the 90 percent of CMV-infected infants who show no symptoms at birth, 10 to 15 percent will develop progressive sensorineural hearing loss. The greatest risk to a fetus occurs with the first infection of the mother. It appears that, when women become infected with CMV in successive pregnancies, the risk to the fetus is low. CMV can be cultured easily from urine or saliva.

Although antiviral drugs are being investigated, there is as yet no specific treatment for CID. Because CMV is a chronic infection and may be shed in body secretions and urine for several years after birth, individuals who have intimate contact with these infants should take proper precautions. It is now known that children, especially toddlers, in group care settings are commonly infected with CMV, though they show no symptoms. Good hygienic practices, especially handwashing and proper disposal of diapers, can stop transmission to adults. Nevertheless, pregnant women must be aware of the risks in these situations, should take special care to wash hands after contact, and might consider avoiding settings where there is high exposure to CMV or contact with known infected children if the pregnant women do not have evidence (i.e., antibodies to CMV in the blood) of previous infection.

HERPES

Herpes simplex is a virus that can produce devastating disease in the newborn infant. In the adult, the type 1 virus typically has been associated with the mouth; type 2, with the genital area. Both types, however, can be found in either location. At times, genital lesions in the mother are visible and may produce pain or other symptoms. At other times, the mother is without symptoms and the condition can be detected only through a culture of the virus. Herpes infection in the newborn is, properly speaking, neonatal rather than congenital; that is, although it is possible for it to be transmitted through the placenta, it is most often acquired during passage of the infant through the birth canal when the mother has active herpes in the genital region. While genital herpes tends to exist in the latent form, it may reactivate periodically. It is at these times that the fetus is susceptible during the birth process.

The incidence of neonatal herpes infection ranges from 0.03 to 0.3 per thousand live births. Typically, the exposed newborn does not show signs of infection until five to nine days after birth. There are two types of neonatal herpes infection: (1) a mild disease of the skin and the mucous membranes of the mouth and eye and (2) a severe, generalized form that involves all organs of the body, including the brain. Many infants with the latter type will die. Survivors may suffer severe aftereffects, such as microcephaly, disease of the retina, intracranial calcifications, seizures, and developmental delay. Infants with neonatal herpes may therefore have significant central nervous system damage requiring intensive educational and therapeutic services.

Herpes infection is now being treated in the newborn period with antiviral drugs. While these appear to reduce effectively the number of deaths from the disease, severe brain damage often occurs, even with treatment. The real answer is prevention. Because herpes simplex is becoming an increasingly common venereal disease, it is important that active herpetic lesions of the genital region be identified during pregnancy. If active lesions are present at the time of delivery, a cesarean section is recommended prior to or shortly after the bag of water ruptures. Infection can be prevented by delivering the fetus before it passes through the birth canal and comes into contact with the infective herpetic lesions.

Occasionally, surviving infants may have periodic herpes skin rashes. The rash, often confined to a small area of the skin, does contain active herpes virus. Children with these active lesions may be cared for safely, provided gloves and good handwashing techniques are used. Covering the rash with clothing or bandages is another way to reduce risk of transmission. When the lesions are crusted over or absent, the child is definitely not infectious. Herpes virus from skin lesions will not cause genital herpes in others unless there is direct transfer of virus from the skin lesions to the genital area of another—a very unlikely occurrence.

ADDITIONAL RESOURCES

American Academy of Pediatrics. *Report of the Committee on Infectious Diseases*, current ed. Elk Grove Village, Ill.: American Academy of Pediatrics.

Andersen, R.D., J.F. Bale, J.A. Blackman, and J.R. Murph. *Infections in Children: A Sourcebook for Educators and Child Care Providers.* Rockville, Md.: Aspen Publishers, Inc., 1986.

Cystic Fibrosis

DESCRIPTION

Cystic fibrosis (CF) is a serious disorder of childhood characterized by the production of abnormal mucus, progressive lung damage, and impaired absorption of fat and protein. Individuals with CF have frequent respiratory symptoms, such as coughing and wheezing. They may require hospitalization and treatment with various medications and therapies aimed at reducing the ill effects of the disease and lengthening the life span.

CAUSE

CF is genetically inherited as an autosomal recessive trait; that is, both parents must be carriers, though neither will have the disease. When both parents are carriers they have—with each pregnancy—a 25 percent chance of producing a child with CF.

INCIDENCE

Among Caucasian children, CF is the most common of the inherited chronic diseases, affecting one in every 2,000 births. It is much less common among other racial groups. It occurs in about one in every 20,000 blacks and in about one in every 100,000 Asians.

DETECTION

Signs of CF include chronic lung disease, increased salt concentration in the sweat, and decreased release of certain digestive enzymes by the pancreas. Certain abnormalities revealed on X-rays or during a physical examination may also indicate the presence of CF; for example, about 5 to 10 percent of children with CF have intestinal blockage at birth. It is usually possible to make the diagnosis of the condition through a properly performed "sweat test." Very young infants may not produce the volume of sweat necessary for this procedure, however, and it is sometimes necessary to repeat the test, which should be done soon after the first one.

Both carrier detection and prenatal diagnosis are possible in families having an affected member.

COURSE

CF may manifest itself in different ways at different ages. There may be intestinal blockage at birth, failure to grow (without any other symptoms), or respiratory problems, which eventually become the predominant symptoms. Chronic cough, wheezing, and recurring pneumonias begin weeks to years after birth and progress to blockage of airflow to parts of the lungs. The resultant reduction in oxygen to the body puts the heart under increasing strain. Prolonged and repeated lung infections, which are common despite intensive use of antibiotics, inhibit oxygen delivery even further. There is risk of lung collapse and massive bleeding into the lungs. The average life expectancy for individuals with CF is currently over 26 years. Death is usually a result of pulmonary complications.

Children with CF may fail to grow properly if they do not receive adequate treatment. Most require enzyme supplements to help them digest proteins and fats. On rare occasions, they may develop diabetes, liver disease (cirrhosis), or a sudden expulsion of part of the bowel beyond the anus (rectal prolapse).

ACCOMPANYING HEALTH PROBLEMS

For persons with CF, the lung symptoms are the most disabling, the heart symptoms the least reversible, and the digestive tract abnormalities the easiest to treat. Intensive treatment of undernutrition—giving substantial nutrients intravenously for several weeks, for example—may improve growth and well-being significantly for several months.

MEDICAL MANAGEMENT

Individuals with CF take some of their medications in an aerosol (mist). They generally receive chest physical therapy in order to loosen secretions that block lung airways; they also take vitamin supplements, enzymes (to assist in proper digestion), and antibiotics (to treat infections). Specific mineral supplements may also become necessary as the condition progresses.

IMPLICATIONS FOR EDUCATION

CF is an incurable disease that produces increasing disability with time. The rate of this progression varies significantly with different individuals. For example, symptoms may be minimal in one five-year-old with CF and severe in another.

Exercise intolerance and heightened susceptibility to infection generally are not problems for preschoolers with CF, even those with moderately advanced disease. It is rare for them to require medications or physical therapy treatments during the several hours per day they may spend in a day care program.

Young adults and some adolescents with CF are susceptible to catastrophic medical problems, such as bleeding into the lungs (pulmonary hemorrhage). Most, however, have a gradual rather than a sudden decline in health. Clinic visits and hospitalizations become more frequent with time; and as the disease worsens and death approaches, the family and child are likely to be under significant emotional stress.

SEE ALSO

Failure To Thrive, Genetics, and *Growth and Nutrition*

ADDITIONAL RESOURCE

Cystic Fibrosis Foundation. *A Guide to Cystic Fibrosis for Parents and Children.* Videotape (38 minutes) available from local chapters of the Cystic Fibrosis Foundation.

Dental Disease

DESCRIPTION

Dental disease is an aggregate of conditions found in and around the mouth that may be due to heredity, congenital defects, infectious diseases, trauma, and neglect. The most frequently encountered dental diseases are cavities (caries), gum (periodontal) disease, and improper contact of upper and lower teeth and jaws (malocclusion). Also prevalent among children with developmental disabilities are enamel and dentin irregularities and fractured teeth.

CAUSE

The cause of dental disease varies with each condition. The two most prevalent conditions, cavities and gum disease, are brought about by the action of bacteria on carbohydrates and other substances. This metabolic activity produces acids and toxins in the plaque, which, when allowed to remain in the mouth for a period of time, demineralize the enamel and produce cavities.

Similarly, toxins irritate the tissues around the teeth, causing inflammation and swelling of the gums (gingivitis). If allowed to continue, the disease progresses to the bone around the teeth (at which point it is referred to as periodontitis). Further loss of bone leads to loss of teeth.

Improper contact of the upper and lower teeth and jaws can result from (1) skeletal discrepancies between the upper and lower jaws, (2) discrepancy between tooth size and available space, (3) the loss of teeth due to cavities or gum disease, or (4) increased pressures on the teeth and jaws due to sucking habits or neuromuscular abnormalities.

Fractured teeth are usually caused by trauma, such as occurs with falls or foreign objects striking the mouth. Occasionally, fractures result from pressure on teeth that have been weakened by cavities or enamel and dentin deficiencies.

INCIDENCE

The incidence of dental disease varies. It is uncommon to find a child who is totally free from one of the dental/oral conditions. With a few exceptions, cavities are no more prevalent among disabled than nondisabled children. They are more prevalent, however, in populations that are not exposed to fluorides. At least one-fourth of the two-year-olds and two-thirds of the three-year-olds in this group have some cavities. Children who have been receiving fluorides since birth, on the other hand, commonly are cavity-free.

Lengthy feedings also affect the incidence of cavities. Nursing caries—decay of the primary upper front teeth and first primary molars—are found in infants and very young children whose nursing sessions have been prolonged, especially those who have been put to sleep with a bottle.

The overall prevalence of gum disease is as high as 90 to 95 percent. (Fortunately, most of the gum disease found in children is of the mild variety caused by plaque and food debris from improper toothbrushing.) The prevalence among children with developmental disabilities is even higher, possibly a result of significantly poorer oral hygiene. Among children with Down syndrome, the prevalence of gum disease is very high and the incidence of cavities very low. There is, to date, no explanation for this finding.

Approximately 50 percent of the children who are receiving phenytoin (Dilantin) for treatment of convulsive disorders may develop gum overgrowth (gingival hyperplasia).

The prevalence of improper contact of upper and lower teeth in children with developmental disabilities is difficult to estimate. In normal populations, 30 percent of people have a receding lower jaw (class II, or retrognathic, type of malocclusion); around 5 percent exhibit a protruding lower jaw (class III, or prognathic, type). Studies have shown that as many as 90 percent of children with neuromuscular disorders have a malocclusion. Anterior open bites—when the top teeth overlap the bottom less than the normal 30 to 50 percent—commonly are found in children with developmental disabilities. This may be partially due to the higher incidence of tongue thrusting and mouth breathing or to weak oral-facial musculature.

DETECTION

Occasionally, an inquisitive parent may notice a mark or a defect in the mouth or on the teeth and bring it to the attention of a dentist. Generally, though, the child is first taken to the dentist because of pain or trauma, to fulfill a school entry requirement, or at the recommendation of a physician. Too frequently, by that time the child already has a dental problem.

It is now recommended that children with developmental disabilities, along with other high-risk children, be seen by a dentist within six months after the first tooth erupts. This way, in addition to examining the teeth and mouth, the dentist can initiate a comprehensive preventive dentistry program that should reduce or eliminate dental disease.

COURSE

Dental disease, especially cavities and gum infections, is progressive. Its effect on both the primary and permanent teeth can be devastating. If primary teeth are lost prematurely, the consequences can include decreased eating ability, interference with speech development, loss of space for the developing permanent teeth, and, possibly, temporomandibular joint disorders.

Cavities that progress to involve the pulp can lead to considerable pain as well as to infection that can rapidly involve many areas of the oral-facial complex. Gum disease does not advance as rapidly in children as it does in adults. Unfortunately, this fact has led to the erroneous notion that gum disease affects only adults and is very unlikely in children.

Fractured teeth that are not properly treated can lead to pulp death (necrosis), with the possibility of infection and tooth loss. Teeth with enamel irregularities not only are aesthetically unpleasing, they also are more likely to fracture or develop cavities.

ACCOMPANYING HEALTH PROBLEMS

Clinical experience suggests that children with serious dental problems may have other health problems as well. Difficulty in chewing frequently leads to a compromised diet, one usually made up of high-calorie carbohydrates at the expense of fresh fruits and vegetables and protein-rich foods. Children with severe dental problems have a high incidence of ear, nose, and throat problems, which often disappear once the dental problems are resolved.

Some reports suggest that children with severe malocclusions may also exhibit temporomandibular joint dysfunction. Too, as mentioned earlier, there seems to be a high correlation of anterior open bite with mouth breathing and tongue thrusting.

DENTAL MANAGEMENT

Managing dental disease in children depends upon making parents aware of the importance of good dental care. Also essential are early examination and the initiation of a comprehensive preventive dentistry program. High-risk children should be seen initially by the dentist six months after the first tooth erupts. At this time, parents will be counseled regarding dental development, methods of cleaning the teeth and massaging the gums, modification of the diet, and optimal use of fluorides.

Cleaning the Teeth

Teeth should be brushed as soon as they begin to erupt. A convenient method is to place the infant in a cradle formed by two adults sitting in a knee-to-knee position: one stabilizes and keeps the child involved while the other wields a small, multitufted, soft brush that effectively cleans the teeth and massages the gums. Toothpaste is not necessary for cleaning and may cause gagging. This cleaning should take place at least once a day, preferably before sleep. As the child grows and becomes more involved in the cleaning process, adults should continue to evaluate and reinforce the child's efforts.

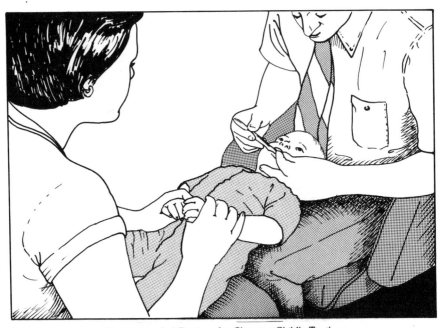

Recommended Position for Cleaning Child's Teeth

Diet

Diet plays a major role in the origin and development of dental disease. A child's diet should be monitored, with restrictions placed on foods—including snacks—that are adhesive or slowly dissolving and on foods that have a high table sugar (sucrose) content.

Fluoridation

Fluoridating community water has brought up to a 70 percent reduction of cavities in children with lifelong exposure. In communities where water is not fluoridated, children should be given fluoride supplements. Professionally applied fluorides are also recommended either annually or semiannually, depending on the child's dental needs. (The suggested dosages may have to be adjusted for the child's disability, dietary habits, and disease patterns.)

Supplemental Fluoride Dosage Schedule (Adjusted Allowance in Milligrams per Day)*

Concentration of Fluoride in Water

Age in Years	Less than 0.3 ppm	0.3 to 0.7 ppm	Greater than 0.7 ppm
Birth to 2	0.25	0	0
2 to 3	0.50	0.25	0
3 to 14	1.00	0.50	0

*2.2 mg of sodium fluoride contains 1 mg of fluoride. Approved by the Council on Dental Therapeutics of the American Dental Association and Committee on Nutrition of the American Academy of Pediatrics.

Use of Pacifiers

Although thumb and finger sucking can have a profound effect on the growth and development of the teeth and jaws, it is common for infants and young children to require additional sucking. Whether a pacifier is less detrimental than finger and thumb sucking to growth and development is still being investigated. Some professionals feel that a pacifier is preferable, partly because it can be withdrawn at the appropriate age.

Even with the most comprehensive preventive dentistry program, dental disease may still occur. Generally, all of the restorative techniques that have been developed are available for use with all children. Unfortunately, children with developmental disabilities may be more difficult to manage in a dental setting. Some may be given general anesthesia, while others may need to be sedated with drugs or stabilized with restraints. Management problems make it even more important that these children visit the dentist frequently in order to intercept problems early and to avoid extensive and complex treatment.

IMPLICATIONS FOR EDUCATION

Children with dental disease may present many problems in the educational setting.

- Pain from the mouth may cause difficulty in chewing food properly. A compromised appetite may lead to either reduced food intake or a modified diet.
- Missing teeth, especially in the anterior segment, can interfere with the proper placement of the tongue and lips, possibly interfering with the speech mechanism.
- Decayed and missing teeth may interfere with social acceptance because of compromised aesthetics and smell.
- Untreated dental disease can lead to pain and discomfort. Children may not be able to cope with pain or understand its management; they may be hyperactive or have decreased attention spans.
- Dental disease may require considerable professional attention, taking time away from the classroom.

Additionally, educators must be careful that children with neuromuscular problems or with uncontrolled convulsive disorders are supervised properly to avoid trauma to the face, mouth, and teeth. During feeding, utensils must be managed carefully so that the child will not bite down on them inadvertently and damage teeth or soft tissues.

Every effort should be made to reduce the frequency of foods, including snacks, that are high in sucrose. These foods have a tendency to remain on the teeth, and the subsequent production of acids may cause cavities.

The classroom can be an excellent environment for teaching proper toothbrushing skills. The physical and/or occupational therapist can use the procedure as a means of developing a systematic approach to personal hygiene and task orientation.

Down Syndrome

DESCRIPTION

Down syndrome, sometimes called trisomy 21 or, less acceptably, mongolism, results from one of the most common chromosomal abnormalities in humans—the presence of an extra chromosome, or extra part of a chromosome, in each cell of the body. This anomaly causes the physical and developmental features of Down syndrome:

- congenital heart disease
- mental retardation
- small stature
- decreased muscle tone (hypotonia)
- hyperflexibility of joints
- speckling of iris (Brushfield spots)
- upward slant to eyes
- extra fold at inner corners of eyes (epicanthal folds)
- small oral cavity, resulting in protruding tongue
- short, broad hands with single palmar crease (simian crease)
- wide gap between first and second toes

The presence and degree of the above characteristics vary with each child. Many other features are associated with Down syndrome, and some of those listed above may be found in children without this condition.

CAUSE

The various physical and mental abnormalities associated with Down syndrome are caused by a genetic imbalance; there is an extra chromosome in all or most cells of the child's body. Normally, every cell of the human body except for the gametes (sperm or ova) contains 46 chromosomes, which are arranged in pairs. With Down syndrome there is one extra, or 47 chromosomes. There are three processes by which this anomaly can occur.

Nondisjunction

Chromosomal pairs are numbered according to size (chromosomes 1 to 22, plus two sex chromosomes). Failure of the chromosome 21 pair to separate accounts for 95 percent of the cases of Down syndrome. This nondisjunction of the chromosome 21 pair takes place prior to conception—during the formation of the sperm or ovum in the parent. The abnormal gamete then joins with a normal gamete at conception to form a fertilized egg with three (a trisomy) of chromosome 21. (This may also occur during the first cell division after conception.) This type of Down syndrome is usually sporadic and has a recurrence rate of 0.5 to 1 percent.

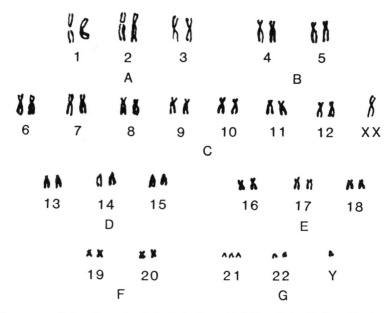

Chromosome Pattern (Karyotype) of a Body (Somatic) Cell in a Male with Down Syndrome. *Notice the extra chromosome 21.*

Translocation

In 4 percent of the cases of Down syndrome, the extra chromosome 21 is attached (translocated) to another chromosome (usually chromosome 14, 15, or 22). About half the time, this type of Down syndrome is inherited from a parent who is a "carrier." The risk of recurrence is therefore much higher than it is with nondisjunction.

Mosaicism

In another 1 to 2 percent of cases, the abnormal separation of chromosome 21 occurs sometime after conception. All future divisions of the affected cell result in cells with an extra chromosome. Therefore, the child has some cells with the normal number of chromosomes and other cells with an extra chromosome. The extent to which the child has the features of Down syndrome depends on the percentage of body cells with the extra chromosome 21. The recurrence risk for this type of Down syndrome is not significantly different from the risk in the general population.

No specific cause for these chromosomal abnormalities has been identified. However, the risk of having a child with Down syndrome increases with advancing maternal age. (Amniocentesis is commonly available for prenatal diagnosis.) In one-third of the cases, the extra chromosome comes from the father.

INCIDENCE

Down syndrome occurs in approximately one in 600 to 800 live births, a figure that does not take into account the large number of affected fetuses that are aborted spontaneously. All races are affected equally. Incidence increases with the age of the mother; one study estimates the rate for women of 40 years of age at one per 110 live births.

DETECTION

The physical characteristics of Down syndrome usually make it evident at birth. The diagnosis is confirmed by growing certain white blood cells in the laboratory and photographing them as they undergo cell division. This chromosomal analysis, called a karyotype, can also be done on fetal cells obtained by amniocentesis, making prenatal diagnosis possible. If the karyotype of an individual with Down syndrome reveals the translocation type, it is important to examine the karyotype of the parents to determine whether they are carriers.

COURSE

With medical and surgical intervention—the correction of heart defects, for instance—and with improved educational opportunities, the prognosis for children with Down syndrome has improved dramatically. Many survive beyond the ages of 50 or 60. The most significant improvements in their physical and mental development have resulted from deinstitutionalization and from training in self-help and work skills.

Children with Down syndrome tend to be hypotonic, that is, to have low muscle tone at birth, making them floppy and poorly coordinated; this improves with age, however. Overall growth is relatively slow, and final height is reached at around age 16. Girls may menstruate and be fertile, but males are usually infertile.

Mental retardation, which is invariably associated with this syndrome, becomes more evident as the child grows older and IQ and social maturity tests include more items calling for abstract reasoning. Performance on adaptive behavior tests, on the other hand, usually improves. (This is true of mentally retarded children in general.)

ACCOMPANYING HEALTH PROBLEMS

Serious health problems that may accompany Down syndrome are congenital heart disease and blockage in the small intestine (duodenal atresia). Because these children have a lowered resistance to infection, they frequently have respiratory infections, runny nose (chronic rhinitis), and conjunctivitis. Also common are eye problems, such as crossing (strabismus) or refractive error (e.g., farsightedness and nearsightedness), and mild-to-moderate hearing loss. Children with Down syndrome are ten to 20 times more likely to develop acute leukemia than would be expected on the basis of chance alone.

Instability of the space between the first two cervical vertebrae (atlantoaxial subluxation) has received more attention. In a small number of affected individuals with this problem, the spinal cord may become damaged. It is recommended that all children with Down syndrome receive an X-ray of the neck before participation in activities (e.g., tumbling) that put pressure on the head and neck.

Other medical problems are summarized well in the review article by Van Dyke cited at the end of this chapter.

MEDICAL MANAGEMENT

To assure survival, major medical problems, such as congenital heart disease and duodenal atresia, require specialized medical and surgical treatment in infancy. After this, health problems associated with Down syndrome are relatively minor and are treated the same as they are with all children.

Periodically treatments for Down syndrome are proposed whose positive effects have not been substantiated in an accepted scientific manner or whose risks may outweigh benefits. An example of the former is sicca cell therapy in which animal neural or endocrine tissue is injected into a child with Down syndrome in hopes that it will be incorporated into the brain. Cosmetic surgery is an example of the latter, where the typical facial features are altered to make the child less Down-syndrome appearing. Parents need support from professionals to evaluate these "treatments" critically. They can divert attention from therapeutic approaches (mostly educational and social) that have proved beneficial.

IMPLICATIONS FOR EDUCATION

While the degree of mental retardation accompanying Down syndrome varies from mild to severe, most affected children are in the moderate range. The retardation, coupled with low muscle tone, leads to delays in development that affect educational performance.

Infants with Down syndrome may seem passive and content to lie quietly, but in order to develop fully they need to be handled, talked to, and played with. They also benefit from exposure to music, colors, textures, movement, and the like. Simple toys and simple tasks reduce frustration and are therefore more conducive to growth. Self-help skills are harder for these children to learn, and they require constant practice to maintain them.

Like all children, children with Down syndrome need discipline. Correction procedures are most effective when used to augment imitation and positive reinforcement.

As infants, these children eat slowly and tend to spit up a mouthful or two after feedings. This may cause them not to grow well when they are young. As they get older, however, many are prone to obesity; therefore, high-caloric snacks should be avoided, and regular exercise should be encouraged. Constipation, too, is common and may be handled with increased amounts of water, fruits, and roughage.

Respiratory infections are frequent, particularly in the very young, and may interrupt the educational process. Adequate humidity in the classroom may help alleviate stuffy noses and upper respiratory problems.

SEE ALSO

Congenital Heart Disease, Genetics, Mental Retardation, and *Syndromes*

ADDITIONAL RESOURCES

Pueschel, S.M. *The Young Child with Down Syndrome.* New York: Human Sciences Press, 1984.

Pueschel, S.M., C. Tingey, J.E. Rynders, A.C. Crocker, and D.M. Crutcher, eds. *New Perspectives on Down Syndrome.* Baltimore: Paul H. Brookes Publishing Co., 1987.

Van Dyke, D.C. "Medical Problems in Infants and Young Children with Down Syndrome: Implications for Early Services." *Infants and Young Children* 1 (1989): 39–50.

Electroencephalography

The electroencephalogram (EEG) is a recording of the electrical signals produced by the brain. Electrodes placed on the scalp surface pick up electrical impulses of millions of nearby nerve cells and carry them to the EEG machine, where they are amplified and combined with signals from other areas of the brain surface. (Signals from deep within the brain are usually too weak to be recorded.)

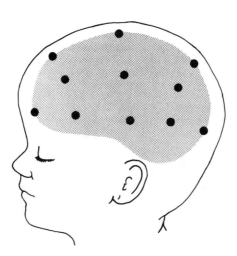

Sites of Electrode Placement

The test causes no pain, though it may frighten the child, making sedation necessary. The normal EEG pattern for adults is not developed until late childhood, and correctly interpreting the EEGs of children—particularly those of newborns—requires specialized knowledge and experience.

The following readouts for a normal child of one month, one year, and four years illustrate how much EEG patterns change as the brain develops:

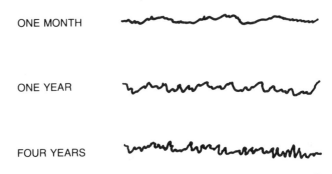

ONE MONTH

ONE YEAR

FOUR YEARS

Normal EEG Patterns at Different Ages

The EEG is the most useful laboratory test for children suspected of having seizure disorders. Various EEG patterns are associated with specific types of seizures. Some children who have seizure disorders, however, may have normal EEGs (although specialized techniques or placements of receiving electrodes sometimes reveal characteristic abnormalities in EEG patterns). Just as a seizure disorder may not be reflected in the EEG, an abnormal EEG does not necessarily mean there is a seizure disorder. About 15 percent of the population have mild EEG abnormalities that are not associated with clinically evident seizures.

NORMAL AT ONE YEAR

ABNORMAL AT ONE YEAR

Normal and Abnormal EEG Patterns

It is best to get an EEG just before and during sleep, the times when seizure patterns are likely to be most evident. For this reason, drugs are sometimes used to produce drowsiness. If a routine EEG does not appear to rule out a seizure, a child may undergo a test in which measurements are taken for up to 24 hours using a device like a small tape recorder to capture the information for later study. During this time the child participates in all the usual activities (except for those involving water) while the parent keeps a record of the child's behaviors.

EEGs are also useful in diagnosing brain malformations, tumors, abscesses, and pockets of blood—all of which alter the normal patterns. They are also useful in determining brain death by detecting the absence of electrical activity—a criterion used by some facilities to determine when to discontinue the use of life-support mechanisms.

Efforts have been made to derive additional information from EEG patterns by using computers. For example, an individual's response to a repeated sound (auditory evoked response) can be assessed by sending certain EEG signals to a computer. This technique, which does not require cooperation by the child, may be useful in assessing hearing in children too young or too developmentally delayed to give reliable responses with other methods. A similar technique, which computes visually evoked responses, can be useful in assessing vision in very young or mentally retarded children. Another recently developed technique, called brain electrical activity mapping, combines EEG data with a computer to produce a visual image of the brain's electrical activity.

SEE ALSO
Hearing Impairment, Seizure Disorders, and *Visual Impairment*

Encephalitis and Meningitis

Encephalitis and meningitis are infections that involve the central nervous system.

ENCEPHALITIS

Description
Encephalitis is an infection of the brain substance.

Cause
Encephalitis is almost always caused by a virus, usually one that can cause infections of other tissues as well (e.g., mumps, influenza). For some unknown reason, in certain individuals the virus attacks the brain. Occasionally, there are epidemics of encephalitis caused by certain viruses, such as the eastern or western equine type. Mosquitoes carry these from birds and domestic and wild mammals to humans.

Incidence
The incidence of encephalitis is hard to determine, since this condition is difficult to diagnose and therefore may go unreported. While any individual can be affected, this disease is more likely to occur in children. Some of the viruses cause encephalitic infections on a year-round basis; others, such as the mosquito-borne viruses, cause infections mainly during the summer months.

Detection

The different locations of the infection result in different symptoms. The initial symptoms of encephalitis include fever, vomiting, various alterations in brain function (confusion, dizziness, headache, drowsiness), and, if the disease is in its more advanced stages, seizures and coma.

Encephalitis is diagnosed primarily from the physical examination, though tests may be done to rule out other conditions.

Course

This condition is usually mild (except in the case of neonatal herpes simplex encephalitis). However, it may progress to coma and, in a very small percentage of children, death. Most children will recover without any aftereffects. A small percentage, however, may incur brain damage, resulting in some degree of mental retardation or learning disability. A rare, slowly progressive form of encephalitis, called subacute sclerosing panencephalitis, causes gradual, ongoing brain damage and, ultimately, death.

Accompanying Health Problems

The primary health problem that can occur with encephalitis is brain damage. This may result in mental retardation, learning disabilities, and/ or a convulsive disorder. Brain damage can also lead to blindness, deafness, hydrocephalus, hyperactive behavior, or paralysis.

Medical Management

Generally speaking, there are no medicines for treating viral infections (though a drug has been used with some success with herpes virus infections). Therefore, in the case of encephalitis, treatment consists of controlling the symptoms until the infection subsides on its own. Fortunately, most viral infections are eventually cleared by the body's own defense mechanisms without any lasting effects.

Implications for Education

Most children who have had encephalitis have no long-lasting effects. Only those children who have incurred brain damage and resultant problems will require special instructional techniques.

MENINGITIS

Description

Meningitis is an infection of the covering (meninges) surrounding the brain and spinal cord.

Cause

Meningitis, like encephalitis, can be caused by a virus. Many times, though, it is caused by bacteria. In the newborn period, when the mortality rate for this condition is highest, meningitis is usually due to organisms normally found in the intestinal tract and vagina of the mother and is acquired by the infant during passage through the birth canal. In children aged two months to three years, the cause is usually one of three organisms: *Haemophilus influenzae*, meningococcus, or pneumococcus.

Incidence

The incidence of neonatal meningitis in full-term infants is 0.13 per thousand births. In preterm babies this figure increases to 2.24 per thousand. Forty in every ten thousand children aged one month to three years are affected by *Haemophilus influenzae*, the leading cause of bacterial meningitis in this age group.

Detection

The signs and symptoms of bacterial meningitis vary with the age and development of the child. Signs and symptoms are likely to include a bulging soft spot (in the infant), fever, stiff neck, irritability, poor feeding, vomiting, and even seizures. The older child may complain also of headache. Meningitis is diagnosed by performing tests on spinal fluid, which is obtained safely and easily by a spinal tap (lumbar puncture). These tests include a culture of the spinal fluid to determine whether the infection is caused by a virus or bacterium, and if the latter, which type. This culture also indicates whether the disease can be treated with antibiotics, and, if so, which ones.

Course

The course meningitis follows depends on which organism causes it. If the disease is due to a virus, the progression is similar to that of encephalitis, and the majority of children will recover on their own without any after-effects. If, on the other hand, the meningitis is caused by a bacterium, it can result in severe brain damage or even death. Fortunately, bacterial meningitis is generally treatable with antibiotics; if these are administered early enough, the child can be cured with no long-term effects. The younger the child and the longer the infection goes untreated (or inadequately treated), the greater the likelihood of serious long-term effects.

Accompanying Health Problems

The primary health problem that can occur with meningitis is brain damage. Neonatal meningitis, usually bacterial, is associated with permanent neurological damage in 30 to 50 percent of its survivors. These problems include hydrocephalus, mental retardation, blindness, hearing loss, motor disability, and abnormal speech patterns. There may also be perceptual difficulties, learning disabilities, and behavioral problems.

Medical Management

If the meningitis is caused by a virus, treatment consists of controlling the symptoms until the infection subsides on its own, usually without any lasting effects. Bacterial meningitis, on the other hand, requires treatment with antibiotics effective in killing the specific bacteria involved. In order to reach the central nervous system in adequate concentrations, most antibiotics must be administered intravenously, at least in the early stages, and the child must be hospitalized.

Implications for Education

Special instructional techniques are required only with those children who have incurred brain damage and resultant problems, including mental retardation, learning disabilities, hyperactivity, hydrocephalus, deafness, and blindness.

SEE ALSO

Hearing Impairment, Hydrocephalus, Mental Retardation, Seizure Disorders, and *Visual Impairment*

Failure To Thrive

DESCRIPTION

Children who weigh significantly less than their peers or who gain weight at a slower-than-normal rate during infancy or early childhood may have growth failure and may be said to "fail to thrive."

Some children are normal but small because of hereditary factors. With others, small size is a sign of underlying problems: the body, for various reasons, either does not receive or cannot properly utilize the nutrients required for proper growth and development. If this malnutrition is prolonged, weight, height, and eventually head size (brain growth) are affected.

CAUSE

The reasons for failure to thrive may be organic or nonorganic or both. Organic causes include numerous disorders, especially central nervous system, cardiovascular, and digestive tract problems. For example, with chronic heart failure, the body has higher-than-normal caloric requirements. With cystic fibrosis, the intestines do not adequately absorb fats and proteins, and the child may fail to thrive despite apparently adequate food intake. However, adequate medical treatment of the underlying disorder will often lead to improved growth rates (catch-up growth).

More common is nonorganic failure to thrive. In many regions of the world this is due mainly to poverty, ignorance, or inappropriate dietary and feeding practices. In the United States this condition is more often associated with neglect, emotional disturbances, or ignorance on the part of parents who are often themselves victims of poor parenting and ongoing stresses. Difficulties in parent-child relationships may result in feeding problems: parents may become impatient with the feeding process; children may refuse to be fed or they may even resort to vomiting. Some cases of failure to thrive involve chronic parental depression or other emotional problems. In other situations there is deliberate neglect, sometimes with accompanying physical abuse.

Failure to thrive is more common among children with developmental disabilities than among nondisabled children. For some developmentally disabled children, growth potential is limited despite adequate feeding practices and food intake. Children with certain chromosomal abnormalities, for example, grow poorly even with greater-than-normal amounts of food. On the other hand, children whose poor growth is due to difficulties with the mechanics of chewing and swallowing may catch up with their peers if they are given adequate nutrients by other routes (a gastrostomy tube, for instance). Some children with disabilities are difficult to feed because of temperament or feeding-time behaviors, common in all children, that lead to stress or conflict. Parents or other caretakers need help in eliminating some of these negative behaviors. At times, hospitalization or assessment by a team of professionals (nutritionists, occupational therapists, psychologists, speech clinicians) may be required to sort out the factors responsible for poor growth and to devise a plan for treatment.

SOME CAUSES OF FAILURE TO THRIVE

Organic causes (rare)*

- Central nervous system abnormalities
- Structural or neuromotor abnormalities of the alimentary tract (e.g., cleft palate, cerebral palsy)
- Gastrointestinal diseases (malabsorption syndromes)
- Congenital heart disease
- Endocrine disorders (e.g., growth hormone deficiency)
- Chromosome defects
- Kidney disease
- Chronic infections
- Malignancies
- Fetal alcohol syndrome

Nonorganic causes (common)*

- Inadequate nutrient intake
- Environmental stress
- Emotional deprivation
- Abuse and neglect

*Nonorganic and organic causes may coexist.

INCIDENCE

Failure to thrive is diagnosed in about 1 percent of hospitalized children. About one-fifth have growth failure due to an organic disease.

DETECTION

Charts giving normal ranges for weight, height, and head size are consulted to determine whether a child is small for age and sex. A series of measurements of more than two standard deviations below the mean over a period of months suggests a diagnosis of failure to thrive, as do gains in weight or height that are much smaller than expected. It is helpful to compare a child's weight and height. A child with growth failure usually has "weight age" (age for which the weight is average) younger than "height age." Once the condition has been considered, a thorough medical history and physical examination will help to find the cause.

The physician may adjust expectations for growth based on parental heights using available studies, obtain a history of intake and feeding practices and behaviors, note signs and symptoms suggestive of organic diseases, and focus on psychosocial factors that can lead to growth failure. At times, hospitalization for observation, testing, and provision of adequate calories and nutrients for *catch-up* growth may be required. If there is no organic cause and the child's growth improves with adequate nurturance, the failure to thrive is likely nonorganic.

COURSE

The course of failure to thrive depends on the timing, cause, and treatment of poor growth. Children with early (occurring in the first year) or prolonged failure to thrive have poorer growth than do children who are malnourished at a later age or for briefer periods.

Delays in gross motor, social, and expressive language skills may accompany failure to thrive. It is sometimes difficult to determine when delays in development are due to failure to thrive or vice versa. When adequate nutrition is restored, improvements in growth usually occur before improvements in developmental skills.

ACCOMPANYING HEALTH PROBLEMS

With organic failure to thrive, the signs and symptoms of the underlying disease tend to predominate. For example, while patients with cystic fibrosis may grow poorly, unless treated, because of impaired digestion of protein and fats, the poor growth is likely to be obscured by the more obvious symptoms of cystic fibrosis, such as coughing, wheezing, and frequent pneumonias.

Children with nonorganic failure to thrive often do not have regular checkups or adequate immunization. They are therefore more likely to have undiagnosed medical problems, such as iron deficiency anemia or impetigo.

IMPLICATIONS FOR EDUCATION

Undernourished children are at risk for learning problems, including mastery of gross motor skills—especially if the malnutrition is severe or prolonged or if it occurs within the first year of life. Children with significant organic failure to thrive during infancy may have reduced abilities in attention and memory. Children with nonorganic failure to thrive sometimes have difficulties with expressive language and social skills; they may have poor listening and attending skills as well.

A comprehensive interdisciplinary assessment of the child's strengths and weaknesses in cognition, language, social skills, and physical capacity, together with an understanding of the child's environment, helps teachers and families to design a program suitable for individual needs. Consultation may be necessary concerning specialized feeding techniques, behavior modification, or dietary manipulation.

SEE ALSO

Child Abuse and Neglect, Cystic Fibrosis, Feeding Problems, and *Growth and Nutrition*

ADDITIONAL RESOURCE

Goldbloom, R.B. "Growth Failure in Infancy." *Pediatrics in Review* 9 (1987): 57–61.

Feeding Problems

DESCRIPTION

Children who are not able to eat enough to grow adequately have feeding problems. Many disabled children do not consume enough calories to support adequate growth. They may remain significantly underweight for their height, or lose weight. Poor growth and malnutrition can adversely affect a child's learning and development.

Feeding problems can be defined objectively by a child's growth chart. Poor growth will first be reflected in weight, then length, and, finally, head circumference. A child's rate of growth is considered abnormal if any of the growth measurements do not follow the normal curve on the chart or if there is a weight-for-length ratio below the fifth percentile. Poor growth can result from insufficient caloric intake or may be an inherent part of a child's underlying medical condition. Children with certain genetic disorders, for example, exhibit growth retardation despite an adequate caloric intake.

Medical, nutritional, developmental, and psychosocial/environmental factors may all contribute to feeding problems. It is often the combination of these factors that creates a complex problem requiring the intervention of an interdisciplinary team of professionals.

CAUSE

Feeding problems in young children that result in insufficient caloric intake occur for a variety of reasons, including

- central nervous system immaturity (e.g., as in a premature infant)
- central nervous system damage (e.g., as in cerebral palsy, causing oral-motor involvement)
- chromosomal abnormalities (e.g., as in Down syndrome)
- cardiac or respiratory disease (e.g., heart defect, bronchopulmonary dysplasia)

- kidney disease
- structural abnormalities (e.g., cleft palate)
- mechanical problems (e.g., gastroesophageal reflux, delayed gastric emptying)
- significant developmental delay
- behavioral resistance
- problems with parent-child interaction

Children with neurological impairment sometimes experience a weak suck, poor lip closure, poor tongue control, difficulty in chewing, or difficulty in swallowing (dysphagia). These children cannot coordinate the oral movements needed for normal feeding. Children who have significantly increased muscle tone may burn calories at a rapid rate and therefore require more food. However, these are often the children who have problems with oral-motor dysfunction and therefore cannot eat enough to meet their caloric needs. Feedings may be long and strenuous, particularly for a child with limited stamina, such as an infant with a cardiac or respiratory problem. Appetite may be irregular because of lack of activity, illness, or constipation. Children in kidney failure may never experience much of an appetite.

Insufficient caloric intake may also occur because of environmental circumstances, such as when a child is fed too frequently, too infrequently, or on an erratic schedule. Some parents may have inappropriate expectations for their child's developmental level. Volumes of food may be too small, thereby not meeting the child's caloric demands, or too large, leading to vomiting. Intake of food may also be affected by behavioral resistance, such as purposeful gagging, vomiting, and tantrums. Temperamental styles, such as excessive passivity or irritability, may also affect feeding.

"Mechanical," or physiological, problems may occur that result in lost calories or decreased appetite. Gastroesophageal (GE) reflux is vomiting or regurgitation that results from a weak muscle between the esophagus and stomach. Repeated GE reflux irritates the esophagus and may cause chronic heartburn, or esophagitis, which can lead to ulcers. Some children experience delayed gastric emptying. Their stomachs do not empty at a normal rate, leaving them feeling full and having no appetite.

Children may also have abnormal feeding patterns that alter their nutritional intake. They may have strong food preferences that limit the variety of nutrients, or they may never indicate hunger. They may have a low fluid intake, or they may drink well but refuse solids. Certain children are intolerant to changes in caretakers, environment, and routine and may refuse to eat in new situations. Children who have significant brain damage may experience "shut-down" periods when they refuse to eat or drink for extended periods of time. Dehydration may result when such children spontaneously wean themselves from the bottle without being effective cup drinkers.

The result of all feeding problems is that a cycle is established wherein poor feeding leads to poor nutrition. This, in turn, decreases motor activity, oral health, and resistance to infection. The child becomes ill and more constipated, which in turn intensifies the feeding problems and the pattern continues.

INCIDENCE

Feeding and growth problems are very prevalent among disabled children. It is estimated that 25 percent of disabled children consume inadequate diets, 90 percent have some type of nutritional problem, and 15 to 25 percent are growth-retarded, or have a weight-for-length ratio below the fifth percentile. At least 70 percent of children who are developmentally delayed, whether or not they have neuromuscular problems, have feeding problems.

DETECTION

The first objective evidence of a child's feeding problem will be seen on the growth chart. If the child's weight-for-length ratio is below the fifth percentile, if any of the measurements have decreased over two percentile lines, or if the growth curve has flattened, a feeding problem exists. A feeding observation can provide additional information.

X-ray studies and other medical tests may be necessary to detect specific mechanical feeding problems. The most common tests are described below.

Barium Swallow

The barium swallow (upper GI) evaluates the function and structure of the throat and esophagus. A child swallows barium solution, and a type of video X-ray is used to show the swallowing process. Physical abnormalities of the throat and esophagus, abnormal swallowing (dysphagia), aspiration, and sometimes GE reflux can be diagnosed.

Chest X-Ray

A chest X-ray may be obtained to look for evidence of pneumonia, which could indicate chronic aspiration, or inhalation of food into the lungs.

pH Probe

A probe is put down the esophagus for 24 hours to measure the pH, or acid-base balance. A low pH means the presence of stomach acids in the esophagus, indicating GE reflux and possible esophagitis.

Gastric Emptying Study

The gastric emptying test measures the rate at which contents are emptied from the stomach. A substance is swallowed and a film is taken of the stomach; computer technology is used to interpret results. If the stomach empties too slowly, the child may always feel full, may not be hungry, and may vomit.

Endoscopy

In endoscopic studies, a tube is placed down the throat to visualize the esophagus. This test is done to confirm the presence of esophagitis and to look for ulcers.

MEDICAL MANAGEMENT

Interventions to increase caloric intake include behavior management, normalizing feeding schedules and volumes (i.e., three regular meals and snacks), and increasing caloric density. Caloric density is increased by adding extra fat or sugar to the child's meals, concentrating formula, or providing food supplements such as "instant breakfast." Children with neuromuscular involvement may also require therapy and/or special equipment to improve jaw closure, sucking, and swallowing. In addition, adaptive positioning may be necessary to maximize a child's potential for oral feeding.

Medical problems such as esophagitis, delayed gastric emptying, and GE reflux can be treated with medications. Rapid gastric emptying is often treated by giving smaller feedings over a longer period of time. An upright posture and thickened feedings are helpful if a child has GE reflux. Some of those children require a Nissen fundoplication, which is surgery to tighten up the muscle between the esophagus and stomach.

If a child has abnormal feeding patterns, steps are taken to normalize the diet and prevent dehydration. Fluids can be mixed with solids; given through foods with a high water content, such as sherbet or gelatin; or given directly by syringe. During periods of illness, such children may require intravenous fluids and/or tube feedings.

If enough food or fluids cannot be taken orally to support a child's nutrition and growth, tube feedings are initiated. Tube feedings may also be necessary if a child aspirates when eating, or inhales food into the lungs. Food is delivered directly to the stomach by means of a tube so that digestion can begin. Tube feedings may be short-term or long-term, temporary or permanent. Children who cannot tolerate feeding through their digestive tracts can be nourished intravenously.

Nasogastric Tube

A nasogastric (NG) tube is a tube that is passed through the nose into the stomach. Through this tube, food is delivered directly into the stomach and therefore bypasses the mouth and esophagus (*see illustration below*).

Nasogastric tubes are used to provide nourishment to children in whom sucking or swallowing reflexes are absent or underdeveloped. Children with respiratory problems or seizures are at greater risk of aspiration (food particles going to the lungs) and may require nasogastric tube feedings. Nasogastric tubes are often used as a temporary measure—if it seems likely that the child will begin to eat orally—as a means of boosting calories prior to surgery or to provide hydration during illness, or while a decision is being made about a more permanent feeding tube. Nasogastric tubes are not recommended for long-term use because they can be very irritating to the nose and throat, and are not cosmetically appealing.

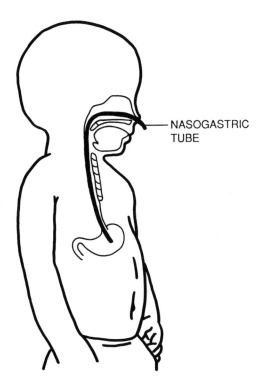

NASOGASTRIC
TUBE

Nasogastric Tube

Equipment

Nasogastric tubes are made of plastic and come in different sizes and lengths. Before inserting a nasogastric tube, one needs to determine the length of tube to be inserted so that the food is deposited in the stomach and not the esophagus or small intestine. This is done by measuring from the tip of the child's nose to the earlobe, then to a point midway between the bottom of the breastbone and the navel. The tube is inserted by gently guiding it through the nostril until the premeasured mark is reached. The tube is then taped to the child's face. A nasogastric tube may stay in place for three to five days, then should be replaced by a new tube in the other nostril. A tube may also be inserted just for the feeding, then removed. A large syringe (50 to 60 cc) is attached to the nasogastric tube during feeding as a receptacle to hold the formula. A plastic feeding bag or bottle may also serve this function. If a child is receiving drip feedings over a prolonged period of time, a mechanical infusion pump is required to regulate the flow of formula.

Feeding Procedure

When feeding a child with a nasogastric tube, the child should always be positioned with the head and chest elevated at a 30 degree angle. This reduces the possibility that the child will aspirate food into the lungs. If possible, the child should also be placed on his or her right side, which facilitates the flow of fluid into the stomach.

Before the feeding begins, the placement of the tube must be verified to make sure it is in the stomach. This is done by inserting 3 to 5 cc of air into the tube with a syringe, while listening with a stethoscope over the stomach. A popping sound is heard if the tube is properly placed. The plunger of the syringe can also be drawn back to withdraw stomach contents. If more than an ounce of undigested formula is left in the stomach, that amount is then deducted from the total feeding volume.

Formula should be warmed to room temperature to prevent cramping. It is inserted into the large syringe that is held about six inches above the child's body. The flow of the formula is adjusted by raising or lowering the syringe. The feeding should go in over about 15 to 20 minutes. Some children cannot tolerate a large volume of formula at one time and are fed by the drip method, or continuous infusion. With this method, a mechanical feeding pump is used to deliver formula by drip over an extended period of time (several hours or all day). Common problems with nasogastric tube feedings are discussed later in this chapter.

Variations

A feeding tube is sometimes placed through the mouth into the stomach. This is called an oral gastric (OG) tube. A nasojejunal (NJ) tube is passed through the nose into the jejunum, or small intestine, so that the stomach is bypassed. The procedure for feeding a child with either an oral gastric tube or a nasojejunal tube is similar to that for a nasogastric tube.

Gastrostomy

A gastrostomy is an opening made through the abdominal wall directly into the stomach. A tube is inserted into this opening for the purpose of feeding. Therefore, food is delivered directly into the stomach and bypasses the mouth and esophagus.

Gastrostomy tubes are used to nourish children who are unable to suck or swallow, are at risk for aspiration, or have abnormalities of the mouth, throat, or esophagus. In short, children who cannot take in enough nourishment by mouth to sustain health and growth are candidates for gastrostomy tubes. Although not necessarily permanent, a gastrostomy tube is used when long-term tube feedings are required.

Gastrostomy tube insertion is a surgical procedure that is often done under general anesthesia. The stomach is sewn to the abdominal wall and an incision is made for the tube. A Nissen fundoplication is frequently done in conjunction with the gastrostomy. The upper part of the stomach is wrapped around the lower part of the esophagus. This narrows the opening and helps to prevent vomiting or GE reflux while allowing the child to swallow formula and saliva as usual. If a Nissen fundoplication is not needed, a gastrostomy can be placed without general anesthesia. The figure below shows the anatomical placement of a gastrostomy tube.

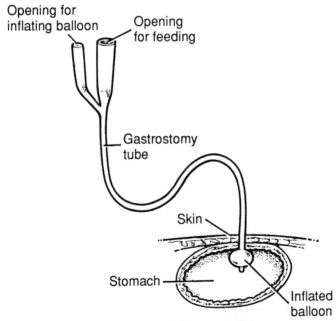

Anatomical Placement of Gastrostomy Tube

Source: Reproduced by permission from *Clinical Handbook of Pediatric Nursing,* 2nd ed., by D. Wong and L. Whaley, The C.V. Mosby Company, St. Louis, © 1986.

Equipment

The most widely used types of gastrostomy tubes are listed below.

Malecot. The end of the Malecot tube looks like a small cage, which helps to hold the tube in the stomach. The tube is stretched out with a probe before insertion.

Pezzer. The end of the Pezzer tube has a mushroom-appearing bulge rather than a cage. It can be difficult for parents to insert.

Foley. The Foley tube has a balloon that is inflated with water after insertion to keep it anchored in place. It is easily inserted by parents but can also be easily dislodged. It sometimes causes problems by migrating down to the small intestine.

Gastrostomy Button. Instead of a tube, the gastrostomy button is a small, flexible, silicone device that has a mushroomlike dome at one end and two flat wings with an attached safety plug at the other end. There is a one-way valve inside the device to prevent reflux of stomach contents. It is a skin-level device, which makes it more cosmetically appealing (see illustration below). The button, however, is more expensive, requires a well-established gastrostomy site, should only be replaced by a physician, and requires special tubing to be attached during feedings. Although the button is not recommended for a child who gags excessively or regurgitates through the tube during feedings, decompression tubing is available to allow air or fluid to exit the stomach.

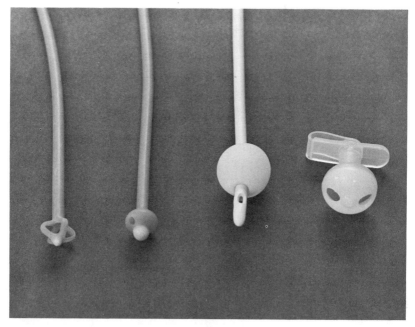

Gastrostomy Tubes (from Left to Right: Malecot, Pezzer, Foley, Button)

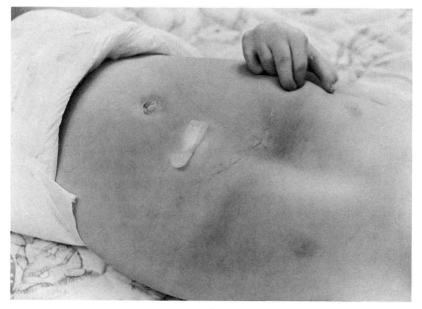

Gastrostomy Button in Child

All of the above tubes, as well as the button, come in different sizes, depending on the size of the child. Standard gastrostomy tubes should be secured to the abdomen with tape. An adhesive dressing (i.e., stomal adhesive) will protect the skin from becoming irritated by the tape. The tube can be pinned or taped to the child's clothes or diapers, or a stretchy cotton netting (i.e., Burn-net) can be placed around the child's abdomen to keep the tube out of the way and prevent the child from pulling it out.

Gastrostomy tubes are often pulled out by children and can come out on their own. If a tube comes out, it is not an emergency situation. The gastrostomy opening will begin to close in two to four hours, however, so a new tube does need to be inserted soon to maintain the opening. A Foley catheter is the easiest type of tube to reinsert. If the tube does not come out accidentally, it should still be replaced every four to six months. The gastrostomy button is replaced when the one-way valve stops working properly, about every nine to twelve months.

Feeding Procedure

The best positions for a child during a gastrostomy feeding are being held upright in the lap, sitting upright in an infant seat, and lying in bed on the right side. These positions help with the emptying of the stomach. Formula should be room temperature or slightly warm. It should take 15 to 20 minutes for the formula to flow in. Formula that is too cold or is fed too quickly may cause cramping.

As with nasogastric tubes, gastrostomy feedings can be done in two ways.

1. *Bolus.* Using a large syringe in the end of the tube, formula is poured directly into the feeding tube (see illustration). Flow is controlled by the size of the tube, thickness of the formula, and the height of the syringe.

2. *Drip.* This method is used if there is a large amount of formula to be given over a long period of time or if the amount must be given very slowly to prevent vomiting. A drip bag with tubing is used, and the flow rate is regulated by means of a mechanical pump.

After a feeding, the tube should be vented or remain unclamped for 15 to 20 minutes to allow for burp time.

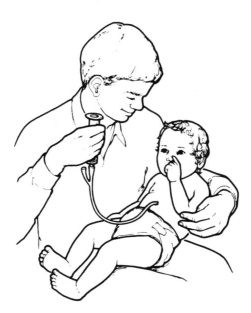

Bolus Gastrostomy Feeding

Source: Reproduced by permission from *Clinical Handbook of Pediatric Nursing*, 2nd ed., by D. Wong and L. Whaley, The C.V. Mosby Company, St. Louis, © 1986.

Medications

Medications can be given through either a nasogastric tube or gastrostomy tube. The medication should be in liquid form or dissolved well in water before being put in the tube. A small quantity of water (5 to 10 cc) should be instilled to rinse the tube after giving medications.

Oral Stimulation

Although children with feeding tubes can still eat by mouth if medically appropriate, many tube-fed children will not accept food orally. Allowing a child to suck on a pacifier during tube feedings (non-nutritive sucking) provides oral stimulation that is then associated with the pleasurable sensation of being fed. Children should also be cuddled and talked to during tube feedings as they would be if fed normally.

Growth

The growth of children being tube-fed needs to be carefully monitored. There is a tendency for children to become overweight after they receive a gastrostomy tube, since feeding becomes easier and caloric intake increases significantly.

Skin Care

The skin around a gastrostomy needs to be checked for drainage, rash, and infection. Leakage of formula and gastric contents around the gastrostomy tube can occur. A small gauze dressing can be placed around the site to collect drainage. The skin around the gastrostomy should be cleansed with soap and water once a day. If drainage or irritation is present, it can be cleansed two to four times a day with half-strength hydrogen peroxide. If the site looks inflamed or has greenish-yellow drainage or a pus exudate, a physician should be contacted since there may be an infection.

Problems

Common tube feeding problems and interventions are listed in the following table.

Common Problems with Tube Feedings

Problem	Cause	Solution
Diarrhea	Feeding too fast	Slow feeding
	Formula too concentrated	Consult dietitian or physician
	Intolerance to formula	Consult dietitian or physician
	Spoiled formula	Clean supplies well; refrigerate formula; hang formula for no more than 8 hours
	Soapy residue on tubing	Rinse well with water
	Improper tube placement	Pull tube back and retape
Vomiting	Feeding too fast	Slow feeding
	Improper tube placement	Reposition tube
	Volume of formula too great	Give smaller amounts of formula more frequently
	Constipation	Relieve constipation
	Breakdown of Nissen fundoplication	Consult physician
Abdominal cramping	Feeding too fast	Slow feeding
	Cold formula	Warm formula to room temperature
	Improper tube placement	Pull tube back and retape
	Tube allowing air in stomach	Unclamp tube to release gas
		Consult physician
Gagging (some gagging is normal)	Feeding too fast	Slow feeding
	Tube allowing air in stomach	Unclamp tube to release gas
	Nissen fundoplication too tight	Consult physician
Plugged tube	Obstruction due to medication or food	Gently milk tube to dislodge obstruction
		Rinse tube thoroughly with water after feedings or medications
		Change tube
Bleeding around tube	Irritation due to changing tube or movement of tube	Secure tube with tape
	Prolapse or protrusion of stomach	Consult physician
Tissue buildup around tube	Normal variation ("granulation tissue")	Consult physician; cauterization with silver nitrate may be necessary

Tube Weaning

Oral feedings can be reinstituted in many children who are fed by gastrostomy tube. The following criteria are used to determine whether a child is ready for oral feedings:

- The medical condition that led to the placement of a gastrostomy tube has been corrected or stabilized for at least six to 12 weeks.
- There are no anatomical or functional problems with swallowing.
- The child is functioning at an adequate developmental level (six months or more) to respond to behavior modification techniques.

Swallowing ability is often assessed by means of X-ray studies, such as a barium swallow test. A child is not a good candidate for oral feedings if he or she has difficulty in swallowing secretions, vomits frequently, or has recurrent pneumonia (signs of aspiration).

Parents often find it difficult to attempt oral feedings at home because of the negative behaviors the child exhibits when they are initiated (i.e., gagging, coughing, crying, fighting). These behaviors result from the child's not having oral feeding experiences during critical periods of development. A therapeutic outpatient or inpatient program staffed by highly skilled professionals often is required to wean a child successfully from tube feedings.

Once a child has been accepting 100 percent of his or her caloric needs for six to eight weeks, the gastrostomy tube can be removed. This can be done easily in a physician's office. The hole will close on its own within a few days, leaving only a small scar.

Central Venous Nutrition

If a child has a problem that interferes with the use of the gastrointestinal tract to digest or absorb nutrients, intravenous feedings may be necessary. Central venous nutrition (CVN), or total parenteral nutrition (TPN), refers to feeding a child solely by intravenous fluids. Central venous nutrition may be necessary for infants and children with Crohn's disease, short-bowel syndrome, inflammatory bowel disease, or malabsorption syndrome, or for children receiving chemotherapy. A long-term central venous catheter, or a tiny, flexible rubber tube, is threaded through a large vein into the heart, and nutrients are put into the blood stream via an intravenous solution. This catheter may be called a Broviac or Hickman catheter. It enters the vein just under the collarbone and exits the skin a few inches below that (see illustration). A mechanical infusion pump is needed to regulate carefully the flow of the intravenous solution. Central venous nutrition is usually started as a continuous infusion over 24 hours but is gradually reduced to ten to 16 hours a day, usually as an overnight feeding.

Because there is a direct entry into the blood stream through the venous catheter, care must be taken to prevent infection. The site at which the catheter is inserted must be cleaned carefully on a daily basis and covered with a bandage or dressing. A solution of heparin (anticlotting medicine) is put in the catheter in between infusions to prevent blood clotting. Parents are taught how to clamp the catheter in case it breaks.

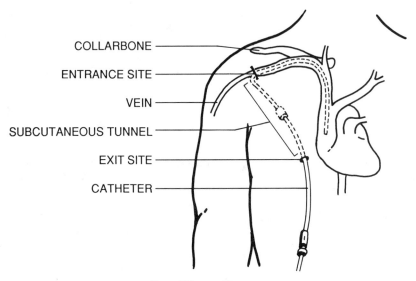

COLLARBONE
ENTRANCE SITE
VEIN
SUBCUTANEOUS TUNNEL
EXIT SITE
CATHETER

Central Venous Nutrition

The catheter needs to be protected from an infant or young child's exploring hands. Therefore, it should be coiled and taped close to the child's body. It is important to prevent the tubing from becoming tangled in toys or furniture. Active play should be limited during infusion time. Parents are encouraged to dress their child in a one-piece jumper or sleeper with snaps in order to prevent the child from handling the catheter while allowing the tubing to be used. A child with a central line can go swimming, but then should have the dressing over the catheter site changed.

If a child has a fever or if the catheter breaks or becomes blocked, a physician should be consulted immediately. Routine medical follow-up is essential to prevent complications.

IMPLICATIONS FOR EDUCATION

The relationship between nutrition and brain growth is well known. A child who is malnourished risks cognitive impairment. Any child who is not receiving sufficient calories for growth may have less energy as well to devote to learning. Other factors associated with feeding problems, such as recurrent illnesses or constipation, may also interfere with educational goals. Difficult or time-consuming feedings create stress for family members, who may not then be able to turn their attention to the child's developmental needs. Professionals in early education can help to identify children who have feeding problems and seek appropriate medical evaluation for them. They may also participate in the management of these problems and can monitor the effects of feeding interventions.

ADDITIONAL RESOURCES

Ahman, E. *Home Care for the High Risk Infant.* Rockville, Md.: Aspen Publishers, Inc., 1986.

American Occupational Therapy Association, Inc. *Problems with Eating: Interventions for Children and Adults with Developmental Disabilities.* Rockville, Md.: American Occupational Therapy Association, Inc., 1987.

Bard Interventional Products. *The Button Replacement Gastrostomy.* Billerica, Mass.: Bard Interventional Products. Videotape. Telephone (800) 826-BARD.

Learner Managed Designs, Inc. *Feeding Handicapped Infants.* Lawrence, Kans.: Learner Managed Designs, Inc. Videotape. Telephone (913) 842-9088.

University of Iowa. *Management of the Child Fed via Gastrostomy Tube: An Oral Feeding Approach.* Iowa City, Iowa: Division of Developmental Disabilities, University Hospital School, University of Iowa. Videotape. Telephone (319) 356-1343.

Wolf, D., and P. Green: *A Practical Guide to Tube Feedings.* Baltimore: John F. Kennedy Institute for Handicapped Children.

Zechman, R., A. Ross, and J. Watkins. *Pediatric Adaptive Technologies: Gastrostomy Tube Feeding.* Seattle, Wash.: University of Washington Child Development and Mental Retardation Center, Media Services. Videotape. Telephone (206) 543-4011.

Fetal Alcohol
Syndrome

DESCRIPTION

Fetal alcohol syndrome (FAS) is a constellation of abnormalities directly related to alcohol ingestion during pregnancy. The major characteristics of FAS include both prenatal and postnatal growth deficiency, delay of gross and fine motor development (often associated with mental retardation), and congenital malformations, some of which result in a characteristic facial appearance.

CAUSE

FAS results from direct exposure of the fetus to the teratogenic effects of alcohol during pregnancy. The exact mechanism by which alcohol damages the developing body tissues is not understood. (Genetic predisposition or poor nutrition—both of which often accompany alcoholism—may be important contributing factors as well.) Since such organs as the brain and the heart are formed during the first trimester, it is clear that the consumption of alcohol during early pregnancy is cause for major concern. Alcohol can injure the fetus throughout the entire pregnancy, however.

There is at present no established amount of alcohol that a pregnant woman can consume without risk to her unborn baby.

INCIDENCE

Incidence rates for FAS vary, ranging from three to six cases per thousand live births. It has been estimated that between 50 and 75 percent of infants born to chronically alcoholic women may be affected with FAS.

DETECTION

Although some children with FAS can be diagnosed in the newborn period, affected children often are not identified until later in infancy or childhood. Presumably, many children with FAS are not identified at all.

ACCOMPANYING HEALTH PROBLEMS

Children with FAS are usually small at birth and continue to grow poorly. In addition, they often have delays in motor and mental development— FAS is one of the most common known causes of mental retardation— and they may exhibit behavior problems, such as hyperactivity. Physical abnormalities associated with this syndrome include small head, eyes, and mouth, as well as droopy eyelids, a wide space between the nose and upper lip, a thin upper lip, and occasionally cleft palate and congenital heart disease.

COURSE

The physical, cognitive, and behavioral difficulties that the vast majority of these children have are often compounded by a poor home environment; the parents commonly have alcohol-related and other personal problems that prevent them from giving appropriate stimulation and nurturance. In many instances, the affected child is removed from the home environment. For some children, unfortunately, this means residing for short periods of time with several foster families rather than being raised in a single, long-term, stable setting.

IMPLICATIONS FOR EDUCATION

Many children with FAS have cognitive limitations and behavior problems that require appropriate adjustments in educational programming.

The ability of the natural parents to provide appropriate care may be limited. On the other hand, if the child is removed from parental custody, the possible lack of a stable, continuing, supportive home may contribute significantly to behavior problems.

SEE ALSO

Mental Retardation and *Syndromes*

Floppy Infant

DESCRIPTION

The floppy (hypotonic) infant, somewhat like a rag doll, assumes atypical postures, has excessive range of motion of the joints, and offers little resistance to passive movement. With young infants, the prominent feature of floppiness may be less than the usual amount of movement; with older infants, it may be delayed onset of motor milestones.

CAUSE

Generalized floppiness is symptomatic of a number of abnormal conditions in various parts of the neuromuscular system—the brain, spinal cord, peripheral nerve, and muscle:

Location	Example Conditions
Brain	Hypotonic cerebral palsy, trauma, malformations, metabolic diseases (e.g., Tay-Sachs disease), Down syndrome
Spinal cord	Spinal musculature atrophy (Werdnig-Hoffmann disease), poliomyelitis, spinal cord trauma
Peripheral nerve	Neuropathies, myasthenia gravis, botulism
Muscle	Muscular dystrophies, metabolic disorders, connective tissue disorders, glycogen storage diseases

DETECTION

Floppiness is usually detected in the following manner (assuming the child is relaxed):

- When the child is held with one hand supporting the abdomen, the head and legs droop.
- When pulled by the hands to a sitting position, the child exhibits poor grasp, little tension of the arm muscles, and significant head lag.
- The child offers little resistance when body parts are moved by the examiner. For instance, an arm that is moved may remain in the new position.
- There may be passive movement beyond the expected range for the child's age. It is sometimes possible, for example, to extend the knees beyond the neutral (straight) position. It may also be possible, when the child lies face up on a table with the hip and knee joints flexed, to spread the legs to touch the knees to the table.

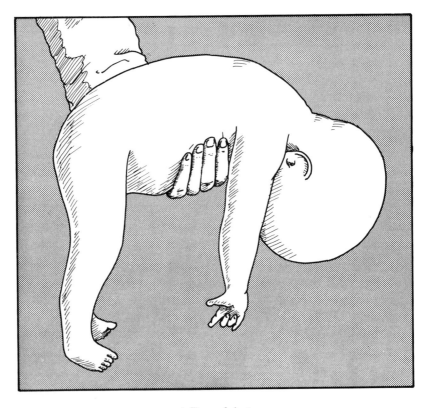

A Floppy Infant

Once floppiness has been noted and demonstrated, it is important to determine the underlying cause. This means looking at the child's history as well as performing a physical examination and other assessments.

History

To explore the possibility of an inherited disease, the parents are asked whether other members of the family have been similarly affected. Details about the pregnancy and birth are sought as well, since they may point to perinatal brain injury. Another important step in tracking down the cause of floppiness is determining whether or not it was present at birth and if it has diminished or increased with time.

Physical Examination

Growth parameters, including head circumference, are assessed. A small head (microcephaly) is an important clue to diagnosis. Particular attention is paid to the neuromotor part of the physical examination, which includes a precise evaluation of muscle function, reflexes, movement, body structure, and gross motor level. Findings in other areas—the skin or bones, for example—may suggest syndromes or diseases of which floppiness is a component.

Other Assessments

The physical examination may point to the need for further laboratory tests (e.g., measuring muscle enzymes), specialized X-ray techniques (e.g., computerized axial tomography), an electromyogram, or even a muscle biopsy.

Input from other professionals is helpful in determining whether the floppiness is an isolated problem or whether the child is delayed in all areas of development.

The following are two examples of how this approach may be used to confirm a particular diagnosis:

Case 1

History	Physical Examination	Test	Diagnosis
Floppy since birth, mother's age at time of birth: 42	Upslanted eyes, flattened back of head, simian creases, wide space between first and second toes	Chromosome analysis	Trisomy 21 (Down syndrome)

Case 2

History	Physical Examination	Test	Diagnosis
Full-term baby, progressively floppy during early months of life	Muscle weakness, absent deep-tendon reflexes, twitching of the tongue	Electromyography, nerve conduction velocities	Werdnig-Hoffmann disease

COURSE

In cases of benign congenital hypotonia—that is, where the floppiness is an isolated problem without other evidence of neurological abnormalities—the child may eventually become completely normal. In most instances of floppiness, however, the course is dependent upon the underlying condition, which may stabilize and remain unchanged or become progressively worse, resulting in death.

IMPLICATIONS FOR EDUCATION

It is important that the "floppy" infant undergo a thorough medical investigation and that early intervention professionals are informed of the diagnosis, prognosis, and accompanying health problems.

Since the hypotonic child will have difficulty moving, the early stages of development, which are dependent upon physical interaction with the environment, may be impeded. It is therefore necessary to bring the environment to the child. This may be done by periodically moving the child to different areas of the room, by putting the child in a semiupright supported position for ease of visual contact, by making certain that toys are within reach, and by making special attempts at interaction. ("Floppy" babies are sometimes left on their own and therefore do not receive appropriate stimulation.)

The amount of physical activity that should be encouraged depends on the diagnosis. The health and educational team need to work together to devise an individualized plan of developmental intervention for the child. Updated information regarding the child's medical condition should be requested frequently and adjustments in this plan made accordingly.

SEE ALSO

Neurological Examination

ADDITIONAL RESOURCE

Dubowitz, V. *The Floppy Infant.* Philadelphia: J. B. Lippincott Co., 1980.

Genetics

PRINCIPLES OF INHERITANCE

Many developmental disabilities—physical, mental, and biochemical—are inherited. The basic unit of inheritance—whether the trait is hair color, height, blood type, or a particular genetic disease—is the gene. There are thousands of genes, which come in packages called chromosomes. In the cells of humans there are normally 46 chromosomes, arranged in pairs (22 pairs called autosomes and one pair called sex chromosomes). Egg and sperm cells (gametes) include half the genetic material, or 23 single chromosomes, of the parent, so that at conception the fertilized egg (zygote) contains 23 pairs of chromosomes.

Chromosome abnormalities are detected by examining and arranging the chromosomes of cells that are typical of the individual, such as a white blood cell. This procedure is called karyotyping.

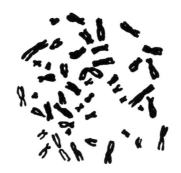

The Chromosomes As They Appear during Metaphase, a Stage in the Cycle of Cell Division

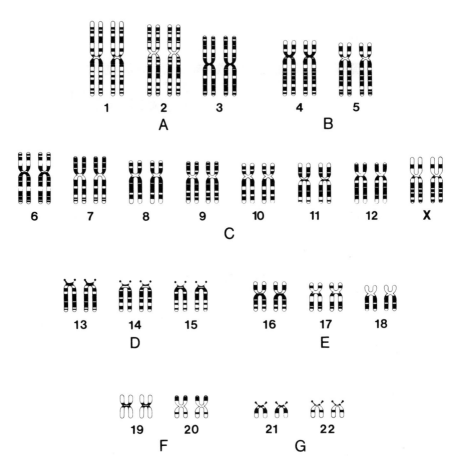

The Individual Chromosomes after Being Cut Out and Arranged Sequentially in Pairs by Size, Shape, and Banding Pattern. *This karyotype of a normal female has 22 pairs of autosomes and one pair of sex chromosomes.*

GENETIC CAUSES OF BIRTH DEFECTS AND MENTAL RETARDATION

Multifactorial Disorders

By far the greatest number of birth defects are caused by an interplay of genetic and environmental factors. Some examples are cardiac malformation, cleft of the lip and palate, and myelomeningocele.

Chromosome Abnormalities

With an inheritance of chromosome abnormality, there is either too much or too little genetic information present. There may be either too few or too many chromosomes, or there may be chromosomes with a piece missing or an extra piece attached.

Some Chromosome Abnormalities

Abnormality	Disorder
• Extra chromosome 21	• Down syndrome (trisomy 21)
• Extra chromosome 18	• Trisomy 18
• Extra chromosome 13	• Trisomy 13
• Girl with only one X chromosome	• Turner syndrome (45,XO)
• Boy with an extra X chromosome	• Klinefelter syndrome (47,XXY)
• Structural abnormality of the X chromosome	• Fragile X syndrome
• Deletion of the short arm of one chromosome 5	• Cri du chat syndrome

Single-Gene Disorders

With the single-gene type of genetic disorder, the amount of genetic material present is adequate. However, within the chromosomes there is an alteration in the genetic material of either a single gene or a pair of genes.

Types of Single-Gene Disorders

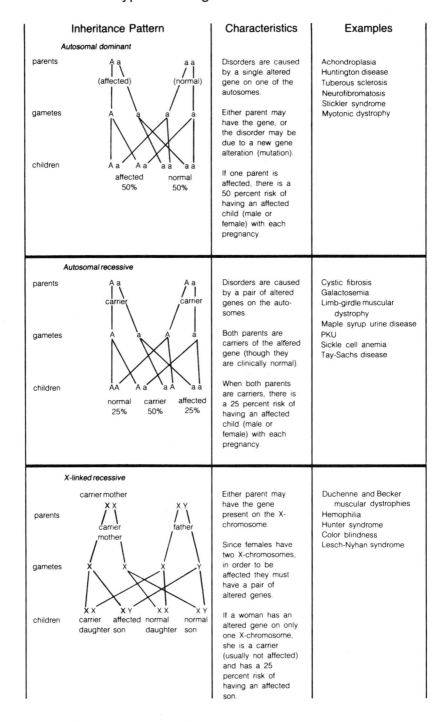

Inheritance Pattern	Characteristics	Examples
Autosomal dominant	Disorders are caused by a single altered gene on one of the autosomes.	Achondroplasia Huntington disease Tuberous sclerosis Neurofibromatosis Stickler syndrome Myotonic dystrophy
parents: A a (affected) — a a (normal) gametes: A a — a a children: A a A a a a a a affected 50% normal 50%	Either parent may have the gene, or the disorder may be due to a new gene alteration (mutation). If one parent is affected, there is a 50 percent risk of having an affected child (male or female) with each pregnancy.	
Autosomal recessive	Disorders are caused by a pair of altered genes on the autosomes.	Cystic fibrosis Galactosemia Limb-girdle muscular dystrophy Maple syrup urine disease PKU Sickle cell anemia Tay-Sachs disease
parents: A a carrier — A a carrier gametes: A a — A a children: AA A a a A a a normal 25% carrier 50% affected 25%	Both parents are carriers of the altered gene (though they are clinically normal). When both parents are carriers, there is a 25 percent risk of having an affected child (male or female) with each pregnancy.	
X-linked recessive	Either parent may have the gene present on the X-chromosome.	Duchenne and Becker muscular dystrophies Hemophilia Hunter syndrome Color blindness Lesch-Nyhan syndrome
carrier mother parents: X X carrier mother — X Y father gametes: X X — X Y children: X X X Y X X X Y carrier daughter affected son normal daughter normal son	Since females have two X-chromosomes, in order to be affected they must have a pair of altered genes. If a woman has an altered gene on only one X-chromosome, she is a carrier (usually not affected) and has a 25 percent risk of having an affected son.	

Types of Single-Gene Disorders *continued*

Inheritance Pattern	Characteristics	Examples
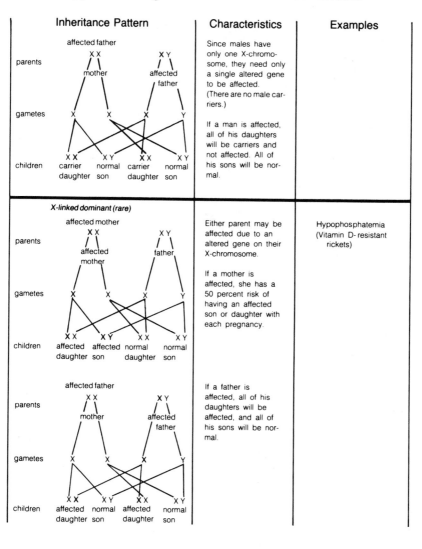	Since males have only one X-chromosome, they need only a single altered gene to be affected. (There are no male carriers.) If a man is affected, all of his daughters will be carriers and not affected. All of his sons will be normal.	
X-linked dominant (rare)	Either parent may be affected due to an altered gene on their X-chromosome. If a mother is affected, she has a 50 percent risk of having an affected son or daughter with each pregnancy.	Hypophosphatemia (Vitamin D-resistant rickets)
	If a father is affected, all of his daughters will be affected, and all of his sons will be normal.	

DETECTION

Any child who is born with a birth defect or is suspected of having a genetic disorder should have a comprehensive genetic evaluation. A genetic evaluation consists of a thorough review of the family history, including obtaining names, ages, and health history of all first- and second-degree relatives. A minimum of a three-generation pedigree is constructed. The racial and ethnic background of the family is determined. Parental age and maternal health history are ascertained. A history of the pregnancy, labor, and delivery is obtained as well as a neonatal history and a history of postnatal growth and development.

Once all of the background data are gathered, the child is evaluated by a clinical geneticist, dysmorphologist (an expert in abnormal body structure), and/or a developmental disabilities specialist. Depending on the results of that evaluation, further testing, and consultation may be recommended. Testing that could be recommended includes chromosome analysis, biochemical or molecular genetic testing, and/or imaging studies (e.g., computerized tomography scan). Consultations that could be requested are ophthalmological, neurological, cardiological, and other specialty examinations.

When the evaluation and testing are completed, a specific diagnosis may be determined. Knowing the specific diagnosis is very useful in order to make an appropriate plan for follow-up care and to provide the family with more specific information about what to expect for their child in the future.

GENETIC COUNSELING

Families who have children with birth defects or who are suspected of having a genetic disorder should be referred to a genetic counseling clinic. Genetic evaluation and counseling can sometimes aid in confirming or ruling out a specific diagnosis. Genetic counselors also help the family to comprehend the diagnosis, prognosis, and available medical management and to understand how the disorder is inherited, the risks of recurrence, and their reproductive options. In a genetic counseling clinic, families are encouraged to consider all available options and to choose what they feel is the appropriate course of action regarding the care of their child and further reproduction. Genetic counselors also try to help the family cope with the grief process and other problems that are inevitable when a child is diagnosed as having a birth defect or a genetic disorder. In addition, the counselors inform families about support groups, and, when appropriate, they make referrals to community agencies.

Families may have difficulty in understanding all of the information provided in a genetic counseling clinic, especially during a time of crisis. To make certain that the information is understood and that it is remembered, counselors see most families more than once. They also attempt to answer new questions as they arise and provide further counseling as other family members who may be at risk are identified.

SEE ALSO
Syndromes

ADDITIONAL RESOURCES

Cohen, F. *Clinical Genetics in Nursing Practice.* Philadelphia: J.B. Lippincott Co., 1984.
Thompson, J.S., M.W. Thompson. *Genetics in Medicine.* Philadelphia: W.B. Saunders Co., 1986.

Growth and Nutrition

Infants and young children with developmental disabilities commonly do not grow as well as they should. Because proper nutrition is critical during early stages of growth—particularly growth of the brain—it must be monitored carefully in infancy and early childhood. Three physical measurements—weight, length, and head circumference—are plotted on standardized growth charts and used as gauges of nutritional adequacy. With each, the rate of growth is more important than the actual measurement at any given time.

WEIGHT

The average full-term newborn weighs approximately 3.4 kilograms (7.5 pounds). The average weight gain per day is 20 grams during the first five months and 15 grams per day throughout the remainder of the first year. Usually, an infant's weight doubles by five months and triples by one year.

The rate of growth slows during the second year, the average weight gain being about 2.5 kilograms (5 to 6 pounds). (This deceleration in rate of growth coincides with a corresponding decrease in appetite, which often worries parents.) In the next few years, annual weight gain is approximately 2.0 kilograms (4.5 pounds). By this time, children appear much leaner than they did as infants.

LENGTH

The average length at birth is 50 centimeters (20 inches). The infant grows about 25 to 30 centimeters (10 to 12 inches) during the first year, 12 centimeters (5 inches) during the second, and 6 to 8 centimeters (2.5 to 3 inches) each year thereafter.

HEAD CIRCUMFERENCE

Head circumference is one of the most important body measurements in that it provides an estimated rate of brain growth. A too rapid rate of increase in head circumference suggests hydrocephalus; a tapering off, potential problems with cognitive development. To find head circumference, a measuring tape is placed along the most prominent part of the back of the head and just above the eyebrows.

The average head circumference at birth is 34 to 35 centimeters. This increases rapidly (by approximately 12 centimeters) during infancy and then much more slowly (by 2 centimeters) during the second year. By the end of the first year the brain is approximately two-thirds of its adult size, and the number of its nerve cells is fixed. Further refinement continues, however, in the organization of brain function. Good nutrition, while not the only environmental factor affecting brain growth, is an essential prerequisite for optimal brain development.

WEIGHT

NATIONAL CENTER FOR HEALTH STATISTICS

Weight by age percentiles for girls aged birth-36 months.

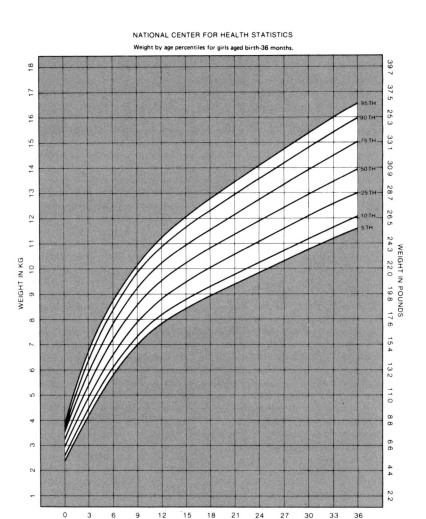

GIRLS

WEIGHT

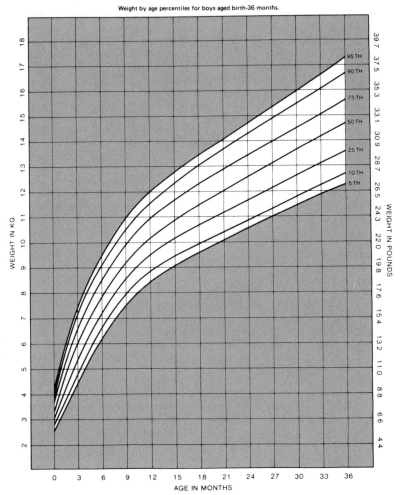

NATIONAL CENTER FOR HEALTH STATISTICS

Weight by age percentiles for boys aged birth-36 months.

BOYS

LENGTH

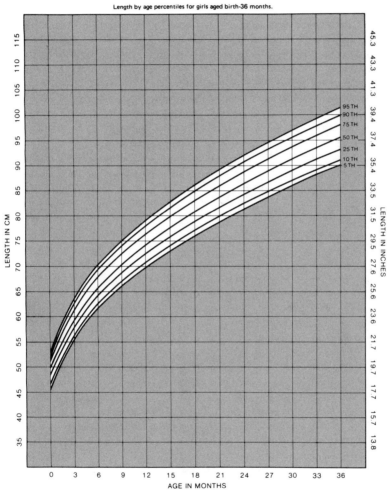

NATIONAL CENTER FOR HEALTH STATISTICS

Length by age percentiles for girls aged birth-36 months.

GIRLS

LENGTH

NATIONAL CENTER FOR HEALTH STATISTICS

Length by age percentiles for boys aged birth-36 months.

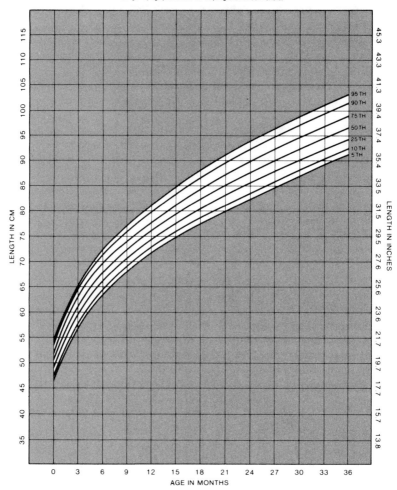

BOYS

HEAD CIRCUMFERENCE

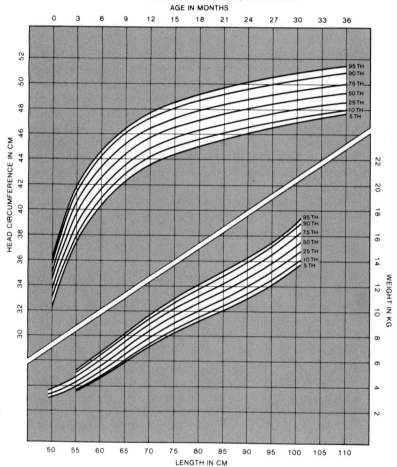

NATIONAL CENTER FOR HEALTH STATISTICS

Head circumference by age percentiles for girls aged birth-36 months.

AGE IN MONTHS

Weight by length percentiles for girls aged birth-36 months.

GIRLS

HEAD CIRCUMFERENCE

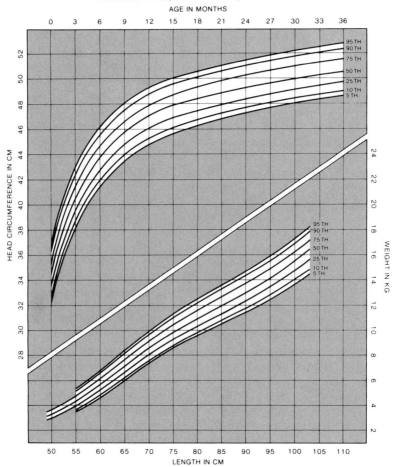

NATIONAL CENTER FOR HEALTH STATISTICS

Head circumference by age percentiles for boys aged birth-36 months.

Weight by length percentiles for boys aged birth-36 months.

BOYS

PROBLEMS AFFECTING GROWTH

When a child is not growing at the expected rate, all growth parameters may be depressed, or there may be a discrepancy between the various parameters. Weight gain may be significantly below linear growth, for example. (Over 50 percent of children under three who were evaluated in a developmental clinic at The University of Iowa showed a weight gain that was low in comparison to their linear growth.)

In all cases of growth failure it is necessary to search for the causes. The following factors should be considered.

Nutrition

How much food is taken in by the child and how much is being retained? The child's usual food, fluid, and nutrient intake should be compared with the norms for children of the same length. Frequent variations in intake due to illness or other factors may account for poor growth. Also, certain dietary habits of parents (such as strict vegetarianism) may lead to the exclusion of important nutrients, as might the child's food preferences or problems with chewing or swallowing.

Parent-Child Interaction during Feedings

Typical childhood behaviors such as food preferences, pickiness, and tantrums may interfere with or complicate intake. Oral-motor problems, too, often result in long and difficult feedings, causing stress for both parent and child. Growth may also be affected by how well the child indicates satiety and how well the caretaker responds.

Innate Response Characteristics of the Child

Temperamental variations must be accounted for. Some children are naturally placid in accepting food, others are resistant.

Physical Growth Expectations

It is true that some children have limited growth potential due to heredity or the nature of the disability. It is sometimes erroneously assumed, however, that because a child has a disabling condition (such as cerebral palsy) he or she cannot be expected to grow well. Such an assumption often masks the real and remediable problem underlying the poor growth: inadequate nutrition.

Structural, Neuromotor, and Sensory Characteristics of the Alimentary Tract

In a large number of cases, intake of sufficient calories and other nutrients for proper growth and motor development is significantly impeded by neuromotor impairment. In other cases, poor growth is due to malabsorption and/or diarrhea.

Stamina

A problem that often goes unrecognized is that children may not eat well because of weakness. Among those whose food intake might be adversely affected by a lack of stamina are children with muscle diseases or congenital heart disease.

Failure to grow adequately may be the end result of any one or a combination of the above factors. Evaluation and treatment of poor growth requires input from a variety of professionals in medicine, psychology, nutrition, occupational therapy, and other disciplines. While some handicapped children's growth potential may be limited despite the best intervention, most can be helped to some degree.

SEE ALSO

Anemia, Failure To Thrive, and *Feeding Problems*

ADDITIONAL RESOURCE

Forbes, G.B., and C.W. Woodruff. *Pediatric Nutrition Handbook.* Elk Grove Village, Ill.: American Academy of Pediatrics, 1985.

Hearing Impairment

DESCRIPTION

The normal auditory system responds to a wide range of sound intensities and frequencies. When hearing is impaired, the range of perception of loudness and pitch is reduced.

Hearing impairment, which can range from mild to profound in degree, is usually classified as one of three types: conductive, sensorineural, or mixed. Conductive hearing loss occurs when there is a dysfunction in the outer or middle ear. Sensorineural hearing loss occurs when damage has been sustained by the inner ear or auditory nerve. If both conductive and sensorineural hearing loss are present, the hearing loss is mixed.

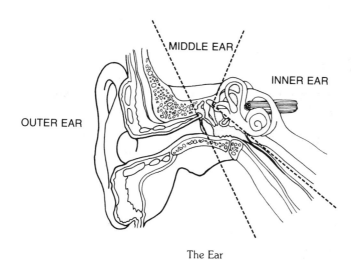

The Ear

With all types of hearing impairment, the perceived loudness of sounds is reduced (or eliminated if the hearing loss is severe enough). Even sounds that are heard may not be heard clearly. With sensorineural and mixed hearing impairments, for example, speech may sound mushy or indistinct; one word may sound like another or like something that has no meaning at all.

Hearing impairment may be unilateral (in one ear only) or bilateral (in both ears). The major effect of bilateral hearing loss is delay and/or deviance in prespeech and language development. Early identification and intervention are crucial; children whose hearing losses are managed appropriately in infancy and early childhood are generally more successful language learners than those whose hearing losses are identified later. The effects of hearing loss on infants and young children who are also developmentally disabled may be even more serious given the potentially additive effects of multiple disabilities. Children with unilateral hearing impairment experience some difficulties, particularly in identifying the source of a sound (localization) and listening in a noisy environment. While they may have fewer problems than children with bilateral hearing loss, it is important that they be identified, treated (if possible), and followed up.

CAUSE

By far the most common cause of conductive hearing impairment in children is middle ear disease (otitis media). Other causes include congenital malformations of the middle ear or a closing off of the ear canal by foreign objects or, occasionally, wax (cerumen).

There are many causes of sensorineural hearing loss. Sensorineural hearing impairment that is present at birth may have been determined genetically, or it may be due to a maternal viral infection or a drug (particularly during the first trimester) that interferes with the normal development of the inner ear. Sensorineural hearing impairment acquired during the birth process itself may be a result of lack of oxygen or other perinatal difficulties. That which is acquired months or years after birth may be caused by disease (such as meningitis or mumps); it may also result from head trauma, exposure to certain drugs or extremely loud noises, or a genetically determined condition that has its onset later in life.

In 1982, a joint committee composed of representatives from the American Academy of Pediatrics, Academy of Otolaryngology-Head and Neck Surgery, American Nurses Association, and American Speech-Language-Hearing Association developed a list of factors that place infants at risk for hearing impairment (see criteria below). These risk factors are frequently used to determine which infants should be screened for possible hearing impairment. However, only 50 to 65 percent of the hearing-impaired population will manifest one of these risk factors. Stated conversely, 35 to 50 percent of the hearing-impaired population will not be identified by this high-risk register only. This occurs primarily because all of the etiologies of hearing loss are not known.

Risk Criteria for Hearing Impairment in Infants

- family history of childhood hearing impairment
- congenital perinatal infection (e.g., cytomegalovirus, rubella, herpes, toxoplasmosis, syphilis)
- anatomic malformations involving the head or neck (e.g., dysmorphic appearance including syndromal or nonsyndromal abnormalities, overt or submucous cleft palate, morphological abnormalities of the pinna)
- birth weight less than 1,500 grams
- hyperbilirubinemia at levels exceeding indications for exchange transfusion
- bacterial meningitis, especially *Haemophilus influenzae*

The joint committee has recently reconvened. Revisions of the risk criteria may be made but new recommendations are not yet available.

INCIDENCE

It has been estimated that 25 to 65 percent of children under the age of two have had at least one ear infection. A significant percentage of these children—and even some children who have never had acute otitis media—experience persistent serous otitis media. Infants and young children who required long-term mechanical ventilation in the neonatal period, who have oral-neuromotor involvement, who have cleft palate, who cannot be fed by mouth, or who are unable to be positioned upright through much of the day are particularly prone to these middle ear problems and the conductive hearing loss accompanying them.

Approximately three in every thousand children below the age of six have a greater-than-mild sensorineural hearing loss in both ears. If we include mild sensorineural hearing loss, the incidence rate is increased 15 to 30 times. Graduates of neonatal intensive care units (who may make up a significant proportion of the population of infants and young children with developmental disabilities) have a particularly high incidence of sensorineural hearing loss; estimates range from one to four in 50.

DETECTION

Because of the relatively high incidence of sensorineural hearing loss, particularly in graduates of neonatal intensive care units, hearing screening prior to initial hospital discharge is increasing. It should also be noted, however, that 50 percent of the population of hearing-impaired infants receive all of their neonatal period care in the well-baby nursery. Overall, nationally, fewer than 5 percent of infants currently are being screened during the neonatal period. Of course, later-onset hearing problems cannot be detected in the neonatal period. This means that parents, physicians, and educational personnel must be alert to signs and symptoms of hearing loss.

Any infant or young child who fails to respond normally to sound or who has delayed prespeech or language development should be evaluated for hearing impairment. Severe or profound hearing loss may be more obvious to an observer than mild or moderate hearing loss. With the former, the child rarely, if ever, responds to voices or environmental sounds. (It is, of course, crucial that all visual, tactile, and vibratory cues be eliminated when such judgments are made.) With mild or moderate hearing impairment, the child's responses to voices and environmental sounds typically are inconsistent; this often gives the erroneous impression that the child hears when he or she wants to. Frequently, too, hearing impairment may be overlooked in children with developmental disabilities, or the behavior is thought to be related to mental retardation or cerebral palsy rather than hearing impairment.

No child is too young for a formal hearing evaluation by an audiologist. While the techniques used and information derived may vary, some information about hearing can be obtained from a child of any age. The most common technique used with children under six months of age is observing their response (e.g., cessation of sucking, widening of the eyes, blinking, quieting, or turning of the head) to sounds of controlled intensities and frequencies.

From roughly six to 24 months, a visual reinforcer is often used. With this technique (visual response audiometry, VRA; or conditioned orientation reflex, COR), a flashing light or animated toy is used to reinforce a head-turn response to sounds of controlled intensities and frequencies.

Children approximately two to five years old are usually tested by a technique called conditioned play audiometry; they are engaged in a play activity, such as putting a block in a box, each time a sound is heard.

Once it has been established that the child has a hearing loss, the type of the hearing loss (conductive, sensorineural, or mixed) must be determined. Hearing evaluation includes assessment of middle ear air pressure and eardrum compliance with acoustic immittance measures (e.g., tympanometry). Abnormal results suggest a conductive component to the hearing impairment. Normal results are typical of a hearing loss that is completely sensorineural. (Normal results in the presence of normal hearing indicate a completely normally functioning auditory system.) It is notable that children who have mixed hearing losses tend to have the identification of their sensorineural hearing loss significantly delayed. It is therefore important to remember that the presence of a conductive hearing loss does not preclude the simultaneous presence of a sensorineural hearing loss. All children with a conductive hearing loss should have their hearing re-evaluated after medical treatment to determine whether hearing is normal or whether there is sensorineural hearing loss.

The testing techniques used depend on developmental rather than chronological age. If the physical or mental condition of the child renders behavioral responses unobtainable or questionable and if sensorineural hearing loss is suspected, electrophysiologic tests typically will be used (auditory brain stem response, ABR; or evoked response audiometry, ERA). This test is a special adaptation of the electroencephalogram (EEG). It measures changes in electrical activity in the brain in response to specific auditory stimuli. The intactness of the inner ear and auditory pathways is assessed. This test provides a highly reliable estimate of hearing loss in infants and young children. It is increasingly being used to screen hearing in the neonatal period as well as to verify behavioral hearing test results suggesting the possibility of sensorineural hearing loss.

MANAGEMENT

All children with hearing impairment should have a medical evaluation to look for signs of underlying diseases, some of which are treatable, and to identify genetic factors for which counseling may be necessary.

In most cases of conductive hearing loss, successful medical or surgical intervention will return hearing to normal. A sensorineural hearing loss, on the other hand, is rarely medically or surgically treatable; it is almost always permanent. The primary management technique for sensorineural loss is amplification, usually with a hearing aid. With a mixed hearing loss, the conductive impairment is treatable whereas the sensorineural impairment is not.

Children of any age, even infants, can use a hearing aid successfully. A hearing aid basically is a miniature, wearable, public address system with a microphone to pick up the sound; an amplifier to increase the sound intensity; and a loudspeaker to deliver the amplified sound to the ear. The hearing aid is coupled to the ear with a custom-made earmold. There are several different styles of hearing aids. The two most commonly used with infants and young children are body-style hearing aids and behind-the-ear hearing aids.

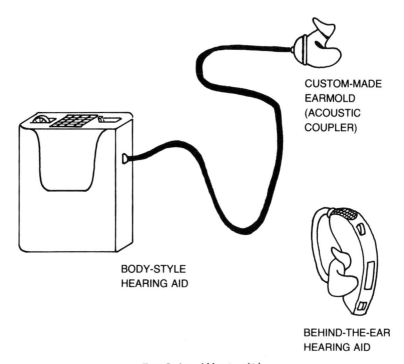

CUSTOM-MADE
EARMOLD
(ACOUSTIC
COUPLER)

BODY-STYLE
HEARING AID

BEHIND-THE-EAR
HEARING AID

Two Styles of Hearing Aids

Unfortunately, a hearing aid cannot correct hearing in the same way that eyeglasses usually correct vision. While the hearing aid increases sound intensity, it does not completely clarify the sound perceived by the impaired inner ear. Furthermore, the hearing aid amplifies all sound, including undesirable noises. It is important, therefore, to have realistic expectations of amplification. While improvement is highly significant, hearing is still far from normal.

While most children with mild and moderate hearing loss are managed adequately with hearing aids, some children with profound sensorineural hearing loss are using vibrotactile devices in addition to their hearing aids. Because of the severity of the hearing loss, even the best hearing aid fitting for these children may provide marginal benefit in hearing conversational-intensity speech and lower-intensity environmental auditory information. Vibrotactile devices change acoustic stimuli to vibratory stimuli; the vibrator portion of the device is worn usually on the sternum or wrist. It functions to provide the child with more information about the auditory environment. Timing information in speech stimuli, such as syllabic patterns, is also provided.

In group educational environments, most hearing-impaired children benefit from the use of a frequency-modulated (FM) auditory training unit. These are two-piece units; the teacher wears a small microphone and miniature FM radio transmitter while the child wears a miniature FM radio receiver. Some receivers are worn in place of the hearing aids; others can be attached to the hearing aids and/or vibrotactile device. In general, FM auditory training units are subject to the same limitations as are hearing aids; however, they have the added benefit of providing more of the teacher's speech to the child while transmitting less of the background noise because of the proximity of the microphone to the teacher's mouth.

The most recent development in management of profound sensorineural hearing loss is the cochlear implant. An electrode is surgically implanted in the inner ear to deliver electrical stimulation to any undamaged sensory cells in the inner ear and the auditory nerve. Cochlear implants in children currently are classified as investigational devices by the Food and Drug Administration. Until more is known about the benefits and risks of these devices in children, patient selection criteria probably will continue to exclude children with developmental disabilities. However, the study of cochlear implants in the developmentally disabled has been identified as an important area for future research.

The primary goal of all management techniques for sensorineural hearing loss is to foster language development. This raises questions in the minds of some professionals regarding management of hearing loss in infants and young children who are also profoundly mentally retarded, given that language development may not be a reasonable expectation. However, other benefits may accrue when providing these children with appropriate management of the hearing loss and thereby some contact with the auditory environment. These benefits may include increased overall alertness, decreased irritability, and decreased self-stimulatory behavior.

IMPLICATIONS FOR EDUCATION

A conductive hearing loss can be treated medically to restore hearing. Until this happens, however, the child experiences significant hearing difficulty. Even though a conductive hearing loss is usually mild in degree, the problems it presents to a child during critical learning years can be severe. Several studies have shown, within the limitations of retrospective data, that older children with learning disabilities had a higher incidence of otitis media with probable conductive hearing loss during early childhood than did children with normal learning abilities. One reason may be the intermittent hearing loss that characterizes episodes of otitis media.

With a sensorineural hearing loss, even one that has been identified and amplified very early, the child has missed many early auditory experiences needed for prespeech and language development; as a result there is at least some degree of language delay. In fact, because of the imperfections of amplification, learning in general can be a struggle. Usually, the more severe the hearing loss the greater the difficulty. Most children with sensorineural hearing loss need the benefits of early intervention programs that are designed specifically for the hearing impaired. Special programming, or at least special supportive services, may be necessary throughout the school years. An audiologist can offer valuable assistance, not only in evaluation, but also in the management of hearing aids and the other assistive listening devices and in developing appropriate communication techniques that will help maximize a hearing-impaired child's learning.

SEE ALSO
Middle Ear Disease (Otitis Media)

Hydrocephalus

DESCRIPTION

With hydrocephalus, there is an imbalance in the production and absorption of cerebrospinal fluid (CSF) in the body, resulting in an enlargement of the fluid-filled spaces in and around the brain. Left untreated, this condition can cause permanent brain damage.

CAUSE

Hydrocephalus is usually caused by blockage in the normal circulation of CSF.

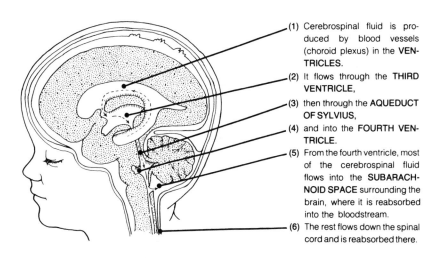

(1) Cerebrospinal fluid is produced by blood vessels (choroid plexus) in the **VENTRICLES.**

(2) It flows through the **THIRD VENTRICLE,**

(3) then through the **AQUEDUCT OF SYLVIUS,**

(4) and into the **FOURTH VENTRICLE.**

(5) From the fourth ventricle, most of the cerebrospinal fluid flows into the **SUBARACHNOID SPACE** surrounding the brain, where it is reabsorbed into the bloodstream.

(6) The rest flows down the spinal cord and is reabsorbed there.

The Normal Flow of CSF

Blockage of the Normal Flow of CSF

If the normal flow of CSF is blocked, there is a backup of CSF in the ventricles. The blood vessels continue to produce fluid, however, causing the ventricles to enlarge and put pressure on the brain. This buildup of CSF causes the infant's head to grow large and the soft spots (fontanelles) to bulge. As the child grows older and the fontanelles close, the head will no longer expand. Untreated hydrocephalus can therefore result in brain damage.

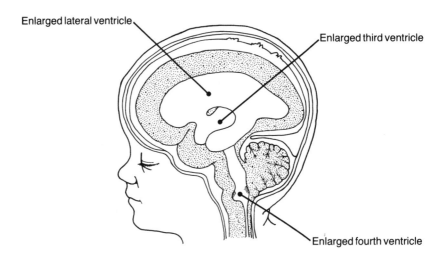

Backup of CSF in the Ventricles

With a condition called noncommunicating hydrocephalus, the outflow of CSF from the ventricles is blocked. This sometimes occurs because the tube through which CSF normally passes from the third ventricle to the fourth is not formed properly (aqueductal stenosis). As a result, the fluid backs up in the lateral and third ventricles. Tumors and other congenital malformations, such as the Arnold-Chiari malformation (common among children with myelomeningocele) can also block the outflow of CSF from the ventricles.

With communicating hydrocephalus, CSF passes readily out of the ventricles but is blocked from being reabsorbed. This condition may result from meningitis, intraventricular hemorrhage in premature infants, or trauma.

Overproduction of CSF

In rare cases of hydrocephalus, the channels for flow and absorption are open, but a tumor within the ventricular system produces more CSF than can be reabsorbed; as a result, the head becomes enlarged.

INCIDENCE

The incidence of hydrocephalus in the United States is approximately 0.8 to 1.6 cases per thousand children.

DETECTION

In children under one year of age, the first sign of hydrocephalus is usually a faster-than-normal increase in head size. As the condition progresses, the child's eyes may begin looking downward so that the white area above the pupil is prominent, a feature referred to as the setting-sun sign. The child may also become listless, irritable, and slow in developing. In older children, whose skulls can no longer expand, the symptoms are more acute; they include headache, vomiting, and coma.

Specialized X-rays, called computerized tomography scans, can show the shape of the brain and dilated ventricles, thereby confirming the presence of hydrocephalus. In young children with open fontanelles, ultrasound can serve the same function. A more recent test, which is particularly good at visualizing the lower back part of the brain (the posterior fossa), is magnetic resonance imaging. This has the added advantage of not using any X-rays, but it is expensive and requires the patient to be still for up to an hour.

COURSE

Left untreated, hydrocephalus produces further brain damage and may even be fatal. With proper medical and neurosurgical management, the majority of affected children will survive, though 60 percent will have significant intellectual and motor handicaps.

ACCOMPANYING HEALTH PROBLEMS

Some children with hydrocephalus also have seizure disorders. If hydrocephalus is accompanied by brain damage or brain malformation, mental retardation may be present as well.

MEDICAL MANAGEMENT

Hydrocephalus is usually treated with a ventriculoperitoneal shunt, which helps to lessen the pressure on the brain. A tube is inserted into the ventricles. This tube is connected to a one-way valve that lets the spinal fluid flow out of, but not back into, the brain. The valve is connected to another tube that is threaded just under the skin down into the cavity of the abdomen. The spinal fluid flows through the shunt and is reabsorbed by the blood vessels in the membranes surrounding the organs there. In rare instances, the tube is threaded into the heart rather than the abdomen; it is then called a ventriculoatrial shunt.

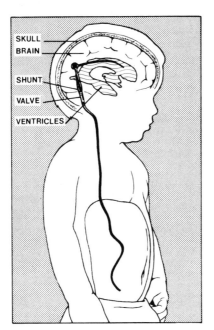
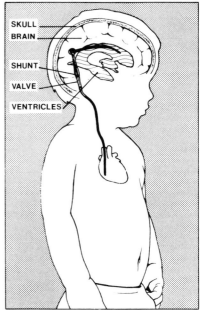

Ventriculoperitoneal Shunt   Ventriculoatrial Shunt

While this system usually works well, the insertion of the shunt may present some difficulties. First, the shunt hardware—a foreign object—provides a place for bacteria to multiply, sometimes resulting in infection. While this does not mean that special restrictions should be placed on the child, it does mean that a physician should be consulted any time the child is sick.

A second potential difficulty with a shunt is that, being mechanical, it is subject to clogging or other malfunctioning, which requires prompt attention. Irritability, vomiting, and fever are the most common signs of infection or shunt malfunction. Unfortunately, these are also the symptoms that children have with the usual childhood illnesses. This is why a physician's advice is always necessary.

Some children may outgrow the need for a shunt as circulation pathways expand, enabling them to maintain the delicate balance between the production and reabsorption of CSF. This balance, however, may be upset by illness, making the shunt necessary to prevent recurrent hydrocephalus.

IMPLICATIONS FOR EDUCATION

While many children with hydrocephalus have no specific educational problems, others may have brain damage that results in motor, language, perceptual, or intellectual disabilities. The damage from the hydrocephalus is more likely to affect reasoning skills than rote memory. It is also likely to make these children hyperverbal. Extreme cases are characterized by the cocktail chatter syndrome—talking incessantly and with little meaning—or by echolalia—copying what other people say. Milder manifestations of this damage are shown by children whose rote memory is strong but who have difficulty with abstractions, particularly mathematics.

Children with hydrocephalus, like all children with disabilities, require a plan of individualized programming.

SEE ALSO

Brain Imaging Techniques and *Myelomeningocele*

Low Birth Weight

A full-term baby usually weighs between 2,500 and 3,800 grams, or 5½ to 8½ pounds. A birth weight of less than 2,500 grams is considered low. A baby may have a low birth weight because of prematurity or intrauterine growth retardation or both. A premature (preterm) baby—one whose period of gestation was less than 37 weeks—is small because of incomplete development. A baby who has suffered intrauterine growth retardation, on the other hand, may be small because of genetic makeup or because of an unfavorable environment in the uterus. The causes, treatment, and outcome of these two conditions may be very different.

PREMATURITY

The usual gestational age—the length of time the fetus is carried in the uterus—ranges from 37 to 42 weeks. (Two techniques for determining gestational age are assessing the newborn's neuromuscular and physical characteristics and counting from the first day of the mother's last menstrual period.) Babies with a gestational age of less than 37 weeks are considered premature, or preterm, regardless of birth weight. While the exact cause of prematurity has not been determined, this condition has been associated with such varied factors as maternal trauma, teen pregnancies, poor prenatal care, and drug abuse.

A preterm baby may be physically normal—though immature—at birth, then develop serious problems during the postnatal period. These complications may, to varying degrees, damage the brain and other tissues, affecting future health and development.

Respiratory Distress Syndrome (Hyaline Membrane Disease)

Normally, the air sacs of the lungs are opened by the newborn's first breaths; they are kept open by a chemical coating called surfactant. If the premature infant does not produce enough surfactant, the lungs collapse after each breath. The result is too little oxygen in the blood and body tissues (hypoxemia) and a disruption of the acid-base balance (acidosis).

Infection

The child's immature defense mechanisms are sometimes unable to combat bacteria that are in the environment or that are introduced through intravenous lines, chest tubes for collapsed lungs, or other invasive equipment. This may result in an infection of the blood (sepsis) or an inflammation of the membranes surrounding the brain or spinal cord (meningitis).

Intracranial Hemorrhage

There may be bleeding into the brain substance or, more commonly, around or into the fluid-filled chambers of the brain (peri- or intraventricular hemorrhage). This may result in the spastic type of cerebral palsy.

Malnutrition

Because many premature infants have difficulty tolerating oral feeding, they may suffer temporary malnutrition. At times, these babies must receive their total caloric and fluid needs by intravenous feeding (hyperalimentation, total parenteral nutrition) or through a nasogastric tube.

Jaundice

Jaundice is a yellowish color of the skin and whites of the eyes caused by an accumulation of bilirubin in the body. Bilirubin, a product of the breakdown of red blood cells, normally is removed by the liver and excreted into the intestines. In preterm babies, the liver may not eliminate the bilirubin from the blood quickly enough. While moderate levels usually are inconsequential (except in sick or very premature babies), high levels may damage the brain permanently, particularly parts called the basal ganglia. Such damage, called kernicterus, may result in athetoid cerebral palsy.

Apnea

Apnea is a prolonged pause in respirations, often accompanied by a slowing of the heart rate (bradycardia) or a blue color to the skin (cyanosis). While this condition may occur in full-term infants, it is particularly common in those who are premature. Apnea must be distinguished from periodic breathing, typical in premature infants, in which a period of rapid breathing alternates with a short period (five seconds or so) of no breathing.

The sudden onset of apnea may indicate a serious illness, such as sepsis, meningitis, pneumonia, intracranial hemorrhage, or low blood sugar (hypoglycemia). Physical stimulation is often adequate to reinitiate breathing. In the absence of serious illness, apnea is treated by environmental stimulation, such as a change in temperature or gentle rocking on a water bed. Medical therapy includes theophylline and caffeine; at times, cardiopulmonary resuscitation is necessary. Occasionally, babies are sent home from the hospital with apnea monitors, which sound an alarm when there is a prolonged period of no breathing.

Necrotizing Enterocolitis

Inflammation, and sometimes death (necrosis), of intestinal wall tissue is a life-threatening complication, the exact cause of which is unknown (though it seems to be related to other problems that beset the preterm infant). In mild cases, conservative medical management is adequate; if a segment of the intestine dies, however, it must be removed surgically, and the shortened bowel may result in temporary—but prolonged—malabsorption of nutrients and diarrhea.

Patent Ductus Arteriosus

During intrauterine life, fetal circulation bypasses the lungs by means of a small blood vessel called the ductus arteriosus. This vessel normally closes at the time of birth. However, in some preterm infants or infants with heart defects, it may remain open, leading to enlargement of the heart and backup of blood in the lungs (congestive heart failure). In some cases, this vessel closes on its own or is closed by the administration of certain drugs; in other instances, it must be tied off surgically.

INTRAUTERINE GROWTH RETARDATION

For every gestational age there is a range of expected weights. An infant whose weight falls below the tenth percentile is considered small for gestational age. The small-for-gestational-age baby has usually suffered growth retardation in the uterus.

Although weight is used in defining intrauterine growth retardation, not all growth parameters are affected in the same manner. Body weight is affected first, then body length, and, last, brain size. For example, if the intrauterine insult occurs late in pregnancy, the infant's weight may be below the tenth percentile while its body length and head size are in the normal range. In contrast, if the cause for poor growth occurs during conception or early pregnancy, weight, length, and head size may be affected equally.

Intrauterine growth retardation may be caused by genetic or inherited factors, or it may be due to an unfavorable environment in the uterus.

Genetic or Inherited Factors

Babies with congenital malformations or chromosomal abnormalities (e.g., trisomy 18 and Turner syndrome) are often small for gestational age. Too, certain families with no other developmental or growth difficulties have a tendency to produce small babies.

Unfavorable Intrauterine Environment

Extreme maternal malnutrition caused by deprivation or disease can affect the growth of the fetus; so can cytomegalovirus infection, rubella, and perhaps other infections as well. Intrauterine growth retardation is also associated with multiple births, cigarette smoking, high altitudes, drug addiction, alcohol abuse, toxemia, and hypertension.

Whereas the premature baby has had a favorable—though shortened—period of gestation, the baby who is small for gestational age has most likely had an unfavorable environment in the uterus. Depending on the nature, timing, and duration of the causal factor, organ systems may fail to develop normally in terms of size, structure, or function. For these reasons, the small-for-gestational-age baby often requires special care during the first few days of life. Insufficient oxygen in the blood at birth (neonatal asphyxia) tends to be more common and accentuated in these babies. The incidence of major congenital anomalies is also more common. Small-for-gestational-age babies often have low blood sugar and may have too many red blood cells (polycythemia).

The baby who is small for gestational age may continue to grow poorly, not catching up as the preterm baby usually does. Whereas preterm babies often catch up during the second year of life, some small-for-gestational-age babies tend to remain smaller than average. In addition to poor growth, some studies have shown a higher than expected prevalence of developmental delay among infants who are small for gestational age.

SEE ALSO

Congenital Infections and *Respiratory Distress Syndrome*

ADDITIONAL RESOURCES

Ensher, G.L., and D.A. Clark. *Medical Care and Psychoeducational Intervention*. Rockville, Md.: Aspen Publishers, Inc., 1986.

Taeusch, H.W., and M.W. Yogman. *Follow-Up Management of the High Risk Infant*. Boston: Little, Brown & Co., 1987.

Mental Retardation

DESCRIPTION

The American Association on Mental Deficiency defines mental retardation as "significant subaverage general intellectual functioning existing concurrently with deficits in adaptive behavior and manifested during the developmental period."

Despite the appropriate reluctance to apply the term *mental retardation* to children under three years old, it is used in this chapter—keeping in mind that the various assessment techniques are limited in their ability to reveal this characteristic in the very young child.

CAUSE

When mental retardation is suspected, the child should have a thorough medical evaluation to try to determine the cause.

Some Conditions or Events Associated with Mental Retardation

Period of Development	Type of Condition or Event	Examples
Pre- and Peri-conceptual	Metabolic disorders	Mucopolysaccharidoses Tay-Sachs disease
	Brain malformation	Encephalocele Hydranencephaly
	Neurocutaneous syndromes	Tuberous sclerosis Neurofibromatosis
	Chromosomal abnormalities	Down syndrome Cri-du-chat syndrome
Prenatal	Teratogens	Chemicals Radiation Alcohol
	Infection	Rubella Cytomegalovirus
	Fetal malnutrition	Mother with high blood pressure or kidney disease
Perinatal	Prematurity	Complications such as poor oxygenation of the brain and intracranial hemorrhage
	Metabolic abnormalities	Asphyxia at birth Hypoglycemia
	Trauma	Misapplication of forceps
	Infection	Herpes simplex encephalitis
Postnatal	Infection	Meningitis
	Trauma	Automobile accident Child abuse
	Lack of oxygen	Near drowning Strangulation
	Severe nutritional deficiency	Kwashiorkor
	Environmental toxins	Lead
	Environmental and social problems	Psychosocial deprivation Parental psychiatric disorders

The physician considers systematically each of the above-mentioned causes for mental retardation. In the majority of cases—particularly when the retardation is in the mild-to-moderate range—the cause will not be identifiable. Even for most known causes there is no known treatment. In the rare instance when the cause is both known and treatable, whatever brain damage has already occurred is irreversible. But despite these depressing odds, parents, educators, and anyone else who is concerned with the child's development and well-being are entitled to the assurance that no condition that might benefit from medical treatment has been overlooked. Also, since some causes may be genetic, proper identification may lead to counseling for parents and other family members regarding the risks of recurrence with future pregnancies.

In some cases, the diagnosis of conditions associated with mental retardation can be made either prenatally, through amniocentesis, or postnatally, through newborn screening programs intended to identify treatable metabolic diseases before permanent brain damage occurs.

The physician usually begins the evaluation with an investigation of the child's history. This includes details of the family tree and of the mother's pregnancy, labor, and delivery, along with information about the child's postnatal period and childhood illnesses or accidents.

A physical examination follows, with attention to signs that may suggest a specific diagnosis, such as peculiar facial features, skin pigment, or urine odor. By this time, many possible causes should be eliminated. Laboratory and radiological procedures are then used either to narrow the possibilities or to pinpoint the diagnosis.

INCIDENCE

Because the label *mental retardation* generally is not used for the birth-to-three age group, actual incidence figures are not available. About 0.5 percent of the preschool population are identified as being mentally retarded. Learning difficulties often are not recognized, however, until the child enters school. It is therefore not surprising that this figure jumps to 10 percent in the six-to-sixteen age group.

Seventy-five percent of mental retardation is mild, 20 percent is moderate, and only 5 percent is severe or profound. Mild retardation is most prevalent among lower socioeconomic groups, whereas moderate and severe mental retardation is more evenly distributed across all socioeconomic levels.

DETECTION

Possible mental retardation is suggested by delays in obtaining developmental milestones and by poor performance on formal cognitive tests. The physician, often the first professional to suspect an intellectual deficit in a very young child, is responsible for initiating referral to an appropriate assessment team.

Performance on standardized psychometric tests that is two or more standard deviations below the mean signals significant delay in cognitive function. There are, however, important cautions in interpreting the results of such tests in very young children.

- Tests predict better as the child gets older. They also predict better with more delayed children, since their behavior is more consistent and less variable over time. Therefore, the predictive value of standard psychometric tests is limited with very young children or children who have mild delays in cognitive development. The tests themselves are not the only reasons for caution. Allowances must be made for the significant variability in the rates of development of young children.
- Many tests are heavily related to sensorimotor function, limiting the performance of children with deficits in these areas. Children with serious chronic diseases may have temporary developmental delays due to poor nutrition, frequent hospitalizations, and lack of appropriate stimulation.
- Performance on developmental tests is to some extent dependent upon the child's experience and may therefore be limited by environmental deprivation.

New assessment techniques involving a child's ability to habituate to a stimulus and recognize a novel stimulus promise more accurate estimates of intellectual functioning, particularly when there is significant sensory and/or motor impairment.

MEDICAL MANAGEMENT

In addition to looking for the cause of mental retardation, the physician has a second important task: that of providing optimal health care, without which the mentally disabled child may not reach his or her highest potential.

Health and development are often closely intertwined, and the physician can help parents integrate the information they receive in these two areas. The physician generally has continual access to parents' perceptions and emotions. Talking with parents at frequent intervals—determining their feelings about their disabled child and providing a resource for ongoing support—is as important a role for the physician as it is for social workers, psychologists, and therapists who work with the child and family.

IMPLICATIONS FOR THE EDUCATIONAL SETTING

While the implications of mental retardation involve primarily educational and psychological development, education-related professionals can also help improve the physical health of these children by encouraging parents to arrange for a medical evaluation (if one has not already been performed) and by helping to identify ongoing health concerns that should be addressed to the child's physician.

SEE ALSO

Cerebral Palsy, Congenital Infections, Down Syndrome, Fetal Alcohol Syndrome, Low Birth Weight, Phenylketonuria and Other Metabolic Diseases, and *Syndromes*

ADDITIONAL RESOURCES

Rubin, I.L., and A.C. Crocker. *Developmental Disabilities: Delivery of Medical Care for Children and Adults.* Philadelphia: Lea & Febiger, 1989.
Wolraich, M.L. *The Practical Assessment and Management of Children with Disorders of Development and Learning.* Chicago: Year Book Medical Publishers, Inc., 1987.

Middle Ear Disease (Otitis Media)

DESCRIPTION

Middle ear disease, or otitis media, is an inflammatory disease of the middle ear, common in children under six years of age. There are two types. The first, called acute otitis media, is characterized by a red, bulging, immobile eardrum, ear pain, and bacteria and pus in the middle ear. The second, called serous otitis media, is a more chronic condition of the middle ear; while it may have some of the same features as acute otitis media, the most prominent characteristic is fluid in the middle ear space, which can result in varying degrees of hearing loss.

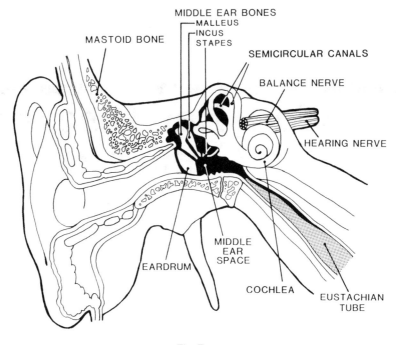

MIDDLE EAR BONES
┌MALLEUS
┌INCUS
STAPES

MASTOID BONE

SEMICIRCULAR CANALS

BALANCE NERVE

HEARING NERVE

EARDRUM

MIDDLE EAR SPACE

COCHLEA

EUSTACHIAN TUBE

The Ear

CAUSE

The eustachian tube connects the middle ear space with the nasal cavity. It equalizes pressure between the middle ear and the atmosphere and permits drainage of secretions. Sometimes this tube does not work well or becomes blocked—most commonly by swelling of the nasal tissues, which accompanies upper respiratory infections. Fluid may then accumulate in the middle ear and allow disease-producing bacteria and viruses to cause an active infection, called acute otitis media.

In many cases, the fluid that accumulates in the middle ear during acute otitis media persists for many weeks after the infection. This accumulation of fluid and accompanying symptoms is known as serous otitis media.

INCIDENCE

Next to colds, otitis media is the most common reason for illness-related visits to the doctor. Ear infections are particularly common in infants and very small children; various studies have indicated that between 25 and 65 percent of children under two years of age have had at least one such infection. The incidence is higher among boys; it is also higher during cold weather months, when upper respiratory infections are common. There are, to date, no conclusive findings regarding the influence of genetic or racial factors.

DETECTION

Children with acute otitis media often complain of earache; they may rub or tug at their ears, have drainage from the ear, and occasionally show signs of hearing impairment. Examination with an otoscope will show a red, bulging eardrum. The most important clue to diagnosis is an eardrum that does not move well. This can be checked either with the otoscope, which can create positive or negative pressure in the ear canal, or with an electronic device called an impedance tympanometer, which can be used in an office, clinic, or school setting to provide a simple, fast, objective measure of eardrum mobility.

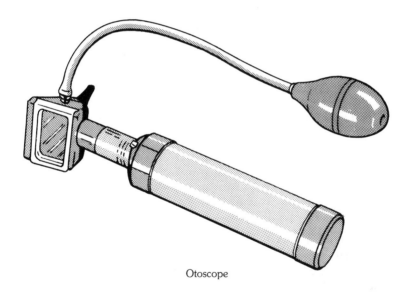

Otoscope

Serous otitis media, the persistence of fluid in the middle ear, is also best detected with either a pneumatic otoscope or an impedance tympanometer. Initially, the eardrum may be bulging because of fluid. If this fluid is absorbed gradually, the eardrum retracts and the thick, gluelike material remaining may need to be drained surgically.

Otitis media is sometimes difficult to detect in young infants. Nonspecific symptoms, such as irritability, fever, and lethargy, should be investigated immediately. Infants and young children with colds should be watched very closely for symptoms of otitis media, as should children who have a history of ear infections and those with conditions that make them prone to ear infections (e.g., cleft palate or Down syndrome).

COURSE

Ear infections usually respond well to antibiotic treatment, but fluid in the middle ear may persist for weeks or even months following the acute infection. Children with eustachian tube dysfunction may be predisposed to recurrent infections and have difficulty eliminating fluid.

ACCOMPANYING HEALTH PROBLEMS

Recurrent otitis media, both acute and serous, can be a major problem. It puts a strain on the family and on the health care system. Even more important is that chronic, severe, and perhaps even moderate middle ear disease affects hearing and, therefore, language development and learning in general. It is still uncertain what effects mild and/or intermittent ear disease have on long-term function.

Otitis media may cause still other complications, including extension of the infection into the mastoid bone, known as mastoiditis—a condition that is difficult to treat. Another possibility is perforation of the eardrum, which, depending on the size of the hole, may or may not heal on its own. While perforation usually is not serious, it can lead to loss of function and increased susceptibility to the formation of cholesteatoma in the middle ear. Cholesteatoma is a condition in which surface cells from the external auditory canal gain entry into the middle ear space, where they begin to grow and form a tumor that can erode the incus, malleus, and stapes and invade the surrounding bones.

MEDICAL MANAGEMENT

Although some ear infections are caused by viruses—against which antibiotics are ineffective—as well as by bacteria, the usual procedure is to treat all infections with antibiotics. This is because distinguishing between the two types of infections involves the uncomfortable and costly procedure of puncturing the eardrum to obtain material for a culture (which may take days to grow). Viral infections tend to be less serious and to clear up with or without antibiotics. If bacteria are responsible and the appropriate antibiotics are administered, the infection will usually clear up in one to two weeks.

Recurrent otitis media is treated by various approaches, including (1) low doses of prophylactic antibiotics, especially during seasons of highest incidence; (2) antihistamines and decongestants; and (3) surgical placement of tubes in the eardrum to allow continuous drainage and provide an alternate route for ventilation of the middle ear space. No one procedure is unequivocally preferred; all three have benefits and liabilities. While antibiotics generally are effective, bacteria tend to develop a resistance to those that are administered repeatedly. Furthermore, unless the antibiotics are taken as prescribed—and often they are not—they are likely to be ineffective.

While various decongestants commonly are used for prevention and treatment, their effectiveness has never been scientifically proven. Presumably, they shrink the swollen membranes of the nose, enabling the eustachian tube to remain open and function properly.

Surgical drainage of the middle ear (myringotomy) and insertion of tubes into the eardrum are also controversial. Although there is as yet no uncontestable research to support their effectiveness, these procedures—when appropriate—appear to improve the function of the middle ear and decrease the number of infections.

The most prudent course at the present time is to treat acute infections with appropriate antibiotics, to follow the status of the middle ear with pneumatic otoscopy or impedance tympanometry, and to consider various treatments for recurrent acute infections and persistent serous fluid in the middle ear.

IMPLICATIONS FOR EDUCATION

Because of the age group served and the types of disabilities encountered, ear infections are very common in children participating in early education and therapeutic programs. It is therefore very important for teachers and therapists to understand the nature of otitis media and to appreciate the impact it has on health and developmental function. Acute infections result in absences as well as in general irritability, either of which may reduce the effectiveness of the educational program.

By noting changes in the behavior of children at high risk for ear infections, education-related professionals can help identify the child with possible ear disease; by watching for signs of improvement (often educational programs have impedance tympanometers), they can aid in proper medical management. Such information is valuable in determining the most appropriate timing and type of therapy for persistent serous otitis media. Health care providers and early intervention staff should work closely together when dealing with diseases of the middle ear.

SEE ALSO

Cleft Lip and Palate, Down Syndrome, and *Hearing Impairment*

Myelomeningocele

DESCRIPTION

Myelomeningocele, also known as meningomyelocele and spina bifida, is a midline defect of the skin, spinal column, and spinal cord.

During the latter part of the first month of pregnancy, when the child is developing in the uterus, the spinal cord (myelo-) and vertebrae around it do not form properly. In the normal child, the spinal cord forms into a straight column, covered first by membranes (meningo-) and then by a bony spine. In the child with myelomeningocele, the membranes pouch out at some point along the back. As the spinal cord develops, it does not follow a straight column but pushes out instead into the membranous sac (-cele), where it does not form in the normal way. Some or all of the nerves coming out of the spine below the sac are not hooked up properly to the spinal cord and thus to the brain.

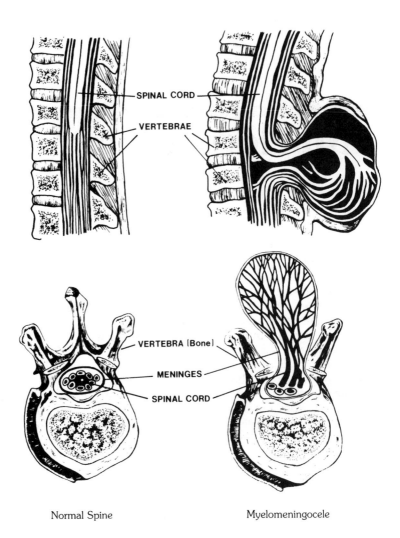

Normal Spine   Myelomeningocele

There are two other types of open spine defect: meningocele and spina bifida occulta. With meningocele, the spinal cord itself does not pouch out, only the membranes surrounding it. With spina bifida occulta, the backs of some of the vertebrae fail to form, but there are no abnormalities in the membranes, spinal cord, or skin.

Children with myelomeningocele may be characterized by hydrocephalus, mental retardation, and, depending upon the location of the defect along the spinal column, lack of control of leg muscles, lack of bladder and bowel control, lack of sensation in the skin, and/or curvature of the spine (scoliosis).

CAUSE

The exact cause of myelomeningocele is not known; it may, in fact, result from a combination of causes. There is no proven major link between this condition and any medication except valproic acid (Depakene), infection, or environmental condition. Nor are parents carriers of a gene that specifically causes myelomeningocele, though they may carry genes that make them susceptible to various nongenetic (e.g., environmental) factors associated with it.

Some preliminary studies have provided suggestive evidence of some possible etiologies. It appears that one of the anticonvulsive medications, valproic acid (Depakene), can induce neural tube defects if taken during pregnancy. Some animal studies have also suggested that high maternal fevers during early pregnancy can induce neural tube defects. Both of these causes explain only a small percentage of the actual cases of children born with neural tube defects. Lastly, some preliminary studies from England suggest that if mothers who are known to be at increased risk for having a child with a neural tube defect (have a previous child born with the defect) take larger-than-recommended doses of vitamins, particularly the B complex vitamins and folate, they decrease the risk of recurrence. However, it is important to note that these findings are very preliminary and that further research is required before they can be confirmed.

INCIDENCE

Myelomeningocele is one of the most common developmental defects of the nervous system; the incidence is about one in every thousand births. The chance of having a second child with this condition is somewhere between one in 20 and one in 40.

DETECTION

Prenatal

Myelomeningocele may be detected in the fetus through amniocentesis by measuring the amount of alpha-fetoprotein and acetylcholinesterase in the amniotic fluid. These proteins are found in high concentration in spinal fluid, which, in the child with myelomeningocele, leaks through the membrane and into the amniotic fluid surrounding the fetus.

Another, easier, method of testing for myelomeningocele in the fetus is measuring the amount of alpha-fetoprotein in the mother's blood. This test, which must be done between the 12th and 14th weeks of gestation, is not as accurate as amniocentesis. However, it is a very effective screening test for pregnant women who do not have an increased risk of having a child with a neural tube defect. It has the advantages of less risk and less cost than amniocentesis.

Sometimes sound waves bounced off the fetus (ultrasonography) make the defect visible. This procedure is not always reliable, however.

Postnatal

Initial diagnosis is not difficult because the spinal lesion is present at birth and easily observed. The extent of the problem can be determined by assessing the lesion itself as well as the muscle groups affected. In rare cases, the defect is covered by skin and goes undetected in the newborn period.

COURSE

Myelomeningocele is a static condition; that is, there is no progression of the defect. However, secondary problems (urinary, for example) can worsen and require intensive management.

ACCOMPANYING HEALTH PROBLEMS

Hydrocephalus

In about 80 percent of children with myelomeningocele, the spinal fluid is prevented from leaving the brain and being absorbed into the blood stream. The resultant increase in pressure may cause brain damage and, hence, mental retardation (see "Hydrocephalus").

Muscle Control

Because the nerves to the lower part of the body are not connected properly to the spinal cord and brain, there may be little or no control of leg muscles. The higher up the defect is on the spinal cord, the greater the paralysis. Most myelomeningocele defects occur in the thoracic, lumbar, or sacral regions of the spine.

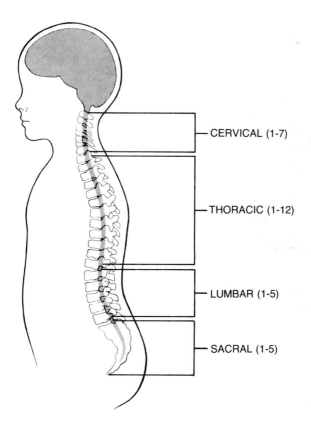

Regions of the Spine

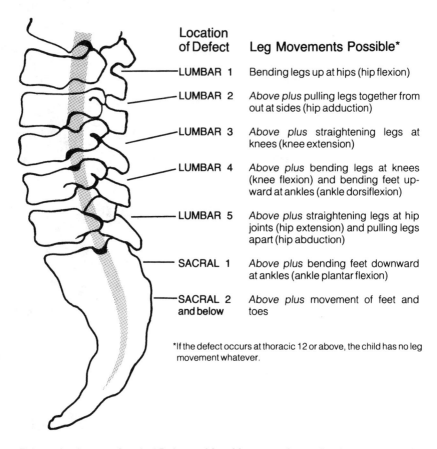

Location of Defect	Leg Movements Possible*
LUMBAR 1	Bending legs up at hips (hip flexion)
LUMBAR 2	*Above plus* pulling legs together from out at sides (hip adduction)
LUMBAR 3	*Above plus* straightening legs at knees (knee extension)
LUMBAR 4	*Above plus* bending legs at knees (knee flexion) and bending feet upward at ankles (ankle dorsiflexion)
LUMBAR 5	*Above plus* straightening legs at hip joints (hip extension) and pulling legs apart (hip abduction)
SACRAL 1	*Above plus* bending feet downward at ankles (ankle plantar flexion)
SACRAL 2 and below	*Above plus* movement of feet and toes

*If the defect occurs at thoracic 12 or above, the child has no leg movement whatever.

Relationship between Level of Defect and Leg Movement. *Incomplete lesions account for variations among children with myelomeningocele.*

Problems with Bladder and Bowel Control

Because the nerves involved in bladder control come from the lower part of the spinal cord (the second, third, and fourth sacral segments), most children with myelomeningocele have neurogenic bladders. This means they may not feel the urge to urinate or have control of the urinary sphincter. A neurogenic bladder, if not cared for properly, may cause damage to the kidneys, either because the urine cannot get out properly (causing pressure on the kidneys) or because not all the urine is emptied from the bladder (causing infections). Treatments, the main one being clean intermittent catheterization, are available to prevent urinary tract infection and subsequent kidney damage.

The nerves involved in bowel control also come from the lower part of the spinal cord, and children with myelomeningocele frequently have neurogenic bowels. This may result in constipation and bowel movement accidents (incontinence).

Curvature of the Spine (Scoliosis)

Because of poor muscle control and the structural defect of the spine, straight alignment is sometimes not maintained. This can lead to a fixed tilt of the pelvis and curvature of the spine, causing poor sitting balance and excessive pressure on certain areas of the skin.

Problems with Psychosocial Development

Both the nature of the defect and the functional difficulties that accompany it may place strains on parent-child relationships. As the child grows older, functional limitations may lead to psychological and social maladjustment.

Pressure Sores (Decubitus Ulcers)

Many children with myelomeningocele lack sensation in their lower extremities, making them prone to pressure sores. The skin should be checked frequently for reddened areas, the first sign of a problem.

MEDICAL MANAGEMENT

The complexity of the dysfunction and the number of organ systems involved demand the participation of many surgical and medical specialists and health-related personnel. An interdisciplinary team frequently is necessary to provide appropriate coordinated care.

Spinal Lesion

To prevent germs from entering the open defect and causing serious infections in the spinal cord and brain, the lesion generally is repaired surgically within the first 24 to 48 hours of life.

Hydrocephalus

To prevent damage to brain tissue, the increased intracranial pressure in hydrocephalus is treated with a shunt, which is surgically placed, usually within the first two months of life.

Urinary Tract

Urological management begins at birth. In the past, various surgical procedures were used to redirect urinary flow and preserve kidney function, but conservative therapies now appear to be effective. These include periodic assessment of urinary tract function and intermittent catheterization to help prevent both urinary tract infections and "accidents."

Orthopedics

Orthopedic evaluation begins at birth. The aims of management procedures are to preserve normal joint structures, to release contractures, to correct deformities, and to facilitate weight bearing and, where possible, ambulation. (Many of these children can learn to walk with the aid of braces and crutches.)

Psychosocial Problems

Support for both child and family must begin with the child's birth and continue throughout his or her lifetime.

IMPLICATIONS FOR EDUCATION

The continual occurrence of acute problems—such as shunt malfunction, urinary tract infection, and repeated hospitalizations and surgery—combines with the socially limiting nature of such problems to affect almost every aspect of the child's performance in an educational setting.

Myelomeningocele generally has no effect on a child's stamina, although the accompanying hydrocephalus may cause attention disorders, learning disorders, and even mental retardation. Educational assessments are necessary to determine what types of learning problems, if any, a child may have.

Because of the damaged nerves along the spine, children with myelomeningocele may not experience the amount of weight bearing necessary for bone development and strengthening; they are therefore more prone to fractures in the lower extremities. Too, they may lack sensation in certain areas of the skin, increasing considerably the risk of burns, abrasions, and pressure ulcers. They may also lack bladder or bowel control and be participating in special bladder and bowel regimens at school. Because these children are less active than normal children, they are prone to obesity and may be following certain nutritional recommendations. Too, the excess weight can impede ambulation and contribute to the development of pressure sores.

The extent of physical and mental problems varies with the location of the defect; some children with myelomeningocele have relatively few of the problems listed here.

SEE ALSO

Bracing, Brain Malformations, Hydrocephalus, and *Mental Retardation*

ADDITIONAL RESOURCE

Wolraich, M.L., and M.H. Lozes. *What You Should Know about Your Child with Spina Bifida,* Second Ed. Iowa City: University of Iowa Campus Stores, 1985.

Neurological
Examination

An essential part of the evaluation of any child with a developmental disability is the neurological examination. This assessment—along with a history of the child's health and development, findings from other parts of the physical examination, and the results of laboratory tests—provides clues to diagnosis and proper treatment.

The infant's response to stimulation (touch, light, sound) varies according to his or her overall level of responsiveness at the time. An infant's typical pattern, including responses to changing stimuli, can be assessed during a nursery examination and may help us understand later patterns of functioning.

MEDICAL HISTORY

Before actually examining the infant, the physician usually collects information about the child's problem—when it was first noticed, whether it has been improving or getting worse, and whether there are any health concerns, such as recurrent ear infections or episodes of vomiting or diarrhea. Information is also sought regarding the family and previous life events that may be linked to the child's current difficulties. Parents or caretakers are questioned about (1) diseases that run in the family; (2) problems the mother may have had during pregnancy, labor, or delivery; (3) unusual behavior or poor health of the child after birth; (4) delay or deviation in development; and (5) possible environmental stresses. Finally, a systematic review of each organ system yields information about hearing and vision, heart and lung function, the skeleton, and so forth.

PHYSICAL EXAMINATION

General Observations

With infants and young children, simple observation may be as revealing (or more so) than the actual hands-on assessment. Hence, the neurological examination begins there. Does the child appear well? Adequately nourished? Of normal body proportions? Is the level of alertness or responsiveness to stimuli significantly heightened?

How much and how well the child moves may indicate whether there is damage to the nervous system and, if so, to what part; for instance, if the arm and leg on the left side appear floppy or stiff, there may be damage to the right side of the brain (which controls movement on the left side of the body).

The Head

Abnormal head size or shape is often associated with abnormal growth and development of the brain. This is especially likely if there is delay in the child's development or if the unusual size or shape is not found among normal family members. Small head size (microcephaly) may be due to defects in brain development, intrauterine infections, postnatal mishaps (such as birth asphyxia), or certain metabolic disorders. An abnormally large head size (macrocephaly), unless it is a familial variation, is usually due to an accumulation of fluid in and around the brain (hydrocephalus).

The Eyes

Examination of the eyes and its movements can provide clues to neurological abnormalities. Unequal eye movements, failure of the pupils to react to light, or rapid, involuntary jerking of the eyes (nystagmus) may be caused by disturbances in the visual pathways or by problems with eye muscle control.

Eye movements can be assessed by observing the infant's reactions to a moving, striped pattern or by having the child track a small, interesting object. Pupil reactions are checked by shining bright lights first in one eye and then in the other. By using small magnifying lenses combined with a light source (ophthalmoscope), the physician can also inspect the retina and the optic nerve at the back of each eye directly. This inspection may reveal signs of pressure in the brain from a tumor or accumulation of fluid, diseases with manifestations in the eye (e.g., toxoplasmosis), or rare genetic conditions (e.g., Tay-Sachs disease).

The Ears

Infants are screened for major problems in hearing by observing their responses to vocalizations or other noises (e.g., a rattle or bell). In addition, the eardrum and middle ear are examined with an otoscope. The child with suspected hearing problems should be referred to an audiologist for formal testing.

Significant hearing impairment usually results from a buildup of fluid in the middle ear. At times, however, it is a result of abnormalities—some of them inherited—in the nerves that transform sound into impulses and then transmit those impulses to the brain.

Nerves of the Head and Neck

Specialized bundles of nerve fibers, called cranial nerves, control specific face and head movements; they also transmit information about sensory stimuli that reach the head. Abnormalities along these pathways may be detected by observing for asymmetry in facial expressions and in movements of the tongue and palate.

Muscle Function

In addition to observing the infant or young child's voluntary activities, the examiner assesses both muscle tone and strength. Muscle tone is the amount of resistance the examiner feels in response to passive movement—to having the arm moved back and forth by the examiner, for example. Stiffness (hypertonia) or floppiness (hypotonia) is often seen with damage to those areas of the brain and spinal cord that control motor activity. Floppiness may also result from abnormalities in the nerves leading from the spinal column to the muscles or from abnormalities in the muscles themselves. The examiner checks tone and strength by working the arms and legs through their range of motion and observes the child's active movements and responses to passive turning of the child's head.

Reflexes

Reflexes are predictable movements in response to various stimuli. For example, an infant of less than three months usually will grasp a finger that is placed firmly in the palm of its hand; or a newborn whose cheek is stroked usually will turn to face that side (this is known as "rooting") and make sucking movements. Other neonatal reflexes involve the infant's whole body. For instance, the child reacts to a sudden noise or change of position by extending the arms and legs briefly, then bringing them back together as though to hug a nearby object (the Moro response).

Many reflexes that are present in the neonatal period normally disappear with time. Their persistence beyond the time of anticipated decline may signal brain abnormalities. As the infant grows older, most neonatal reflexes are replaced by new automatic responses (e.g., righting and equilibrium), which can be elicited during examinations. These are prerequisites for new skills, such as sitting, crawling, and walking. The appearance of new responses is often delayed, however, if the earlier, "primitive" reflexes continue.

Deep tendon reflexes are important indicators of the function of the neurological system. One such reflex is the knee jerk. A heightened response—an excessive knee jerk—suggests the possibility of damage to the brain itself or to the nerve that travels along the spinal cord from the motor cortex of the brain (the corticospinal tract). A poor or negative response suggests one of three things: problems with the nerve running from the spinal cord to the muscle, problems with the muscle itself, or general central nervous system dysfunction.

The Babinski response is elicited when the bottom of the child's foot is stroked. Except for young infants, the expected response is a downward bending of the big toe; if the toes bend upward and fan out, the response is abnormal.

Yet another response that suggests problems in the central nervous system—particularly in the motor cortex or in the corticospinal tract—is clonus. Clonus is the repeated muscle jerking that occurs when the muscle is suddenly stretched (as happens, for instance, when the foot is bent upward).

Other Findings

Findings in other organ systems may suggest nervous system dysfunction. For example, children with neurofibromatosis, a disease that affects the skin as well as the nervous system, generally develop areas of increased pigmentation on the skin (café au lait spots), which may suggest the diagnosis of this disease before neurological symptoms are evident.

Another rare condition with important neurological manifestations is the Sturge-Weber syndrome. Abnormal growth of blood vessels in early fetal life produces a purplish, nonelevated area of the skin, commonly on one side of the face. Similar blood vessel abnormalities may also occur in the brain covering (meninges) below the affected facial skin, producing faulty brain growth and development with resultant seizures, mental retardation, and motor disability.

Abnormal findings in the physical examination or a history of delayed developmental milestones (particularly in the motor area) during early infancy must be viewed in light of an objective measure of the child's general developmental level. A general developmental screening test is done to determine whether there is need for a more complete, interdisciplinary evaluation.

Depending on what has been learned from the patient history and physical examination, selected laboratory studies may help pinpoint the trouble. The most commonly employed tests include blood analyses, X-rays, computerized tomography scans, and electroencephalograms. The physician generally tries to gain the most information with the fewest tests and the least discomfort to the child.

INTERPRETATION

The greatest skill of the examiner lies in interpreting and integrating the information obtained from all of the above techniques. All physicians are trained to perform a neurological assessment and to interpret the findings; with difficult cases, however, it may be necessary to rely on the expertise of a specialist in this field—the pediatric neurologist.

SEE ALSO

Brain Imaging Techniques, Brain Malformations, Cerebral Palsy, Electroencephalography, and *Floppy Infant*

Orthopedic Problems

Infants may be born with or acquire problems with bones, joints, and muscles. This chapter describes some of the more common orthopedic disorders of the foot, knee, hip, spine, and other areas of the body.

THE FOOT

Metatarsus Adductus

In metatarsus adductus, the forefoot turns inward but the ankle and heel are in their normal positions, a problem that may be related to the compression of the fetus in the uterus. Mild and flexible cases are treated with stretching exercises; rigid deformities may require casting in early infancy. Generally, the longer treatment is delayed, the more difficult it is to remold the foot into a normal position.

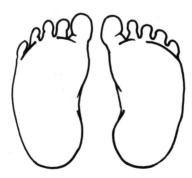

Metatarsus Adductus

Clubfoot (Talipes Equinvarus)

With clubfoot, certain muscles are shortened, and the tissues surrounding the joints are fixed, causing the foot to turn inward and upward. Treatment, which includes passive correction and prolonged casting, should begin as soon after birth as possible.

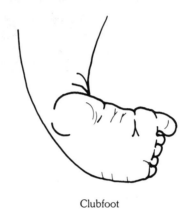

Clubfoot

Calcaneovalgus

With calcaneovalgus the bones of the foot are usually in normal alignment, but the foot is turned outward, the ankle upward. This deformity is flexible; if treated soon after birth by daily passive stretching of the soft tissue, it may improve spontaneously.

Flatfeet (Pes Planus)

Babies' feet tend to look flat because of a thick layer of fat tissue on the bottoms. With time, this layer disappears and the arch usually becomes evident. In the otherwise normal child, treatment for flatfeet is necessary only rarely—corrective surgery almost never. Children beyond the age of three who experience discomfort may use arch supports to distribute weight evenly.

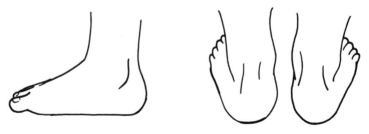

Flatfeet

Toeing In

Toeing in—that is, turning inward of one or both of the lower extremities—is caused by a condition or combination of conditions involving the foot, the larger bone between the knee and ankle (tibia), and/or the bone between the hip and knee (femur). Toeing in is commonly caused by metatarsus adductus (discussed above). If the child has a flexible foot, it usually corrects itself; otherwise, cast treatment may be necessary. A twisting inward of the tibia (tibial torsion) can cause severe or persistent turning in of the entire foot; this is commonly treated by night splints, although there is some disagreement about their effectiveness. A third cause of toeing in is a turning inward of the femur (femoral anteversion). Present in all babies, this generally corrects itself with age and is helped little by shoe corrections. Even in persistent cases, no treatment is necessary except encouraging long- or crossed-leg sitting rather than "W" sitting.

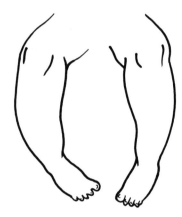

Toeing In

Toeing Out

Toeing out is normal when children begin to walk, and in most cases correction is spontaneous. If, however, toeing out persists after a period of independent walking, orthopedic consultation is recommended; the condition may be due to a twisting outward of the large bone between the knee and ankle (external tibial torsion) or it may be caused by flatfeet.

Congenital Rocker-Bottom Foot (Vertical Talus)

Congenital malposition of the bones of the foot results in a characteristic rocker-bottom shape to the underside of the foot, a problem that requires orthopedic consultation.

THE KNEE

Knock-Knees (Genu Valgum) and Bowlegs (Genu Varum)

Knock-knees and bowlegs generally do not require treatment, although at times wedges (lifts) in the shoes are prescribed. Mild bowing of the lower extremities is typical in the infant and very young child and usually corrects itself spontaneously by 18 months to two years. If not, the physician will search for specific causes, such as abnormal muscle tone, nutritional deficiencies (rickets), abnormal bone growth, or other diseases.

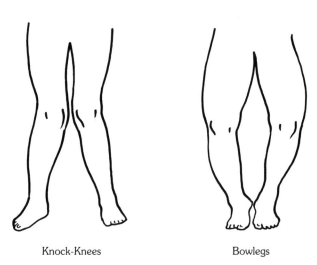

Knock-Knees   Bowlegs

Abnormal Hyperextensibility of the Knee Joints (Genu Recurvatum)

Normally, straightening of the knee stops when the bones of the upper and lower leg are in alignment. Lax joint support tissues (as found in Ehlers-Danlos syndrome) or abnormal muscle tone (spastic diplegia) may cause children to stand with their knees hyperextended. In severe cases bracing may be necessary.

THE HIP

Congenital Dislocation of the Hip

Congenital dislocation of the hip (CDH) results from abnormal development of some of the components of the hip joint. At times, the head of the thigh bone (femur) may be totally out of the hip socket, or the supporting tissue may be lax and allow this bone to move in and out of the socket when manipulated by a physician. The cause of this problem, which affects females more often than males, is not known, though it is very likely that a number of factors are involved, including breech delivery, hormonal changes in the mother during late pregnancy, and positioning of the hip after birth (CDH occurs more frequently in some culture groups that swaddle their infants or wrap them to cradle boards).

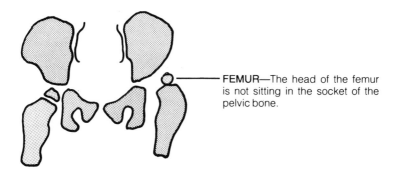

FEMUR—The head of the femur is not sitting in the socket of the pelvic bone.

Congenital Dislocation of the Hip

Children are checked for CDH during the regular physical examination in the newborn period and repeatedly during the first year of life. The examiner attempts to move the femoral head gently in and out of the hip socket. Normally this is not possible. X-rays are not useful in the newborn period but may help to confirm the diagnosis in older infants. Children with spina bifida and certain types of cerebral palsy are prone to dislocation of the hip at any age and are therefore monitored closely for this problem.

The goal of treatment is to return the femoral head to its normal position within the hip socket (acetabulum). To prevent joint inflammation (arthritis), treatment should begin as soon as possible. Newborns are treated with splints, older babies with casting or surgery.

THE SPINE

Infantile Scoliosis

Many times, curvature of the spine (scoliosis) in children ages birth to three is idiopathic; that is, the cause is unknown. This condition—which is very rare in the United States—is more common among boys and children with low birth weight and muscle disorders. In about 85 percent of cases, idiopathic scoliosis disappears on its own, but in the remaining 15 percent the curve may worsen and lead to severe deformity.

Congenital Scoliosis

Another type of scoliosis is caused by abnormal development of the bony parts of the spine (vertebrae). Children born with this type (which is confirmed by X-rays) need close follow-up; if the defect is progressive, they may require surgery.

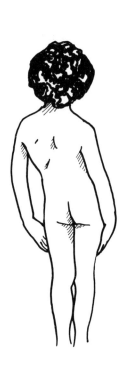

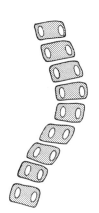

INFANTILE SCOLIOSIS

CONGENITAL SCOLIOSIS

Neuromuscular Scoliosis

A third type of scoliosis occurs as a result of neuromuscular disease. With cerebral palsy, for example, the degree of muscle tone may be greater on one side than on the other, causing unequal forces on the spine. This and other conditions that are characterized by abnormal muscle tone allow the child to sit or stand with the spine out of alignment, resulting in curvature. With neuromuscular scoliosis, attention should be given to the underlying disease. Treatment includes proper positioning, bracing, and, occasionally, surgery.

MULTIPLE JOINT CONTRACTURES

Babies are sometimes born with various joints compressed and positioned at abnormal angles (arthrogryposis). This congenital deformity is caused by neuromuscular problems in the fetus, too little amniotic fluid, or structural abnormalities of the uterus—all of which inhibit the fetus from moving in the uterus.

Arthrogryposis multiplex congenita is a severe form of this disorder characterized by many involved joints as well as by other types of bony and muscular abnormalities.

Mild cases of both of these conditions are treated by passive exercises; more severe cases may require gradual correction of deformities by splints, casts, or surgery.

ORTHOPEDIC PROCEDURES FOR CEREBRAL PALSY

Procedures around the Feet

The purpose of procedures around the feet is to foster better function by allowing the feet to assume a more normal position.

Heelcord (Achilles Tendon) Lengthening

The Achilles tendon, which attaches the gastrocnemius and soleus muscles to the calcaneus, is cut in order to reduce the increased stretch reflex and to lengthen the muscle. This procedure is used when the child has difficulty pointing the feet upward and, if ambulatory, walks on the toes. This procedure allows the foot to be placed in a neutral position.

Lengthening and Transfer of Posterior Tibial Tendon

This procedure will correct ankle varus (the bottoms of the feet point inward).

Procedures around the Hip

Hip Adductor Release

The muscles and/or their tendons that adduct the thighs (pull them toward each other) are cut to lengthen them, relieving the contracture (shortening), diminishing scissoring, and preventing progressive hip dislocation. Sometimes the nerves to these muscles are severed as well (obturator neurectomy).

Varus Derotation Femoral Osteotomy

The shaft of the femur is cut to realign the head and neck of the femur with the acetabulum (hip socket).

SEE ALSO

Bracing, Cerebral Palsy, Myelomeningocele, and *Positioning and Handling*

Perinatal Injury

Jason B. was a 4,200-gram, full-term infant, born to a gravida 3, para 2, abortus 1, 29-year-old woman. The pregnancy was complicated by preeclampsia and gestational diabetes. Labor was induced because of maternal high blood pressure. The amniotic sac was artifically ruptured, and the fluid contained thick meconium. Monitoring indicated fetal distress, and so delivery was by emergency cesarean section. The Apgar score was 1/5 at one and five minutes. Jason required vigorous resuscitation. Problems in the early newborn period included aspiration pneumonia, hypoxia, hypoglycemia, and jaundice. Seizures appeared on the second day of life. He had continuing feeding problems and was hypotonic at the time of discharge.

This is a typical, though abbreviated, case history of a difficult perinatal period that will have a profound impact on the child's future growth and development. This report and others like it contain certain terms commonly used by medical professionals, many of which are defined in this chapter. (The information presented here is not all-inclusive; some of the terms may be found in other relevant sections of this manual.)

TERMS APPLIED TO A WOMAN TO SIGNIFY HER PREGNANCY AND BIRTHING HISTORY

Gravida

Gravida is Latin for a pregnant woman; she is called gravida 1 during the first pregnancy, gravida 2 during the second, etc.

Para

Para, also Latin, means a woman who has borne a live child. A para 2 is a woman who has borne two live children, etc.

Abortus

Abortus is a miscarriage or delivery of a fetus with no chance of survival.

Stillborn

A *stillborn* child, though mature enough to survive outside the uterus, is born dead.

MATERNAL CONDITIONS THAT AFFECT THE GROWING FETUS

Prenatal Care

Studies have shown a higher incidence of prematurity and complications in newborns whose mothers did not receive adequate medical supervision. Contact with a physician early in the pregnancy facilitates the detection of conditions that may affect adversely the fetus and newborn child; it also allows treatment that may ameliorate, if not prevent, complications.

Maternal Disease

All acute and chronic diseases are potentially harmful to the fetus. Asthma, seizure disorders, and hypertension in the mother are a few of the diseases whose inadequate treatment may produce adverse effects. Careful monitoring of these diseases during pregnancy is essential to fetal well-being.

Rh Disease

A woman with Rh-negative blood may have an infant with Rh-positive blood. If minute amounts of blood from the infant enter the mother's circulation—which usually happens at the time of delivery—they are recognized as foreign by the mother's system; her body reacts by developing an immunity to that type of blood. Antibodies against Rh-positive blood remain in the mother's circulatory system and, in subsequent pregnancies, pass through the placenta to the fetus. Unless the unborn child has Rh-negative blood like the mother, these antibodies will destroy the child's red blood cells, causing severe anemia. A mother with Rh-negative blood should be given a special injection immediately after the first and each subsequent delivery to blunt her antibody responses to Rh-positive blood cells from the baby, thereby preventing Rh disease with subsequent pregnancies.

Diabetes Mellitus

Part of the routine testing for a newly pregnant woman is a urine check for sugar. This is because women with diabetes must have their blood sugar levels carefully controlled during pregnancy to ensure proper growth of the fetus. Certain women who show no signs of diabetes prior to pregnancy may do so during pregnancy. A special diet and, at times, insulin may be necessary to control blood sugar.

Toxemia

Toxemia of pregnancy, the cause of which is unknown, appears to affect the kidneys, resulting in varying degrees of high blood pressure, protein in the urine, and fluid retention. Most likely to be affected are young women during their early pregnancies. Management consists of careful observation, control of blood pressure, and, in the case of uncontrollable high blood pressure or seizures, prompt delivery to save both the baby and the mother. The early, milder, stage of this disease is sometimes called preeclampsia, eclampsia being the later, severe form, which is characterized by grand mal seizures. High blood pressure, a symptom of toxemia in the mother, can result in poor fetal growth as well as separation of the placenta from the uterine wall with resultant hemorrhage (abruptio placentae).

Teratogens

There are many agents in the environment—some recognized, others not—that may injure the fetus. Among these, in all probability, are environmental pollutants over which the pregnant woman has no control. Agents that are known to have adverse effects, however, can and should be avoided. Among these are certain drugs, alcohol, cigarettes, and unnecessary irradiation.

CONDITIONS AND TERMS THAT APPLY TO THE INFANT DURING LABOR, DELIVERY, AND THE EARLY NEWBORN PERIOD

Fetal Monitoring

Recent techniques make it possible to monitor the heart rate of the infant during labor. An electrode may be attached externally (to the mother's abdomen) or internally (directly to the baby's scalp) to observe the infant's response to uterine contractions and to detect early signs of fetal distress. Another electrode generally is used (either internally or externally) to monitor the length and intensity of the intrauterine contractions.

Cesarean Section

Cesarean section is the delivery of the fetus through incisions in the abdominal and uterine walls. The indications for a cesarean section are inability of the fetus to pass through the pelvic outlet of the mother; prolonged labor; placenta previa, in which the placenta overlies the opening of the uterus; severe toxemia; and fetal distress. Other situations—including a previous cesarean section or breech (other than head first) presentation—may also be viewed as cause for a cesarean section, depending on the physician and/or local custom.

Apgar Score

The Apgar score is the score given to a newborn infant by a nurse or physician, usually at one and five minutes following delivery. It is a useful means of communicating the newborn's general status and adaptation to extrauterine life. The maximum Apgar score is 10.

Efforts have been made to correlate the Apgar score with future developmental and neurological states. While very low scores do not invariably lead to significant future problems, they suggest significant distress during labor and delivery and warrant close observation of the infant.

Criteria for Apgar Scores

Criterion	Apgar Score		
	0	1	2
Color	Blue-pale	Extremities blue, rest of body pink	Completely pink
Heart rate	Absent	Below 100	Over 100
Respiratory effort	Absent	Weak, irregular	Good, crying
Muscle tone	Limp	Some flexion of extremities	Active motion
Reflex irritability (catheter in nostril)	None	Grimace	Cough/sneeze

Resuscitation

Low or absent heart and/or breathing rates in the newborn require immediate measures to stimulate or mechanically provide circulation and respiration. Delays in instituting such procedures may result in permanent neurological damage.

Asphyxia

Failure of the newborn to begin breathing after delivery is a major manifestation of asphyxia, a condition characterized by too little oxygen in the blood, elevated levels of carbon dioxide in the blood and tissues, and disturbance of the acid-base balance. Circumstances that may lead to asphyxia include (1) compression of the umbilical cord, (2) premature separation of the placenta, (3) sustained contraction of the uterus, (4) an umbilical cord that is wrapped tightly around the neck or body, (5) damage to the head and brain during the birth process, and (6) depression of the infant's breathing caused by drugs administered to the mother during the late stages of labor. The longer the baby has gone without sufficient oxygen, the longer it will take for him or her to respond to resuscitation. Thus, the quicker the response, the better the chances for a fast and full recovery.

Meconium

Meconium is a thick, sticky, brown substance that normally is passed in a bowel movement during the first few days of life. Passage of this material before delivery is one sign of fetal distress (insufficent oxygen, for example, may cause various negative reactions in the child, including the passage of meconium). Furthermore, the meconium may get inside the mouth as the child moves through the birth canal, then enter the trachea and lungs with the first breath. Meconium is highly irritating and can cause severe inflammation of the lungs (pneumonitis). When this substance cannot be removed from the baby's mouth prior to the first breath, it must be sucked out of the upper air passageway (trachea) as quickly as possible.

Jaundice

Jaundice is a yellowish color of the skin and whites of the eyes caused by an accumulation of bilirubin, a byproduct of the breakdown of red blood cells. Normally, bilirubin is picked up by the liver and passed into the intestine through the bile ducts of the liver and gallbladder. The liver in the newborn, however, is slow in removing this substance from the blood. Moreover, the trauma of the birth process may bring about an increase in the breakdown of red blood cells.

While mild jaundice requires no treatment, there are instances in which it may be necessary to reduce the amount of bilirubin in the blood. For example, Rh disease and other maternal-infant blood incompatibilities may cause the red cells to break down at a rate far exceeding the liver's ability to remove the bilirubin; also, in some infants, especially those who are preterm, the liver may not be able to remove this substance efficiently. Excess bilirubin is therefore quite common in newborns and not usually cause for concern. Very high levels, however, are known to cause damage to the brain (kernicterus) and resultant cerebral palsy. There are two common treatments: when the degree of elevation is moderate, special-wavelength fluorescent lights are used to break down the bilirubin in the skin; in more severe cases, it is necessary to exchange the baby's blood with donor blood.

Sepsis/Meningitis

Newborns, particularly preterm babies, have a lowered resistance to infection, making them susceptible to various bacterial, fungal, and viral organisms. The insertion of tubes (e.g., for intravenous feeding) provides an avenue of entry for infectious organisms. Since infection of the blood, spinal cord, and brain can have a devastating effect on the baby, most infants in intensive care units have, at one time or another, "septic workups," in which the blood, urine, and spinal fluid are examined for infection. If found, the infection is treated with antibiotics.

Hemolytic Disease of the Newborn

Red blood cells have surface markers, a type of "fingerprints," which characterize each individual. The most widely recognized markers are the ABO and Rh systems. There are many others that are less familiar but nonetheless important. If the markers of the mother and fetus are different, the blood cells of the fetus may gain entry into the mother's circulation, where they induce an antibody response. If subsequent fetuses have the same markers, the antibodies from the mother may pass through the placenta and into the fetus, where they attack the red blood cells and break them down. Such a sequence of events may result in varying degrees of anemia and jaundice in the newborn period. One of the best known and most serious types of hemolytic disease relates to the Rh system. The ABO and other blood group systems may result in significant, but less severe, anemia and jaundice.

Low Blood Sugar (Hypoglycemia)

The brain and heart are highly dependent upon adequate amounts of sugar. Preterm babies, growth-retarded babies, infants of diabetic mothers, and sick infants may have difficulty in maintaining appropriate blood sugar levels, making them particularly prone to brain damage due to hypoglycemia.

Seizures

Seizures do not constitute a disease; rather they are manifestations of some disease process. In the newborn they are ominous signs of two serious problems: (1) metabolic abnormalities (such as low blood sugar) or (2) injury to the brain caused by trauma or insufficient oxygen. Seizures are treated by correction of the metabolic disturbance (if it exists) and by anticonvulsants.

Intravenous Feeding (Hyperalimentation, Total Parenteral Nutrition)

Intravenous feeding is a process of administering complete nutrients directly into the blood stream. Very premature infants, very sick infants, or infants who have had intestinal tract surgery may not tolerate oral feedings, which ordinarily provide adequate nutrition for growth and recovery from illness.

Infants of Diabetic Mothers

While infants of diabetic mothers are not born with diabetes, they may undergo stress during pregnancy because of the complications associated with diabetes in the mother (such as kidney problems and inadequate control of blood sugar). Some studies suggest a higher incidence of congenital birth defects (congenital heart disease, for example) in this group than in the population as a whole. Infants of diabetic mothers are more likely to be large, although preterm; as newborns, they are likely to have significant difficulties in maintaining normal blood sugars.

THE EFFECTS OF PERINATAL INJURY ON FUTURE DEVELOPMENT

In the early 1960s, Great Britain established perinatal risk registers in order to determine what effects unfavorable perinatal events might have on future development. The predictive validity of such registers has been inconsistent, varying with the criteria for inclusion in the high-risk groups. The literature on the subject is extensive, and there are many areas of controversy and confusion.

In 1979, Nelson and Ellenberg studied forty thousand infants and reported on signs of neonatal neurological dysfunction that were predictive of future motor dysfunction.* Increases in the risk of cerebral palsy were observed in children with any one of the characteristics listed in the table below.

Factors Associated with Increased Risk

Factor	Relative Risk
Overall impression of abnormality of brain function by the attending physician	99*
Neonatal seizures	71
Apgar score of three or less at ten minutes or later	54
Multiple apneic episodes	36
Need for nasogastric feedings	22
Head circumference three standard deviations above or below the mean	21–26
Five-minute Apgar score of three or less	21
Diminished activity or diminished crying lasting more than one day	19–21
Birth weight less than 2,000 grams	16
Thermal instability	13
Hypertonia or hypotonia	12–15
Bilirubin equal to or greater than 20 mg/100 ml	12
Hematocrit less than 40 percent	11

*That is, children with apparent brain dysfunction at birth are 99 times more likely than other children to have or develop cerebral palsy.

When an older child has significant developmental problems, it is not unusual to find that there were complications in the perinatal period. On the other hand, many children who have complications in the newborn period turn out to be normal, and many children with cerebral palsy had

*Nelson, K.B., and J.H. Ellenberg. "Neonatal Signs as Predictors of Cerebral Palsy." *Pediatrics*, 64 (1979): 225.

no problems as newborns. Further work is needed to define those events or combinations of events that predict unfavorable outcomes so that identification resources can be focused on these high-risk groups.

SEE ALSO

Cerebral Palsy, Low Birth Weight, and *Respiratory Distress Syndrome*

Phenylketonuria and Other Metabolic Diseases

PHENYLKETONURIA

Description

Phenylketonuria (PKU) is one of the best-studied inherited errors of body metabolism. Untreated PKU almost always results in severe mental retardation; it may also cause convulsions, behavior problems, severe skin rash, and a musty odor of the body and urine. With early diagnosis and appropriate treatment, all of these manifestations of the disease can be prevented.

Cause

PKU results from the body's inability to convert phenylalanine, an essential amino acid found in high-protein foods, to another amino acid called tyrosine. This conversion, which takes place in the liver, depends on the presence of the enzyme phenylalanine hydroxylase. Children with PKU do not have this enzyme, and as a result the phenylalanine levels in their body tissues become markedly elevated. Phenylalanine is then converted to phenylketones by a little-used chemical process. (The excretion of phenylketones in the urine is what led to the name "phenylketonuria.") It has been presumed—though never proven in laboratory experiments— that the very elevated levels of phenylalanine (or one of its byproducts) are toxic to the body's tissues and therefore cause the clinical features of PKU.

For a child to inherit PKU, both parents must be carriers. That is, while neither parent has the clinical features of PKU, both have one gene for PKU, and both pass it on to the child. (There are, at present, no completely reliable laboratory tests to detect carriers.)

Incidence

PKU occurs in approximately one in 10,000 to one in 20,000 live births, depending on the ethnic background of the population. The occurrence rate is higher among groups of European ancestry. When both parents are carriers, the chances of having a child with PKU are one in four with each pregnancy.

Detection

Since 1964, mass screening of newborn infants has been adopted by most states and many foreign countries. A drop of blood is taken from the child's heel just prior to hospital discharge. If the blood test shows elevated levels of phenylalanine, the test is repeated for confirmation. Diagnosis must be prompt, since treatment should begin as soon after birth as possible.

Course

Left untreated in the first few months of life, PKU can lead to severe mental retardation and serious behavior problems. Formerly, many persons with PKU lived in residential institutions. Today, with appropriate diagnosis and dietary treatment, children with PKU can grow and develop normally.

Accompanying Health Problems

Children with appropriately diagnosed and treated PKU are as active and healthy as children without PKU. However, women with PKU—treated or untreated—are at increased risk for bearing children with microcephaly, congenital heart disease, and mental retardation. Presumably these impairments result from the high levels of phenylalanine to which their babies are exposed during pregnancy. There is some speculation that in the future these abnormalities may be prevented by restricting the mother's phenylalanine intake prior to conception and during pregnancy.

Medical Management

Once the diagnosis of PKU is confirmed, the infant is put on a special phenylalanine-restricted diet. It is important that the child's dietitian be experienced in dietary treatment of children with PKU. Most of the caloric intake is in the form of a special formula (e.g., Lofenalac or Phenyl-Free), from which nearly all of the phenylalanine has been removed. A certain amount of phenylalanine must be added to the diet, however, to allow for normal growth. As the child becomes older, limited amounts of cereals, fruits, and vegetables are usually permitted. Meats, dairy products, and other high-protein foods are prohibited because of their high phenylalanine content. (The formula provides most of the dietary protein.) Blood phenylalanine levels must be monitored frequently so that necessary adjustments can be made in the diet. PKU clinics have different policies regarding how long a phenylalanine-restricted diet should be continued. Most clinics recommend it for at least the first six years of life. Some clinics recommend allowing the children to eat a normal diet after age six; other clinics permit a wider variety of foods but continue some restriction of phenylalanine; still other clinics continue the phenylalanine-restricted diet. Many clinics have found it difficult to ensure strict adherence to the diet when the child reaches school age.

Implications for Education

Provided that children with PKU are appropriately diagnosed and treated with a phenylalanine-restricted diet, they are no different from normal, healthy children and should be treated accordingly. There is no evidence of motor, perceptual, language, or attentional problems that interfere with the educational process. Symptoms of illness will be unrelated to the PKU and should be dealt with according to normal procedures. Nearly all children with PKU who are in early education programs will be following a phenylalanine-restricted diet. It is essential that educators communicate with parents to ensure the child's compliance with the crucial dietary treatment.

OTHER METABOLIC DISEASES

Early detection is important for a number of other metabolic disorders, including congenital hypothyroidism, galactosemia, and branched-chain ketoaciduria. Like PKU, these conditions can be screened for in the newborn period. Positive test results should be confirmed immediately, since infants with galactosemia and branched-chain ketoaciduria can become seriously ill in the first week of life, with a substantial risk of death or long-term disability. Also, since all of the conditions screened for can produce brain damage, it is well to begin treatment as early as possible.

Congenital Hypothyroidism

With congenital hypothyroidism, the thyroid glands fail to develop normally. As a result, there is little or no thyroid hormone, a substance necessary for normal growth and development in childhood. This condition, which affects 1 in 5,000 newborns, occurs sporadically and is not inherited from parents.

Children who are hypothyroid during early infancy have poor growth and little appetite. They are also sluggish and constipated. As newborns, they are likely to have jaundice, large protruding tongues, and poor muscle tone, with resultant umbilical hernias. Not every child with congenital hypothyroidism has these signs and symptoms, however.

With proper treatment, children with congenital hypothyroidism are healthy and without serious medical problems. Prior to newborn metabolic screening, many children with this condition were not detected early enough for treatment to be effective. Generally speaking, if significant mental impairment is to be prevented, treatment with replacement thyroid hormone must begin in the first three months of life. Children who began treatment with thyroid hormone before three months of age have shown normal intellectual functioning at five years. Their continued long-term functioning is also expected to be normal.

Galactosemia

Galactosemia occurs with an absence of the liver enzyme galactose-1-phosphate uridyltransferase. Without this enzyme, galactose reaches high levels in the blood and tissues, with resultant liver disease, kidney disease, blindness (due to cataracts), and mental retardation.

Galactosemia, which occurs in one in every 50,000 births, is passed on through autosomal recessive inheritance. That is, both parents must be carriers of a gene for the disease. At present, many clinics are recommending that women who have previously given birth to children with galactosemia undergo amniocentesis. If the fetus has galactosemia and the pregnancy is continued, the mother may be advised to restrict her intake of galactose during the latter part of pregnancy.

Children with galactosemia are treated with a special diet free of galactose (a substance found in both human and cow's milk). They are generally given one of the soy-based formulas (Isomil, Neo-Mull-Soy, Nursoy). Later, as they grow older and begin eating solid foods, they must avoid foods containing milk or milk products. Children treated early with a galactose-free diet are generally healthy and able to avoid serious medical problems. Whether early treatment results in completely normal intellectual ability and overall functioning, however, remains to be fully documented.

Branched-Chain Ketoacidura

Children with branched-chain ketoaciduria (maple syrup urine disease) are unable to metabolize three amino acids—namely, valine, leucine, and isoleucine. This is a very rare condition, occurring in only one in every 150,000 births; both parents must be carriers of a gene that causes it.

Affected children are fed a specially manufactured formula from which valine, leucine, and isoleucine have been removed. Since these three amino acids are essential for growth and development, small amounts of regular milk are given as a supplement. As the children begin eating solids, foods containing protein are prohibited or introduced only in small, carefully measured quantities. At the present time, it is recommended that children with branched-chain ketoaciduria continue on a protein-restricted diet throughout childhood and into adulthood.

Although early treatment of branched-chain ketoaciduria has certainly reduced medical problems, there are as yet insufficient data to predict how early treatment of this disease will affect intellectual capabilities and overall functioning in adult life.

Children with branched-chain ketoaciduria may become suddenly and seriously ill with what in normal children would be a mild viral illness, such as a cold or stomach flu. They may then require further modification of their diet or possibly artificial removal (peritoneal dialysis) of the branched-chain amino acids valine, leucine, and isoleucine (and the products of their metabolism) from body tissues. It is important that these children be treated at a medical center with expertise in the management of branched-chain ketoaciduria.

SEE ALSO
Genetics

Positioning and Handling

POSITIONING

Positioning is the process of securing a child with developmental disabilities in adapted or specially designed equipment to facilitate better posture and performance.

Why Position a Child with Disabilities?

Standard, unadapted child care equipment frequently does not provide the necessary postural support for the individual with developmental disabilities. Lacking normal control of the body, the child may lean to one side, arch the back, or fall forward. Over extended periods, this may lead to joint contractures, scoliosis, hip dislocations, and other structural problems. Poor positioning can also block motor function and cause skin irritation.

The child who is properly positioned in adapted or specially designed equipment is more comfortable, may perform better, and has less chance of developing deformities. Proper positioning has advantages for the caretaker as well, making the child easier to feed, transport, and otherwise manage.

Poorly Positioned Child. *Note leaning to one side.*

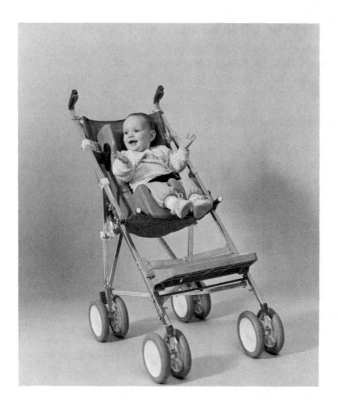

Properly Positioned Child

Evaluating the Child's Positioning Needs

Because body alignment can affect the whole spectrum of a child's learning and development, a team of professionals is usually involved in evaluating the child prior to ordering adaptive equipment; typically, (1) physical therapists and occupational therapists determine motor and adaptive function levels; (2) a nurse or physician evaluates general health status; (3) a speech pathologist reviews language comprehension and speech motor skills; (4) a psychologist measures social and intellectual abilities; (5) a teacher determines educational goals; (6) an audiologist assesses hearing; and (7) a social worker identifies individual family needs—which must be considered if the equipment is to be put to proper use. When these evaluations are completed and reviewed by team members, the therapists are ready to measure the child and to select, order, and fit the appropriate equipment.

Positioning Equipment

Maintaining the best possible position for everyday functioning may include (1) adapting available child care equipment, such as a stroller, car seat, highchair, potty chair, or classroom chair; (2) utilizing commercial therapeutic equipment, such as a wheelchair; or (3) constructing equipment from original designs. While such equipment is usually used for sitting, devices are also used for side lying, standing, and other positions. Depending on the needs of the individual, adaptive equipment may have inserts for maintaining specific angles and inclines as well as head and neck supports and appropriate restraining straps.

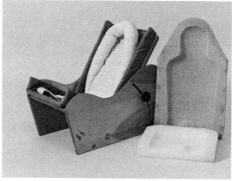

Commercial Floor Sitter

Constructed Floor Sitter with Commercial Insert Options

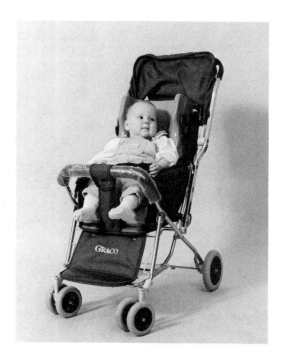

Commercial Seating Support Placed in Standard Stroller for Transportation and Support of Posture

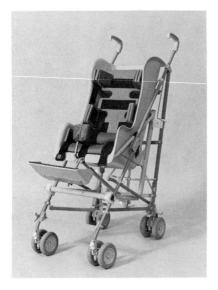

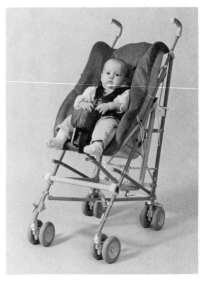

Commercial Infant and Young Child Transportation Equipment Designed with Adjustable Pads for Supporting Good Posture

Child Seated in Same Chair with Cover Applied Over the Pads. *The seat is removed from the frame for use as a car seat. The frame collapses, similar to an umbrella stroller, for easy transporting.*

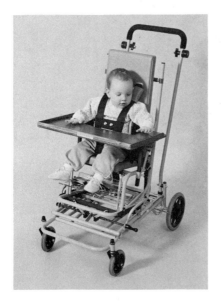

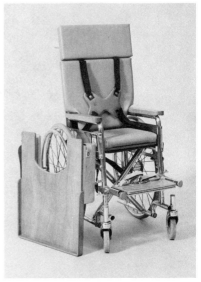

Commercial Stroller/Infant Wheelchair Raises for Use as a Highchair. *The seat can also be removed from the frame for use as a car seat. The frame collapses.*

Standard Wheelchair with Specially Constructed Wood and Foam Inserts and Lap Tray

The Importance of Follow-Up

A child needs to build up skin or behavioral tolerance to the adapted equipment gradually. A specific program for increasing tolerance is recommended. Once positioning is completed, the child should be re-evaluated and the equipment examined at regular intervals. Changes in growth and motor abilities often require changes in the adaptive device.

HANDLING

Handling is the process of picking up and carrying a child with a developmental disability.

Why Use Special Handling Techniques?

Children with motor handicaps have less control than other children. For this reason, it is advisable to offer them the support they need to feel secure. Proper handling techniques can also prevent undesirable responses, such as too much extension in the child's posture.

Techniques in Handling

INCORRECT. *Avoid lifting the child under the arms without supporting the legs. The child with high muscle tone (hypertonicity) may "scissor" the legs. The child with low muscle tone (hypotonicity) may slip through your hands.*

CORRECT. *Bend the child's legs before picking up. Provide good support for both the trunk and legs.*

Gather the Child with Low Muscle Tone Close to You To Give a Feeling of Stability

For Distances, You May Want To Have the Child Straddle Your Hip

SEE ALSO
Bracing, Cerebral Palsy, and *Myelomeningocele*

Respiratory Distress Syndrome

DESCRIPTION

Respiratory distress syndrome (RDS) is a pulmonary disorder commonly encountered in premature infants. It is among the most frequent causes of death in the premature infant as well as the most common illness in many neonatal intensive care units. The usual signs are labored, grunting respirations, poor oxygenation of body tissues in room air, and characteristic findings on chest X-ray examinations.

CAUSE

RDS is caused by a deficiency of a material called surfactant, which is needed to keep the air sacs (alveoli) in the lungs open. When surfactant is absent or when it is present in inadequate amounts, the air sacs collapse, and hence the entire lung collapses (a condition known as atelectasis). The tremendous energy then required to breathe leads to exhaustion and the above-mentioned signs of RDS.

A fetus seldom produces adequate amounts of surfactant before 36 weeks of gestation. RDS is therefore common among premature infants. This condition rarely occurs in full-term infants unless the lungs are particularly immature, as they may be, for example, in infants born to women with diabetes.

INCIDENCE

RDS occurs in 1 percent of newborns, making it the most common severe respiratory problem in the first few days after birth. The incidence of RDS varies greatly with gestational age; it is rare in full-term infants and extremely common in infants born prior to 32 weeks of gestation.

DETECTION

Generally speaking, RDS is not difficult to detect clinically. Usually within a few hours after birth, the premature baby audibly grunts on expiration, breathing frequently and with great effort, flaring the nostrils and retracting the muscles between the ribs and just below the rib cage. The infant is also lethargic and has a bluish color due to decreased oxygen concentration in the blood.

COURSE

Depending on the prematurity of the infant, the duration of RDS may be one to two days, or it may last more than a week. This condition usually improves when the infant begins producing adequate amounts of surfactant.

ACCOMPANYING HEALTH PROBLEMS

Premature infants suffering from RDS are vulnerable to other health problems associated with prematurity. One of the most important of these is bleeding into the fluid-filled spaces of the brain (intraventricular hemorrhage), a condition often associated with later disabilities.

Infants with very severe RDS, especially those who are on mechanical ventilators for prolonged periods or those who receive high concentrations of oxygen, are at risk for developing a chronic lung disorder known as bronchopulmonary dysplasia.

MEDICAL MANAGEMENT

Neonatal intensive care units, anticipating RDS in premature infants, routinely monitor pulse and respiration, along with the amount of oxygen in the blood. At the first clinical sign of RDS, treatment is begun. Initially this may take the form of increasing the concentration of inspired oxygen. Often, constant distending pressure through the nose or mouth (continuous positive airway pressure) is applied to keep the alveoli and lungs from collapsing. Some infants require a mechanical ventilator, which essentially breathes for them. Infants with RDS usually are not able to nurse or drink formula from a bottle; they must either be fed intravenously or given formula or breast milk through a tube that is passed through the mouth or nose and into the stomach.

IMPLICATIONS FOR EDUCATION

Today, approximately 90 percent of infants with RDS survive. Of these, the majority will develop normally and do well in regular classes. A small group, however, particularly those who have experienced intraventricular hemorrhage or other medical complications during the early days of life, may have developmental disabilities including cognitive and/or physical impairment. Some may have continuing problems with respiratory illness, especially during the first year. Breathing difficulties, cough, or fever should always be evaluated by a health provider.

SEE ALSO

Low Birth Weight

Routine Health Care

When children are receiving care and treatment for developmental disabilities or impairments, routine health care may be neglected. This is especially problematic for two reasons: (1) some children with disabilities may be more prone to certain common illnesses, such as colds, ear infections, or diarrhea, and (2) with these children it is often more difficult—though particularly important—to distinguish routine illnesses from more serious ones.

THE HEALTH CARE PROVIDER

It is essential that every child be seen regularly by a health care provider. This is especially true of a child with disabilities, since chronic disease, poor nutrition, and medications all influence developmental progress. Also, any leveling off or regression in development may be a sign of specific neurological disease. Therefore, although most handicapped children are involved with developmental assessment and treatment agencies, it is important that the primary health care provider keep abreast of the child's developmental progress as well.

One important function of the primary health care provider is to counsel parents regarding proper diet, including adequate calorie intake as well as a proper balance of protein, fats, and carbohydrates. This medical professional should also teach parents how to monitor their child's health and recognize early signs of illness, including

- change in personality or habits
- fever
- change in appetite
- change in bowel or urinary habits
- irritability
- lethargy
- vomiting
- diarrhea

Schedule of Preventive Health Care Recommended by the American Academy of Pediatrics

AGE	INFANCY						EARLY CHILDHOOD				
	By 1 mo.	2 mos.	4 mos.	6 mos.	9 mos.	12 mos.	15 mos.	18 mos.	24 mos.	3 yrs.	4 yrs.
HISTORY Initial/Interval	●	●	●	●	●	●	●	●	●	●	●
MEASUREMENTS Height and Weight	●	●	●	●	●	●	●	●	●	●	●
Head Circumference	●	●	●	●	●	●					
Blood Pressure										●	●
SENSORY SCREENING Vision	●	●	●	●	●	●	●	●	●	●	●
Hearing	●	●	●	●	●	●	●	●	●	●	●
DEVEL./BEHAV. ASSESSMENT	●	●	●	●	●	●	●	●	●	●	●
PHYSICAL EXAMINATION	●	●	●	●	●	●	●	●	●	●	●
PROCEDURES Hered./Metabolic Screening	●										
Immunization		●	●	●			●	●	●		
Tuberculin Test	←———————————●▶					←———————		●	———————→		
Hematocrit or Hemoglobin	←———————				● ——→		←———————		●	———————→	
Urinalysis	←———————		●	——→			←———————		●	———————→	
ANTICIPATORY GUIDANCE	●	●	●	●	●	●	●	●	●	●	●
INITIAL DENTAL REFERRAL										●	

Recommended Immunization Schedules

Recommended Age	Immunization(s)
2 months	DTP,[a] OPV[b]
4 months	DTP, OPV
6 months	DTP (OPV)
15 months	MMR[c]
18 months	DTP,[d,e] OPV,[e] PRP-D[f]
4–6 years[g]	DTP, OPV
14–16 years	Td[h]

[a]Diphtheria and tetanus toxoids with pertussis vaccine.
[b]Oral poliovirus vaccine.
[c]Live measles, mumps, and rubella viruses.
[d]Should be given 6–12 months after the third dose.
[e]May be given simultaneously with MMR at 15 months of age.
[f]Haemophilus b conjugate vaccine.
[g]Up to the seventh birthday.
[h]Adult tetanus toxoid (full dose) and diphtheria toxoid (reduced dose) in combination.

The primary health care provider should also counsel parents on how a disability may affect their child's behavior and development. Otherwise, misunderstandings may occur. For example, a behavior syndrome that is caused by hypersensitivity to environmental stimuli—a result of central nervous system damage—may be mistaken for prolonged, severe colic. Likewise, the sudden and abnormal rigidity in infants suffering spasticity may be misconstrued by anxious parents as rejection.

In addition to counseling parents, the primary health care provider should advise other professionals on the child's health limitations as well as on how to recognize new or recurrent health problems. This physician—the pediatrician or general practitioner—should also facilitate communications among parents, medical subspecialists, and nonmedical professionals. It is the primary health care provider with whom the education-related professional should discuss both the child's general health and specific disability-related concerns.

SEE ALSO
Dental Disease and *Growth and Nutrition*

Seizure Disorders

DESCRIPTION

Seizures, also called convulsions, are characterized by involuntary motor activity or a change in consciousness of behavior. These are symptoms of underlying abnormalities of the brain. Normally, minute electrical impulses travel along specific nerve pathways in a controlled fashion and at appropriate times. A seizure occurs when bursts of unorganized electrical impulses interfere with this normal brain functioning. Electrical bursts of different types or in different locations of the brain result in different kinds of seizures. Epilepsy is a chronic condition of the nervous system that is characterized by recurrent seizures.

Grand Mal Seizures

Grand mal seizures, which account for 60 percent of all convulsive disorders, are generalized throughout the body. Prior to onset of a grand mal seizure, the child may experience a very brief warning, or aura; this can take the form of numbness, noise, taste, smell, or other unusual sensations or feelings. The seizure itself has two phases: tonic and clonic. During the tonic phase there is usually loss of consciousness, stiffening of the body, heavy and irregular breathing, drooling, skin pallor, and occasional bladder and bowel incontinence. After a few seconds, the clonic phase begins. The clonic phase is characterized by alternating rigidity and relaxation of the muscles. The tonic and clonic phases are usually followed by a period of drowsiness, disorientation, or fatigue (the postictal state).

Focal Seizures

Focal seizures are caused by abnormal electrical impulses in a localized area of the brain. These can occur in the motor strip of the right frontal lobe, for example, in which case there may be involuntary, repetitive jerking of the left hand and arm.

Focal seizures may become generalized and result in loss of consciousness.

Infantile Spasms

Also called infantile myoclonic seizures or jacknife epilepsy, infantile spasms usually begin when a child is three to nine months old. Episodes, characterized by dropping of the head and flexion of the arms, may occur hundreds of times a day. The developmental prognosis of infants with this type of seizure is generally (though not always) poor; while the spasms may abate after several years, other types of seizures may replace them. Infantile spasms may indicate the presence of an underlying disorder, such as tuberous sclerosis. They are associated with a typical electroencephalographic pattern called hypsarrhythmia.

Myoclonic-Akinetic Seizures

Myoclonic seizures, not to be confused with infantile myoclonic seizures (see above), are characterized by brief, involuntary jerking of the extremities, with or without loss of consciousness. Akinetic seizures, on the contrary, are characterized by loss of tone. These two types of seizures may be related to fixed neurological damage or to a degenerative process. They are often very difficult to control.

Psychomotor Seizures

Sometimes referred to as temporal lobe seizures, psychomotor seizures are caused by abnormal electrical bursts in the temporal lobe of the brain. They are usually characterized by involuntary, repetitive behaviors, such as chewing, lip smacking, or rubbing of the hands or legs. Affected individuals may have unusual sensory experiences or undergo emotional changes, becoming fearful or angry. The seizure may last from a few seconds to a few minutes—with the child in an altered state of consciousness. It is commonly followed by confusion.

Petit Mal Seizures

Petit mal seizures occur most commonly between the ages of four and 12 years and usually disappear as the child reaches maturity. About one-third to one-half of the individuals who have petit mal seizures will also have (or eventually develop) grand mal seizures. Petit mal seizures are more difficult to recognize: the child usually appears to be staring absent-mindedly, sometimes repetitively blinking the eyes or smacking the lips. The episodes are brief, usually lasting from five to 30 seconds. There is loss of consciousness without loss of muscle tone; this means that the child does not fall down, yet has no memory of the episode and is unaware of the passage of time. These types of seizures also are likely to have a characteristic electroencephalographic pattern (three per second spike and wave).

Simple Febrile Seizures

Perhaps the most common type of seizure—occurring in 5 to 10 percent of children under the age of five—is one that is precipitated by fever. This type of seizure, which typically lasts less than ten minutes, tends to occur during a febrile illness in a child between the ages of one and six. It is characterized by loss of consciousness and involuntary, generalized jerking. (It is, in fact, a grand mal seizure.)

There is some controversy about whether to treat children with febrile seizures; most physicians, however, feel that it is not necessary to treat the child who has only one uncomplicated febrile seizure. The vast majority of children who have simple febrile seizures are not harmed by them and do not develop epilepsy. However, children who have focal or prolonged febrile seizures and children who have a history of abnormal development or abnormal findings on a neurological examination are more likely to have epilepsy triggered by fever rather than by febrile seizures.

CAUSE

The reasons for seizures are as varied as the types. In most cases the cause is unknown; that is, the seizure is idiopathic. At times it is possible to identify a hereditary component. Also, any injury to the brain can bring about a seizure disorder. A severe head injury or brain hemorrhage can cause scarring in the brain, where abnormal bursts of electricity may originate. Scarring can also be caused by meningitis or encephalitis or by congenital infections, such as rubella. Other conditions associated with seizures include cerebral palsy, hydrocephalus, and metabolic disorders.

INCIDENCE

Seizure disorders occur in 0.5 percent of the general population.

DETECTION

Most seizures are easy to detect because of their obvious clinical manifestations. However, psychomotor and petit mal seizures can sometimes have atypical clinical signs that make the diagnosis more difficult.

When seizures have occurred, a brain wave test (electroencephalogram [EEG]) is usually obtained. Electrodes placed on different areas of the scalp record the electrical impulses caused by the brain activity. In most circumstances, the EEG provides helpful confirming evidence of a seizure disorder. For example, if a grand mal seizure is coupled with a characteristic pattern on the EEG, the physician has a clear diagnosis. The EEG alone, however, is not sufficient to diagnose a seizure disorder. The seizure disorder may not show up in the EEG pattern, or the EEG pattern may be abnormal when there is no clinical evidence of seizures.

Both children with petit mal seizures and infants with infantile myoclonic seizures have a very specific disorganized pattern on their EEGs. EEG patterns do not always correlate with clinical seizure types, however. In some instances the location rather than the pattern of abnormal electrical discharges can be significant. For instance, children with psychomotor seizures show an abnormal EEG in those electrodes that are placed over the temporal lobe region of the brain.

COURSE

Without anticonvulsant medications, most children with seizure disorders will have recurrences of seizures. In the majority of cases—particularly with grand mal, focal, petit mal, and psychomotor seizures—anticonvulsants can prevent recurrence once the appropriate dosage requirement has been determined, provided the child receives the medication regularly. With some children, however, seizures are not easily controlled; they may require multiple changes in medications and dosage. With a few children, it is impossible to control seizures totally. While this can be true of any type of seizure disorder, it is more frequently the case with myoclonic or mixed seizure disorders or when there is severe brain damage or severe mental retardation.

Seizures may disappear or decrease in frequency as the child gets older, but it sometimes happens that one type of seizure is replaced by another type (e.g., infantile spasms may be replaced by grand mal seizures). There can be a recurrence of, or increase in, seizure activity around puberty, when hormonal changes may inhibit the brain's ability to restrict the abnormal bursts of electricity. Many times, after a number of years have gone by without a seizure—and provided there is no cause to suspect a continuing disorder—physicians will try taking children off anticonvulsants to see whether seizures will recur.

ACCOMPANYING HEALTH PROBLEMS

Seizure disorders frequently accompany other disorders, including cerebral palsy, myelomeningocele, encephalitis and meningitis, and mental retardation.

MEDICAL MANAGEMENT

Seizure disorders are treated with anticonvulsant medications. The three most commonly used medications are phenobarbital (Luminal), carbamazepine (Tegretol), and phenytoin (Dilantin). These are the first-line medications for grand mal seizures. If they are not effective, primidone (Mysoline) or valproic acid (Depakene) may be added. Ethosuximide (Zarontin) is used with petit mal seizures, carbamazepine and primidone with psychomotor seizures, and clonazepam (Clonopin) with myoclonic seizures. Anticonvulsants frequently are ineffective with infantile myoclonic seizures, and both steroids and ACTH (a hormone secreted by the pituitary gland) have been tried with varying degrees of success.

Anticonvulsant Medications and Their Side Effects

Name	Types of Seizures Treated	Side Effects or Treated Adverse Reactions
Carbamazepine (Tegretol)	Grand mal Focal Psychomotor	Vomiting, headache, drowsiness, blood dyscrasia, ataxia
Clonazepam (Clonopin)	Petit mal Myoclonic (minor motor)	Hyperactivity, short attention span, impulsive behavior, drowsiness, ataxia, vertigo or dizziness, confusion, excessive weight gain, drooling
Corticosteroids (adrenocorticotropic hormone [ACTH])	Infantile myoclonic	Moon face, elevated blood sugar, susceptibility to infections, thinning of the bones, muscle weakness
Phenytoin (Dilantin)	Grand mal Psychomotor Focal	Gingival hyperplasia, hirsutism, dermatitis rash (in approximately 5–10 percent of patients; drug should be discontinued), drowsiness, gastric distress, nystagmus, ataxia, dysarthria, blood dyscrasias
Ethosuximide (Zarontin)	Petit mal	Dizziness, gastrointestinal distress: nausea, vomiting, anorexia; leukopenia, kidney dysfunction
Phenobarbital (Luminal)	Grand mal	Rash (Stevens-Johnson syndrome), ataxia, hyperactivity, questionable effect on cognitive performance, blood dyscrasias
Primidone (Mysoline)	Grand mal Psychomotor	Drowsiness, dizziness, abnormal behavior, ataxia, rash, blood dyscrasias, diplopia, nystagmus
Valproic acid (Depakene)	Petit mal Grand mal, mixed Myoclonic-akinetic	Nausea, vomiting, drowsiness, incoordination, dizziness, skin rash, liver toxicity, hair loss, weight gain

Uncomplicated seizure disorders frequently are managed by pediatricians and family physicians. More complex cases, however, require consultation with a neurologist. Ongoing follow-up is required because seizures can change in intensity and type with time. The medication and dosage also need to be checked as the child grows. Also, the child should be monitored for adverse side effects.

IMPLICATIONS FOR EDUCATION

Grand mal seizures in and of themselves usually are not harmful unless they are very prolonged or recur in rapid succession (status epilepticus), in which case immediate medical care is needed. Otherwise, the main concern is that the child does not become injured from falling. During the seizure, breathing frequently is irregular. It may even appear to stop, but this is rarely the case. Usually, the only first aid required is preventing self-harm. It is best to keep the child on his or her side to prevent food from getting into the lungs should vomiting occur. Contrary to popular notions, it is not necessary to prevent the child from swallowing the tongue. In fact, trying to put something in the mouth can result in the loss of the child's teeth or injury to the first aid provider's fingers. In the rare case where breathing has actually stopped, as might occur if regurgitated stomach contents are aspirated, standard cardiopulmonary resuscitation techniques should be employed immediately.

Both a poorly controlled seizure disorder and the side effects of many of the anticonvulsant medications can affect alertness and academic performance. Changes in behavior should be reported to the child's physician. It is also important for teachers to take note of the child's behavior just prior to and during a seizure and to report this as well.

**FIRST AID
FOR EPILEPTIC SEIZURES**

A major epileptic seizure is often dramatic and frightening. It lasts only a few minutes, however, and does not require expert care. These simple procedures should be followed:

- REMAIN CALM. You cannot stop a seizure once it has started. Let the seizure run its course. Do not try to revive the child.
- If the child is upright, ease him to the floor and loosen his clothing.
- Try to prevent the child from striking his head or body against any hard, sharp, or hot objects; but do not otherwise interfere with his movement.
- Turn the child on his side to prevent choking.
- DO NOT INSERT ANYTHING BETWEEN THE CHILD'S TEETH.
- Do not be alarmed if the child seems to stop breathing momentarily.
- After the movements stop and the child is relaxed, allow him to sleep or rest if he wishes.
- It isn't generally necessary to call a doctor unless the attack is followed almost immediately by another seizure or the seizure lasts more than five minutes, or this is a first seizure in a child with no known diagnosis of epilepsy.
- Notify the child's parents or guardians that a seizure has occurred.
- After a seizure, many people can carry on as before. If, after resting, the child seems groggy, confused, or weak, it may be a good idea to accompany him home.

Courtesy of:
Iowa chapter Epilepsy Foundation of America and
Epilepsy Association of Area 10,
Cedar Rapids, Iowa.

SEE ALSO
Electroencephalography

Syndromes

DESCRIPTION

Medical syndromes are various signs and symptoms that occur together commonly enough to warrant giving the pattern a specific name. Down syndrome, for example, is associated with the following characteristics: decreased muscle tone, short stature, a small oral cavity, an upward slant to the eyes, an extra fold at the corner of the eyes, wide spaces between the first and second toes, and short, broad hands with a single palmar crease.

A medical syndrome commonly gets its name from the person who first reports the description of the syndrome. Examples include Down, Marfan, and Potter syndromes.

CAUSE

The causes for many syndromes have been identified. It is known, for example, that Down syndrome results from the presence of an extra chromosome 21. Hurler syndrome results from the absence of the enzyme alpha-L-iduronidase in the body cells, without which certain substances accumulate in large amounts, causing physical and mental impairment. The physical and mental abnormalities that characterize fetal alcohol syndrome are caused by the effects of alcohol on the brain and other developing organs of the fetus. Finally, Potter syndrome, which is associated with poor lung development, a flat nose, and multicystic kidneys, may occur when there is an unusually small amount of amniotic fluid surrounding the fetus.

The cause of some syndromes is still unknown; an example is Cockayne syndrome, which is associated with poor growth, intellectual impairment, hearing loss, visual impairment, and premature aging.

DETECTION

Most syndromes are diagnosed by observing the abnormalities present and then identifying the pattern. Recognizing a syndrome is important for a number of reasons: it may lead to the identification of potential medical problems, some of which may be treatable; it can also provide parents and educators with information helpful in the planning of individualized instruction or home management. Identifying Waardenburg syndrome, for instance, may lead to the discovery of a hearing loss, which calls for special types of instruction. The identification of certain hereditary syndromes can lead to parental counseling regarding the risks of having another child with the same condition.

Because intellectual limitations characterize many syndromes—Down, Williams, Noonan, and Prader-Willi, to name a few—it is especially important that children with this disability be examined for signs and symptoms of particular syndromes.

COURSE

Once a particular syndrome is identified, it may be possible to ascertain the likelihood of certain problems developing in the future. Children with Hurler syndrome, for example, should undergo frequent eye and heart examinations, since problems are encountered commonly in these two organs. Children with Prader-Willi syndrome need to have their caloric intake closely monitored because of the rapid and severe obesity that can occur with this condition.

ACCOMPANYING HEALTH PROBLEMS

Serious health problems are a common feature of many medical syndromes. Congenital heart defects, for example, occur frequently with Noonan, Down, Williams, Marfan, and Turner syndromes; kidney abnormalities occur in Turner, Zellweger, and Lowe syndromes. Knowing which health problems are associated with a given syndrome aids in prompt recognition and treatment.

IMPLICATIONS FOR EDUCATION

While certain problems are common with a given syndrome (most children with Down syndrome have intellectual limitations; most with Hurler syndrome have visual, hearing, or cardiac impairments), it is important to keep in mind that not all children with a particular syndrome are identical. For example, although most children with Prader-Willi syndrome have intellectual limitations, some do have average abilities. Because a child may have some—but not all—of the features associated with a syndrome, each child must be evaluated individually.

The following is an annotated list of selected syndromes. The most common identifying features are included, although many are variable and there are often many other abnormalities present that affect health, growth, and development. When known, the pattern of genetic transmission is stated. Further details of each of these and other syndromes can be found in the resource identified at the end of this chapter or in general pediatric references.

Apert: Autosomal dominant; premature fusion of skull bones, poor growth of facial bones, wide-spaced eyes; fused fingers and toes; mental retardation.

Bardet-Biedl (Laurence-Moon-Biedl): Autosomal recessive; retinitis pigmentosa with early night vision loss and eventual blindness; obesity present from infancy; extra or fused fingers or toes; mild to moderate mental retardation.

Beckwith-Wiedemann: Large tongue; large body; low blood sugar in early infancy; omphalocele (abdominal contents protrude through a defect in the abdominal wall at birth); occasional mild to moderate mental retardation.

Coffin-Lowry: X-linked; downslanting eyes; coarse facial features; hypotonia; tapering fingers; severe mental retardation.

Cornelia de Lange: Continuous eyebrows, small or malformed hands and feet; excessive body hair; mental retardation.

Cri du chat: Missing part of chromosome 4; small head; catlike cry in infancy; mental retardation.

Diencephalic syndrome of infancy: This rare cause of failure to thrive is caused by a tumor (glioma) of the anterior hypothalamus (where appetite is controlled). Affected children appear emaciated yet hyperalert. They do not grow despite seemingly adequate caloric intake; and, when encouraged to eat more, they will refuse forcefully. Treatment, though not totally satisfactory, is irradiation of the tumor.

Down or Trisomy 21: See "Down Syndrome."

Ehlers-Danlos: Autosomal dominant; hyperextensible joints and skin; poor wound healing.

Ellis-van Creveld (chondroectodermal dysplasia): Autosomal recessive; short extremities; poorly formed nails; cardiac defects; occasional mental retardation.

Erb's palsy: When traction is exerted on the head, neck, or shoulders during delivery, the brachial plexus may be injured. In Erb's palsy, the injury is limited to the fifth and sixth cervical nerves with resultant loss of power to abduct the arm from the shoulder, to rotate the arm externally, to supinate the forearm, or to flex the forearm. It is important to differentiate this injury from cerebral palsy and fractures of the clavicle or humerus. Treatment consists of initial partial immobilization followed by splinting to prevent contractures and gentle range of motion exercises. It may be six months to one year before the degree of impairment is fully appreciated.

Fetal alcohol syndrome: See "Fetal Alcohol Syndrome."

Fetal hydantoin (Dilantin): Caused by use of phenytoin (Dilantin) during pregnancy for seizure control; poor growth; depressed nasal bridge; wide-spaced eyes; bowed upper lip; cleft lip and palate; abnormalities of fingers, toes, and their nails; mild to borderline mental retardation.

Fragile X: X-linked; large head; prominent forehead and ears; occasional autisticlike behaviors; large testes (may not be evident until puberty); mental retardation.

Goldenhar: Poor growth of facial structures; lateral cleftlike extension of the corner of the mouth; skin tags or pits in front of the ears; outer and inner ear defects with possible deafness; malfunction or clefts of the palate; spinal column abnormalities; occasional mental retardation.

Hurler: Autosomal recessive; accumulation of mucopolysaccharides and lipids in various tissues; coarse facial features; cloudy corneas; short stature; excessive body hair; severe mental retardation with failure of advancement by two to five years.

Lowe (oculo-cerebral-renal): X-linked, recessive; hypotonia; cataracts; kidney abnormalities; failure to thrive; hyperactivity; mental retardation.

Menkes (kinky hair): X-linked, recessive; progressive brain deterioration; seizures; feeding difficulties; twisted and fractured hair; mental retardation.

Neurofibromatosis (Von Recklinghausen disease): Autosomal dominant; areas of excessive or diminished pigmentation on the skin; connective tissue tumors under the skin, along nerves, and sometimes in eyes or membrane around the brain or spinal cord; occasional seizures; mental retardation is not typically present.

Osteogenesis imperfecta: Usually autosomal dominant, bluish sclerae (whites of the eyes), fragile bones, possible deafness.

Pierre Robin: Small jaw; relatively large, protruding tongue; cleft palate.

Prader-Willi: Rounded face, almond-shaped eyes, strabismus; low forehead, hypogonadism, hypotonia, mental retardation, poor growth in infancy but obesity later with excessive appetite and compulsive eating behavior.

Riley-Day (familial dysautonomia): Autosomal recessive; most common in Ashkenazi Jews; disturbance in autonomic and peripheral sensory functions; problems with swallowing, aspiration pneumonia, excessive salivation and sweating, temperature regulation, absence of taste sensation, diminished pain sense, dysarthria, emotional lability, and mental retardation.

Rubinstein-Taybi: Slanting eyes, small head, broad thumbs and toes, mental retardation.

Sanfilippo: Autosomal recessive; excessive accumulation of mucopolysaccharides in tissues; mild coarse facial features; mild stiff joints; slowing mental development by age three followed by deterioration.

Seckel: Autosomal recessive; short stature; small head; prominent nose; low-set ears; moderate to severe mental retardation.

Sjögren-Larrson: Autosomal recessive; spasticity (especially lower extremities); ichthyosis (dry, rough, scaly skin); mental retardation.

Smith-Lemli-Opitz: Autosomal recessive; upturned nostrils; drooping eyelids; fusion of second and third toes; abnormalities of genitalia; feeding problems; irritability; mental retardation.

Trisomy 18: Extra chromosome 18; small mouth; narrow eye openings; clenched hands; mental retardation.

Tuberous sclerosis: Autosomal dominant; brownish facial skin nodules; whitish patches on the skin elsewhere; tumors of the brain resulting in seizures and occasionally mental retardation.

Turner: Missing X chromosome; webbing of neck; low hairline in back; short stature; broad chest with widely spaced nipples; infertility; sometimes mental retardation, although average IQ is 95 with performance lower than verbal scores.

VATER Association: Vertebral anomalies and ventricular septal defects; anal atresia (absent anal opening); tracheoesophageal fistula (opening between esophagus and trachea); radius (bone in the forearm) abnormality; renal (kidney) abnormality.

Waardenburg: Autosomal dominant; wide spacing between eyes; white hair forelock; deafness.

Williams: Small size; prominent lips; hoarse voice; heart abnormalities; in infancy may be fretful and have feeding problems; during childhood outgoing and loquacious; mild mental retardation with better verbal than perceptual motor skills.

SEE ALSO

Down Syndrome, Fetal Alcohol Syndrome, Genetics, and *Phenylketonuria and Other Metabolic Diseases*

ADDITIONAL RESOURCE

Jones, K.L. *Smith's Recognizable Patterns of Human Malformation: Genetic, Embryonic, and Clinical Aspects.* Philadelphia: W.B. Saunders Co., 1988.

Teratogens

Teratogens are agents in the environment of the developing embryo and fetus that cause structural or functional abnormalities. About 8 percent of birth defects are clearly linked to teratogens. The percentage of birth defects due to teratogens may actually be much higher, however, since the causes of most congenital anomalies are unknown.

**Causes of Developmental Defects in Man—
Estimates Based on Surveys and Case Reports in
the Medical Literature**

Known genetic transmission		20%
Chromosomal aberration		3–5%
Environmental causes		
Ionizing radiations		<1%
Therapeutic	Nuclear	
Infections		2–3%
Rubella virus	Varicella virus(?)	
Cytomegalovirus	Toxoplasma	
Herpes virus hominis	Syphilis	
Maternal metabolic imbalance		1–2%
Endemic cretinism	Phenylketonuria	
Diabetes	Virilizing tumors	
Drugs and environmental chemicals		4–5%
Androgenic hormone	Anticonvulsants	
Folic antagonists	Oral hypoglycemics(?)	
Thalidomide	Few neurotropic-anorectics(?)	
Oral anticoagulants	Organic mercury	
Maternal alcoholism		
Combinations and interactions		?
Unknown		65–70%

Source: Reprinted from *The Handbook of Teratology*, Vol. 1, by J.G. Wilson and C. Fraser (Eds.) with permission of Plenum Publishing Corporation, © 1977.

Several factors interact to determine the occurrence and severity of a teratogenic effect. Among them are the timing of exposure (stage of pregnancy), the genetic makeup of the fertilized egg, genetic and environmental factors in the mother, and the type and dosage of the teratogen itself. The time at which susceptibility is greatest varies with the different developing organ systems. In general, exposure during the first two weeks of pregnancy either results in spontaneous abortion or has no effect at all. Exposure during weeks three through seven is likely to result in the abnormal growth and development of a body part. Later exposure may produce disturbances in the functioning of certain organs though their general structure appears normal.

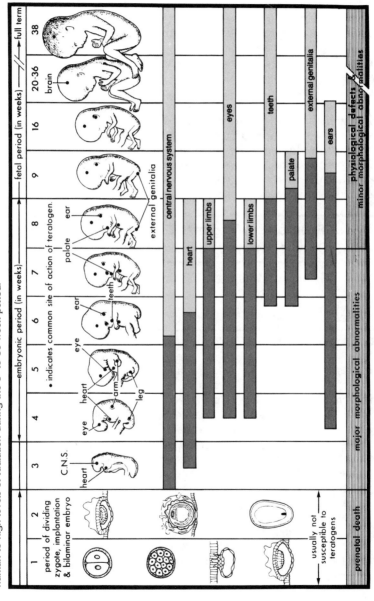

the light band indicates stages that are less sensitive to teratogens. Note that each organ or structure has a critical period during which its development may be deranged, and that physiological defects, functional disturbances, and minor morphological changes are likely to result from disturbances during the fetal period. Severe mental retardation may result from exposure of the developing human to high levels of radiation during the 8- to 16-week period.

Source: Reprinted from *Before We Are Born: Basic Embryology and Birth Defects*, 2nd ed., by K.L. Moore, p. 111, with permission of W.B. Saunders Company, © 1983.

Substances may be teratogenic for some animals and not for others. While many drugs and chemicals have resulted in birth defects when administered to animals in large doses, it is not certain what significance such studies have for humans receiving much smaller doses. On the other hand, thalidomide, believed to be safe on the basis of initial animal studies, was later found to cause abnormal arm and leg development in humans.

A few agents that are known to cause abnormalities in humans are listed below. While some of these high-risk substances (alcohol, for instance) can be avoided, there are situations in which it is difficult or impossible to avoid exposure to a potential teratogenic agent. For example, a drug to control seizures or high blood pressure may be teratogenic yet necessary for maternal health; if medication is discontinued, the fetus as well as the mother could be harmed by the maternal disorder. While it is sometimes possible to reduce the dosage or to switch to equally effective but less teratogenic medicines, there are instances in which such changes are not possible. Also, there are circumstances in which neither the woman nor her physician is aware of exposure to a known teratogen.

Examples of Agents Capable of Causing Developmental Abnormalities in Humans

Class	Example	Common Effect	Time of Maximal Chance of Harm	Chance of Harm
Radiation (high doses)	Radiotherapy	Mental retardation Small head Skeletal abnormalities	First trimester of pregnancy	High
Infection	Rubella (German measles)	Cataracts Congenital heart disease Deafness	First 5 weeks of pregnancy	15–20 percent
Maternal metabolic imbalance (untreated)	Phenylketonuria	Mental retardation Congenital heart disease	Unknown	95 percent
Drugs and environmental chemicals	Ethanol (alcohol)	Small head Mental retardation Poor growth	Unknown	Unknown

Visual Impairment

While newborns can see quite well, a normal adult level of visual acuity is not present at birth; rather, it develops gradually and depends upon proper functioning of all structures of the visual system. For normal vision to occur, images must first be transmitted accurately to the brain, as illustrated below.

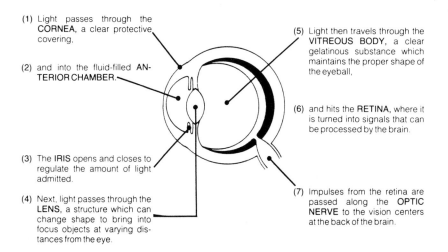

(1) Light passes through the CORNEA, a clear protective covering,

(2) and into the fluid-filled ANTERIOR CHAMBER.

(3) The IRIS opens and closes to regulate the amount of light admitted.

(4) Next, light passes through the LENS, a structure which can change shape to bring into focus objects at varying distances from the eye.

(5) Light then travels through the VITREOUS BODY, a clear gelatinous substance which maintains the proper shape of the eyeball,

(6) and hits the RETINA, where it is turned into signals that can be processed by the brain.

(7) Impulses from the retina are passed along the OPTIC NERVE to the vision centers at the back of the brain.

How Light Is Transmitted to the Brain

Primary visual impairment may arise from problems at any step in this process, or difficulty seeing may be due to the brain's failure to process information from the eyes appropriately. Also, improper image reception during infancy can result in secondary—and often permanent—abnormalities.

CAUSES

Light Is Blocked from the Retina

Sometimes the structures that normally transmit light from the eye surface to the retina—the cornea, anterior chamber, lens, and vitreous body—act instead to block the image. Abnormalities in one or more of these structures may result from exposure during pregnancy or birth to certain viruses or bacteria, from chemical eye burns or eye trauma, or from increased pressure within the eye that is present at birth (congenital glaucoma). In some cases, a clouding of the lens (cataract) may accompany certain infections or inherited disorders, such as rubella or Down syndrome.

Images Are Not Focused on the Retina

Vision is also impaired if the image is not focused clearly on the retina. This occurs with nearsightedness (myopia), farsightedness (hyperopia), and uneven focusing of the image on the retina (astigmatism). These are referred to as refractive errors.

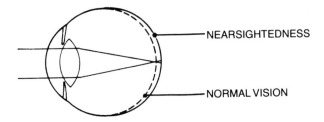

Nearsightedness

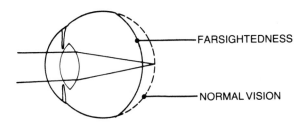

Farsightedness

Nerve Impulses Are Blocked from Reaching the Brain

Disorders that can block the path of nerve impulses from the retina to the vision centers of the brain include tumors of the retina, brain injury, and retinopathy of prematurity. (Retinopathy of prematurity,is a disease of the retina that occurs in some premature infants who required oxygen for treatment of respiratory distress. Mild cases may resolve completely without visual impairment. More severe cases, however, may result in retinal damage and loss of vision. Retinopathy of prematurity may be accompanied by strabismus and refractive errors.)

The Brain Fails To Process Information from the Eyes

Some children may have problems with "central processing" of visual information. That is, the structures that transmit visual information to the brain are intact, but the information reaching the brain is not processed or interpreted in a meaningful way. This may occur in children with damage to the visual cortex in the occipital lobes or in children with generalized cerebral dysfunction that produces significant intellectual defects.

Strabismus

With strabismus, sometimes called "squint," the eyes do not work together. One eye consistently may turn inward (or outward), or the eyes may alternate in their deviation from proper alignment. Strabismus may result from weakness of the muscles that control eye movement, from ocular defects such as cataracts or a damaged retina, or from poor visual acuity.

Since sensory input is necessary for proper development of the visual system, untreated strabismus may result in further loss of functional vision. Therefore, infants who continue to show signs of strabismus by six months of age are referred to an ophthalmologist for evaluation. In every case, the most important goal of treatment is to preserve the best possible vision. If possible, the underlying cause is treated. With poor visual acuity, for example, cataracts are removed or glasses are prescribed. At times, a child may be forced to use the weaker eye by patching the normal eye. Occasionally, surgery may be necessary to correct alignment.

INCIDENCE

Blindness occurs in about one in four thousand children. Less severe yet significant visual defects occur in about one child in 20. The rate of visual impairment is much higher among children with multiple handicaps; one study found significant visual abnormalities in 30 percent of multiply handicapped children whose primary diagnosis did not involve vision.

DETECTION

Screening for actual or potential visual abnormalities in children is important. During infancy or early childhood—the optimal time for preventing or minimizing visual impairments—most children are not aware (or cannot communicate) that their vision is faulty. A child's eyes should be examined for abnormalities and muscle imbalance at birth, at three, six, and 12 months, and annually thereafter. At these intervals the parents should be asked whether they have noticed the child crossing the eyes involuntarily, holding objects close to the face, failing to focus on faces or objects, exhibiting poor eye-hand coordination, or performing any other acts that suggest possible visual problems.

Visual acuity testing becomes more precise as the child develops. With various commonly used tests, preschool children may be asked to name objects (STYCAR) or pictures (Allen), or to point in the direction of the "legs" of the letter *E*. Children under 12 months may be observed as they track brightly colored objects. Another method of assessing vision in very young children or in children with significant developmental delays uses an electroencephalogram in combination with a computer to assess the brain's response to a flashing light (visual evoked responses).

While vision screening is important for all children, it is especially valuable for those with a history of visual problems or for those who have had certain infections around the time of birth. Other events, such as exposure to prolonged supplemental oxygen following premature birth, are serious enough to warrant an examination during the first few months of life by an ophthalmologist, a physician with specialized training in disorders of vision.

MEDICAL MANAGEMENT

Many children in the birth-to-three-year age range who have strabismus due to unequal visual acuity in the two eyes can be treated successfully with patching of the stronger eye, while older children often will need glasses or surgery to correct "squint" from this or other causes. Surgery may also be necessary to treat cataracts or glaucoma. Even very young children may be able to wear glasses successfully.

Poor eyesight has been blamed for certain learning problems, especially reading disabilities. The American Academy of Ophthalmology, however, has found the incidence and spectrum of learning problems to be the same among children with and without learning disabilities. This organization doubts that there are improvements in learning arising out of eye muscle, visual tracking, or other visual training techniques advocated by some.

IMPLICATIONS FOR EDUCATION

Because visual impairment is common and rarely produces signs or symptoms readily traceable to the visual system, children must have regular vision system assessments. At high risk for vision problems are children with disabilities, children who were born prematurely or who suffered intrauterine growth retardation, and children with family histories of visual impairment. Early detection, combined with appropriate referral and effective treatment, can improve vision significantly among affected children.

Frequent squinting, rubbing of the eyes, lack of attention, or irritability may be associated with visual problems and should be reported to the child's parents.

Whenever possible, the activities and experiences of children with visual impairment should be accompanied by verbal expression and tactile interactions.

SEE ALSO

Cerebral Palsy, Congenital Infections, and *Low Birth Weight*

ADDITIONAL RESOURCES

Zambone, A. "Serving the Young Child with Visual Impairments: An Overview of Disability Impact and Intervention Needs." *Infants and Young Children* 2, no. 2 (1989).

Helpful References

Batshaw, M.L., Y.M. Perret. *Children with Handicaps: A Medical Primer.* Baltimore: Paul H. Brookes Publishing Co., 1986.

Bleck, E.E., and D.A. Nagel, eds. *Physically Handicapped Children: A Medical Atlas for Teachers.* New York: Grune & Stratton, 1982.

National Center for Education in Maternal and Child Health. *Reaching Out: A Directory of National Organizations Related to Maternal and Child Health.* Washington, D.C.: National Center for Education in Maternal and Child Health, March 1989.

Index

A

Abduction splint, 38
Abnormal hyperextensibility of knee
joints, 214
ABO, 224
Abortus, 220
ABR, see Auditory brain stem response
Abuse, 67–70, see also specific types
reporting of, 70
Academy of Otolaryngology-Head and
Neck Surgery, 169
Accompanying health problems
Acetabulum, 215
Achilles tendon lengthening, 217
Acidosis, 182
Acquired immune deficiency syndrome
(AIDS), 91–92
ACTH, 255
AFO, see Ankle-foot orthoses
Agenesis of corpus callosum, 50
AIDS, see Acquired immune deficiency
syndrome
Akinetic seizures, 252
Alcohol
low birth weight and, 184
maternal use of, see Fetal alcohol
syndrome (FAS)

teratogenic effects of, 141, 268
Alimentary tract characteristics, 165
Allen test, 272
American Academy of Ophthalmology,
272
American Academy of Pediatrics, 169
Task Force on Pediatric AIDS of, 91
American Association on Mental
Deficiency, 185
American Nurses Association, 169
American Psychiatric Association, 7
American Speech Language Hearing
Association, 169
Anemia, 1–6, see also specific types
causes of, 1–2
classification of, 3
cytomegalic inclusion disease and, 94
defined, 1
iron deficiency, 1, 2, 4, 5, 124
sickle cell, 2
syphilis and, 89
toxoplasmosis and, 90
Anencephaly, 49
Angiography, 46
Ankle-foot orthoses (AFO), 31–33, 37,
43
Anomalous pulmonary venous return, 84
Antibiotics, see also specific types